CAMBRIDGE LIBRARY COLLECTION

Books of enduring scholarly value

Philosophy

This series contains both philosophical texts and critical essays about philosophy, concentrating especially on works originally published in the eighteenth and nineteenth centuries. It covers a broad range of topics including ethics, logic, metaphysics, aesthetics, utilitarianism, positivism, scientific method and political thought. It also includes biographies and accounts of the history of philosophy, as well as collections of papers by leading figures. In addition to this series, primary texts by ancient philosophers, and works with particular relevance to philosophy of science, politics or theology, may be found elsewhere in the Cambridge Library Collection.

Caliban

Having acquired a Shakespeare folio for a few shillings, anthropologist Daniel Wilson (1816–92) found in *The Tempest* a source of scientific intrigue. Writing more than two hundred years before Darwin propounded his theory of evolution, in his final play Shakespeare had created a missing link caught between the animal and the human. In this monograph, first published in 1873, Wilson uses the strange and unfortunate character of Caliban as a means through which to explore the principles of evolution. He traces many of the play's plot devices back to real events that perhaps inspired them – from storms in Bermuda to records of semi-human creatures around the world – and brings literary commentary into science as he links the relationships set out in the play to anthropological principles. This interdisciplinary approach makes the book both an entertaining exegesis of the play and a uniquely accessible explanation of contemporary scientific theories.

Cambridge University Press has long been a pioneer in the reissuing of out-of-print titles from its own backlist, producing digital reprints of books that are still sought after by scholars and students but could not be reprinted economically using traditional technology. The Cambridge Library Collection extends this activity to a wider range of books which are still of importance to researchers and professionals, either for the source material they contain, or as landmarks in the history of their academic discipline.

Drawing from the world-renowned collections in the Cambridge University Library and other partner libraries, and guided by the advice of experts in each subject area, Cambridge University Press is using state-of-the-art scanning machines in its own Printing House to capture the content of each book selected for inclusion. The files are processed to give a consistently clear, crisp image, and the books finished to the high quality standard for which the Press is recognised around the world. The latest print-on-demand technology ensures that the books will remain available indefinitely, and that orders for single or multiple copies can quickly be supplied.

The Cambridge Library Collection brings back to life books of enduring scholarly value (including out-of-copyright works originally issued by other publishers) across a wide range of disciplines in the humanities and social sciences and in science and technology.

Caliban

The Missing Link

Daniel Wilson

CAMBRIDGE
UNIVERSITY PRESS

University Printing House, Cambridge, CB2 8BS, United Kingdom

Cambridge University Press is part of the University of Cambridge.
It furthers the University's mission by disseminating knowledge in the pursuit of
education, learning and research at the highest international levels of excellence.

www.cambridge.org
Information on this title: www.cambridge.org/9781108063678

© in this compilation Cambridge University Press 2014

This edition first published 1873
This digitally printed version 2014

ISBN 978-1-108-06367-8 Paperback

CALIBAN:

THE MISSING LINK.

a

CALIBAN:

THE MISSING LINK.

BY

DANIEL WILSON, LL.D.

PROFESSOR OF HISTORY AND ENGLISH LITERATURE, UNIVERSITY COLLEGE,
TORONTO.

London

MACMILLAN AND CO.

1873

OXFORD:

By T. Combe, M.A., E. B. Gardner, E. Pickard Hall, and J. H. Stacy,

PRINTERS TO THE UNIVERSITY.

To Jane Sybel,

MY SHAKESPEARE SCHOLAR,

THIS VOLUME IS DEDICATED

VERY LOVINGLY

BY HER FATHER.

CONTENTS.

PREFACE.

'I'll believe as soon
This whole earth may be bored, and that the moon
May through the centre creep, and so displace
Her brother's noontide with the Antipodes.
It cannot be.'—*A Midsummer Night's Dream.*

THE Antipodes, in Shakespeare's day, were beings
for whom the world, and all which pertains to it, were
turned upside down. The ideas entertained of them
were of the very vaguest kind ; the capacity of belief
in regard to them was restrained by no ordinary limits
of experience or analogy. The most that could be affirmed with any confidence in regard to them, seemed
to be that they must exist under conditions in all respects the reverse of our own ; and with their heads, if
not absolutely where their heels should be, yet somewhere else than on their shoulders. The sun was below,
and the earth above them. They were manifestly beings
with which fancy had free scope to sport at will.

'The cannibals that each other eat,' concerning whom
Othello discoursed to his admiring auditors, are now
very familiar to us. Of that other class of 'anthropophagi, whose heads do grow beneath their shoulders,'
ocular testimony seems more remote than ever. 'When

we were boys,' says Gonzalo, in 'The Tempest,' 'who
would believe there were such men whose heads stood in
their breasts ; ' of which, nevertheless, now every New
World adventurer 'will bring us good warrant.' Later
explorations, either in the regions of actual travel, or in
those of scientific research, have failed to confirm such
warranty. But somewhere outside the old world of
authenticated fact, Shakespeare found, or fashioned for
us, a being which has come, in our own day, to possess
an interest, undreamt of either by the men of the poet's
age, or by that profane generation for which Dryden
and D'Avenant revived 'The Tempest,' with changes
adapted to the prurient court of the later Stuarts.

It will need no apology to the appreciative student
of Shakespeare that 'the missing link' in the evolution
of man should be sought for in the pages of him 'whose
aim was to hold as 'twere the mirror up to nature ;' nor,
if it is to be recovered anywhere, will he wonder at its
discovery there. Ben Jonson said truly

'He was not of an age, but for all time.'

Much that he wrote was imperfectly appreciated even by
the men of his own day. It was too refined, too noble,
too lofty in its marvellous range of thought and feeling,
for later generations of the Restoration and Revolution
eras. It will ever fail of adequate comprehension by a
frivolous or a faithless age. Shakespeare is indeed capable of proving the source, not merely of pastime, but
of supreme delight to the mere pleasure seeker. But

there are not only passages, but whole characters in his dramas, the force of which is wholly lost on him who turns to them in no more serious mood than to an ordinary tale or novel. When such a mere dallier, as the youthful reader is apt to be, has become a loving student, and learned to enter into true sympathy with the poet, he discovers a depth of meaning undreamt of before, and catches at length the just significance of his first admiring editors' advice 'to the great variety of readers':—'Read him, therefore, and again and again; and if then you do not like him, surely you are in some manifest danger not to understand him.'

The dramas of Shakespeare have been studied by the present writer under very diverse circumstances. He became possessor of the old 1632 folio in youthful days, when it could be bought on an Edinburgh bookstall for a few shillings. He was already accustomed to resort to Shakespeare's pages as a source of rare enjoyment; and in this and other editions the great dramatist was read, in the only way in which the spirit of his writings is to be caught by a venerating, loving student. In more recent years, it has been his pleasant duty to read some of the great master's choicest works with Canadian undergraduates, as part of the Honour Work of the University of Toronto; and thus—in what was, in days greatly more recent than those of Shakespeare, an unexplored wild of the New World,—to fulfil the behest of his first editors: who, having commended the reading and re-reading of the great dramatist as

indispensable for the true understanding of him, thus
conclude—'And so we leave you to other of his friends,
who, if you need, can be your guides. If you need
them not, you can lead yourselves and others ; and such
readers we wish him.'

In such a study of Shakespeare, his many-sidedness,
his universality, his ever-renewing modernness, startle
the reader afresh, when he has vainly fancied that he
already appreciates him at his highest worth. The
sympathies of the man seem all-embracing. He com-
prehends every phase of human character, every im-
pulse and passion of the human soul, every conceivable
stage of development of the human mind.

In this age, which, not altogether without justification, claims for itself a more adequate appreciation of
England's greatest poet than he has before received,
there are engrossing themes, alike in the departments
of faith and science, undreamt of in Shakespeare's day;
and, above all, there is that one in which science and
faith alike claim a share, which professes to furnish
entirely novel revelations of the origin of man and the
evolution of mind. By Shakespeare, I imagine, the old
narrative of what was done 'in the beginning,' was received undoubtingly as true. As to Sir Thomas Browne,
who is accepted in the following pages as, in some
respects, the representative of a later and very different
age, his mode of affirming his faith in the primitive
story is in this quaintly characteristic fashion : 'Whether
Eve was framed out of the left side of Adam, I dispute

not; because I stand not yet assured which is the right
side of a man, or whether there be any such distinction in nature. That she was edified out of the rib
of Adam I believe, yet raise no question who shall
arise with that rib at the resurrection.'

Of such a theory or system of human descent as now
challenges universal acceptance, Shakespeare entertained
as little thought as Bacon did. The elements of its conception lay remote from every theme with which his
mind delighted to dally ; and far apart from all those
deeper thoughts on which he mused and pondered, till
they assumed immortal embodiment in his own Hamlet.
And yet he had thought out, and there sets forth with
profoundest significance, the essential distinctions and
attributes of humanity :—

> ' What is a man,
> If his chief good and market of his time
> Be but to sleep and feed ? a beast, no more.
> Sure he that made us with such large discourse,
> Looking before and after, gave us not
> That capability and god-like reason
> To fust in us unused.'

He had not only sounded all the depths of the human
soul, but he had realised for himself the wholly diverse
motives and cravings of the mere animal mind. The
leading purpose of the following pages is, accordingly,
to shew that his genius had already created for us the
ideal of that imaginary intermediate being, between the
true brute and man, which, if the new theory of descent
from crudest animal organisms be true, was our prede-

cessor and precursor in the inheritance of this world of
humanity. We have in 'The Tempest' a being which is
'a beast, no more,' and yet is endowed with speech and
reason up to the highest ideal of the capacity of its lower
nature. A comparison between this Caliban of Shakespeare's creation, and the so-called 'brute-progenitor of
man' of our latest school of science, has proved replete
with interest and instruction to the writer's own mind ;
and the results are embodied in the following pages, for
such readers as may care to follow out the same study
for themselves.

The main theme is accompanied with a commentary
on two plays of Shakespeare, 'The Tempest,' and 'A
Midsummer Night's Dream,' chiefly appealed to in the
course of the preceding argument. Some of the conjectural readings and other subjects touched on in this
supplement may be of interest to Shakespeare students.
Corrupt as the text of Shakespeare's plays undoubtedly
is, the author is far indeed from thinking that they stand
in need of any great amount of note or comment. The
loving student of his dramas, even with the most imperfect text, learns to enter so thoroughly into their
spirit and the personality of their characters, that he is
scarcely conscious of obscurity. He catches, as it were,
the sense of the whole ; and in many a controverted
passage, has never thought of obscurity, or felt any
difficulty in enjoying it, till he has turned to the commentators, and learns how sorely they have been perplexing themselves over its riddles.

Yet commentators have done good service in this, if in no other respect. They have led to the diligent study of Shakespeare, even if it were at times only 'of envy and strife.' But for the well-timed, though indiscriminate censures of Jeremy Collier, in his famous 'Short View of the Immorality and Profaneness of the English Stage,' published in 1698, and the controversies which they provoked, the study of Shakespeare, on which his true appreciation depended, might have been long delayed. The Rev. Joseph Hunter, in his 'Disquisition on Shakespeare's Tempest,' wonders 'that so much respect has not been paid to Dryden as to find a place in the prolegomena of this play for the portion of the prologue to his own and D'Avenant's transversion of it, in which he pays so fine a compliment to Shakespeare.' But no one who has any regard for the fair fame of Dryden will seek to recall, in association with the name of Shakespeare, the authorship of a 'transversion' which is without exception the most contemptible evidence of the utter incapacity of the Restoration era to comprehend Shakespeare. It is not as a dramatist that Dryden takes rank among England's poets ; and least of all would it be a tribute of respect to his memory to revive a prologue appended to one of the most chaste of all the great master's creations, in which the later poet descends to a grossness only too characteristic of the audience for which Miranda and Caliban had to be despoiled of that on which the innocence of the one, and the simple naturalness of the other, mainly depend. If the name

of the great satirist to whom we owe the 'Absolom and
Achitophel' is to be associated with Shakespeare's, it
can be done with a better grace, where he writes to
Sir Godfrey Kneller in acknowledgement, as is believed,
of a copy of the Chandos portrait :—

> 'Shakespeare, thy gift, I place before my sight;
> With awe I ask his blessing ere I write;
> With reverence look on his majestic face ;
> Proud to be less, but of his god-like race.'

It was not till the eighteenth century that Nicholas
Rowe, the first textual critic of the Shakespearean
drama, appeared ; and but for the bitter wars of Pope
and the dunces,— with Warburton, Johnson, Steevens,
Malone, and all the learned brood of commentators
following,— Shakespeare might have long been left to
the mercy of such playwrights as D'Avenant and
Dryden in the seventeenth, and Garrick and Cibber in
the eighteenth century. Yet let it never be thought, as
has too frequently been assumed, that Shakespeare is
only now for the first time adequately appreciated ; or,
as others even more grossly affirm, that it was not till
German critics had revealed his power, that English
readers learned how great a poet their own Shakespeare
is. However notorious the failure of his friends and
literary executors, Heminge and Condell, may have
been as editors,— and had they executed their task in
the way it was in their power to have done, with original manuscripts, stage copies, the memories of living
actors, and the texts of earlier quartos, to appeal to,

the race of commentators would have had no pretext
for textual recension ;—yet in high estimation of their
author's works, it is not easy for any later critic to
surpass them.   There, too, in the same folio, where
their appreciative preface proves that Shakespeare was
a true hero even to his fellow players, surly Ben Jonson,
forgetting all his old irascibilities, writes of his 'star
of poets '—

> ' Soul of the age,
> The applause ! delight ! the wonder of the stage !
> My Shakespeare.'

Another contemporary, Leonard Digges, in laudatory
verses of inferior power, but no less sincerity, prefixed
to a spurious edition of Shakespeare's poems published
in 1640, bears witness to the delight with which his
plays were welcomed before all others.   His 'Cæsar'
could ravish the audience, when they would not brook
Jonson's tedious 'Catiline.'   His Othello and Falstaff, his
Beatrice, Benedick, and 'Malvolio, that cross-garter'd
gull,' would crowd cock-pit, galleries, and boxes, till
scarce standing-room remained ; when even the choicest
of Ben Jonson's plays, 'The Fox and subtil Alchymist,'
could only at long intervals command their merited ova-
tion ; and so he concludes with the comparison of 'his
wit-fraught book' to old coined gold, which by virtue
of its innate worth will pass current to succeeding ages.
Shakespeare's writings are indeed a mine of wealth, from
which the more they are studied the less it will surprise
us to draw forth treasures new and old ; and here, in his

Caliban, we recover a piece of 'old coin'd gold,' with its Elizabethan mint-mark, but with a value for us such as Shakespeare himself was unconscious of: like some rarest numismatic gem, whose worth in the artistic beauty of its die, far exceeds all its weight of sterling gold.

UNIVERSITY COLLEGE, TORONTO,

July 3, 1872.

CHAPTER I.

IN THE BEGINNING.

'We do but learn to-day what our better-advanced judgments will
unteach us to-morrow; and Aristotle doth but instruct us, as Plato
did him: that is, to confute himself.'—*Religio Medici.*

IN the 'Medley' of the Poet-Laureat, when the tale
of the Princess is closed, with its mock-heroics, its
bantering burlesque, and its real earnestness, and the
little feud begins

> 'Betwixt the mockers and the realists,'

Lilia joins entirely with the latter. 'The sequel of the
tale had touched her,' she sate absorbed, perplexed in
thought, till

> 'Last she fix't
> A showery glance upon her aunt, and said,
> You—tell us what we are; who might have told,
> For she was cramm'd with theories out of books;'

but that the crowd, who had been making a sport of
science, were swarming at the sunset to take leave;
and ere all was quiet again, the stillness gave its fitter
response to the question, unanswerable by 'theories out
of books.'

> 'So they sat,
> But spoke not, rapt in nameless reverie,
> Perchance upon the future man; the walls
> Blacken'd about us, bats wheel'd, and owls whoop'd,
> And gradually the powers of the night,
> That range above the region of the wind,
> Deepening the courts of twilight, broke them up
> Through all the silent spaces of the worlds,
> Beyond all thought, into the Heaven of heavens.'

B

But this question, 'Whence, and what are we?' is not
to be repressed, either by shouting crowds or by brooding silences. The activity of the reasoning mind within
us is in no respect more manifest than in the irrepressible
inquiry into our own origin and that of the universe of
which we form a part. Every philosophy and every
faith undertakes some solution of the problem; and
childlike as are the fables of primitive cosmogonists,
they all concur in recognising the evidence of design,
and so the necessity of a preexistent designer. The
eternity of matter has indeed had its advocates, as in
the philosophy of Democritus; but matter was with
him no more than the formless void that preceded
creation. Time began when the universe was called
into being; and its evolution out of chaos was in
accordance with a purposed plan, and the work of a
presiding will.

The order of the universe, as thus recognised, is first
a supreme infinite intelligence, then lesser finite intel-
ligences. But the gulf which lies between the finite
and the infinite is very partially diminished to us by
any conception we may form of highest finite in-
telligences, such as antique poetry and mythology
impersonated in a multitude of fanciful idealisms; and
which to our own minds are acceptably presented as
ministering spirits, symbolised by indestructible fire:
beings in whom the intellectual element predominates,
and to whom is committed the ministration of the
supreme, intelligent, divine will. With such spiritual
essences science may reasonably disclaim counsel, as
with things lying wholly beyond its province. But
man, too, is an intelligent being, in some by no means
obscure sense made, as such, in the image of God.
It is indeed well to avoid as far as possible, in scientific

discussion, the use of terms which have been appropriated by the theologian. But the human element, which Shakespeare calls 'God-like reason,' however we may designate it, cannot be ignored; though by some modern lines of reasoning it is made to assume a very materialistic origin. From very early times of philosophical speculation, mind and matter have marshalled their rival champions to the field. As Byron jestingly puts it: when Berkeley and his followers have said there is no matter, the profane realist has responded, it is no matter what they say! But the rival creeds are not to be so fused. The feud between the idealists and realists, the metaphysicians and the naturalists, is as far as ever from being settled; nor can science limit its bounds within any absolute materialism. As soon as we take up the question of the origin and descent of man we are compelled to deal with the spiritual no less than the material element of his being, whatever theories we may be tempted to form in accounting for the origin of either.

In attempting to follow up the track of time through the field of space, to that point when the universe, which was not always there, began to be, two contradictory hypotheses seem to offer themselves to the theorist. The eternity of matter may be assumed, with its imagined elements in incoherent chaos, awaiting the evolution of law and the beginning of organisation. But out of this can come no directing or informing will. It may seem but a step beyond this, but it is a very long one, to start as Lady Psyche does, in her introductory harangue to the fair undergraduates of the university of the future :—

> ' This world was once a fluid haze of light,
> Till toward the centre set the starry tides,

And eddied into suns, that, wheeling, cast
The planets; then the monster, then the man:
Tattoo'd or woaded, winter-clad in skins,
Raw from the prime.'

On the other hand, if the ancient maxim holds good, that nothing can come out of nothing, it seems not less but more scientific to start with the preoccupation of the mighty void with the Eternal Mind. The conception of such a Supreme Divine Intelligence seems to commend itself to finite reason. It is easier to conceive of the eternity of God than of His coming into being. But if 'first mind, then matter,' be thus the order of the universe, how are we to reconcile with it the inductions of modern science, in such a total reversal of this order in the process of creation of mind as is implied in the development of the intellectual, moral, and spiritual elements of man, through the same natural selection by which his physical evolution is traced, step by step, from the very lowest organic forms ?

The contrast which this hypothesis presents to older theories of evolution, is nowhere better shown than in the musings of the old sage of Norwich. In his 'Religio Medici' he deals, after his own quaint fashion, with the oracles of antiquity, the supernatural of popular belief, and the spiritual beings set forth in revelation. For angelic natures he entertains a reverent regard undreamt of in our age of positivisms and spiritualisms. He doubts not that 'those noble essences in heaven bear a friendly regard unto their fellow-natures on earth ;' and therefore he believes that 'those many prodigies and ominous prognostics which forerun the ruin of states, princes, and private persons, are the charitable premonitions of good angels.' It was due, no doubt, to such calm philosophisings, that, in the very crisis of England's and Charles the First's fate, he left the state and its prince to the charity of such good angels, and busied himself with his ' Pseudodoxia Epidemica ' or inquiries into many commonly presumed truths, and vulgar and common errors. But having in this tranquil fashion mused on the character and functions of angelic essences, he passes to a refinement of the Platonic idea of ' an universal and common spirit to the whole world,' the Divine Source by whose almighty fiat the void was filled, the darkness made light, and the light responded to by a world of life. The quaint medicist then refers anew to the angelic beings who owe their existence to the same divine source, as certainly the masterpieces of the Creator, the flower, or perfect bloom of ' what we are but in hopes and probability ; for,' he adds, ' we are only that amphibious piece between corporal and spiritual essence, that middle form that links those two together, and makes good the method of God and nature, that jumps not from extremes, but unites the incompatible distances by some middle and participating natures.'

The mystical fancies of the old physician reflect ideas of an elder time, when faith had in it much of refined simplicity and somewhat also of credulity ; and in which genius dealt reverently yet fearlessly with many problems that anew invite our solution. Sir Thomas Browne is as one born out of due time. He presents in unique combination some of the most characteristic features of the previous age : the age of Camden, Hooker, and Donne ; of Bacon and Hobbes ; of Spenser, Sidney, Lilly and Shakespeare. He is especially noticeable for a learned conceit in his choice of words, and a quaintness of phrase, such as Lilly had commended, and Shakespeare ridiculed, even while turning it to account. But still more does he link the age that preceded with the

one to which, in point of time, he belonged, by the
singular interblending of scepticism with a devout credulity: as where he declines to dispute the question
as to whether Eve was formed out of the left side of
Adam ; or whether 'Adam was an hermaphrodite, as
the Rabbins contend upon the letter of the text, because
it is contrary to reason that there should be an hermaphrodite before there was a woman.' In this and
like manner he glances in inconsequential fashion at
thoughts which are now presented to all minds in
clearest definition : accepting without difficulty what
no one will now credit, and rejecting unhesitatingly
what is now assumed as indisputable.

It was a transitional age, in which liberty was running
into licence, and nonconformity was persecuted rather
because its austerity offended the licentiousness of the
times, than that its creed ran counter to any recognisable
belief of the new era. The nonconformity which re-
ceives least toleration in our own day lies under the ban
of science far more than of theology. The Church has
grown so broad, that it becomes a puzzle to define what
might constitute heresy, or may not prove to be orthodoxy within its pale. But outside of its consecrated
bounds science has established its accredited beliefs,
as by a new Council of Nice ; and woe to the heretic
who ventures to question its dogmas. Its new hypotheses
are pronounced by most of its exponents to be infinitely
probable, and by many of them to be absolutely demon-
strated. With a generous denouncement of all intoler-
ance, the modern evolutionist presents his axioms to
the questioner, and passes on. Infallibility has deserted
the chair of St. Peter, and finds itself at home on a
new throne. It is perilous to mediate in the inquiries
which now occupy a foremost place in deduction, in-

duction, and scientific research. There are indeed among the leaders of thought, men of calm judicial sobriety, whose decisions are presented in so attractive a form as to invite from the thoughtful mind the most careful examination before they are rejected. But it is otherwise with the crowd of followers, who have been dazzled by the novelty of the new theory of evolution, and are animated with all the zeal of young converts. We own to being charmed with the theory of the origin of species, to having recognised in it the key to a thousand difficulties in natural history; but all is vain, unless the whole hypothesis of the descent of man, the evolution of mind, and every step in the pedigree by which he is traced back to the remotest of his new-found ancestry, be accepted as indisputable fact.

In such a stage of argument it is advantageous to be able to appeal on any point to an impartial umpire; and it may prove of value to compare the poetical imaginings of an age rich in genius of the highest order with the matter-of-fact realism of our own day. It suited the quaint philosophic mysticism of Sir Thomas Browne to conceive of man as the intermediate link between spiritual essences and mere animal life; but M. Louis Figuier puts forth, in his 'Day after Death,' with all the gravity of a pure induction of science, the latest scheme of psychical evolution, in which he traces a refining and sublimated humanity from planet to planet in ever-renewing resurrection, until, freed from its last earthly taint in the final solar abode of perfected souls, it shall there 'lie immortal in the arms of fire.' This demonstration of 'our future life according to science,' is neither offered to us as religious musings, like those of Sir Thomas Browne; nor as the sport of scientific fancy, such as the dying philosopher, Sir

Humphrey Davy, wrought into the ingenious day-
dream which beguiled his last hours. The Frenchman
belongs to a scientific age; writes in an era of revolution,
in which many old things are passing away; imagines
himself strictly inductive ; and publishes to the world
his fanciful speculations on a whole cycle of evolutions,
as a new gospel : the latest revelation of science and
the most comprehensive scheme of future development.
It has one special use at least, in which it is, so far,
a counterpart to Sir Humphrey Davy's 'Last Days
of a Philosopher.' It suffices to illustrate the barrenness
of the most ambitious fancy, with all the aids that
science can command, in every effort to realise that
other life, which 'it hath not entered into the heart
of man to conceive.'

But what imagination utterly fails to do as an induction based on supposed scientific foundations, the
creative fancy of the true poet, working within its own
legitimate sphere, has accomplished to better purpose.
Not, indeed, that the unseen world, and the spiritual life
beyond the grave, are any nearer to the gifted poet
than to the humblest believer to whom the realities of
that higher state of existence are objects of faith : but
in those stages of real or hypothetical evolution, and the
transitional states of being which their assumption involves, fancy has to play its part under whatever severe
restraints of scientific judgment. The comprehensive
faith which his novel doctrines involve, makes ever new
demands on the cultivated imaginings of the man of
science ; and it requires a mind of rare balance to pre-
serve the fancy in due subordination to the actual demonstrations of scientific truth. But if it were possible
to free the imagination from the promptings, alike of
seductive hypotheses and of the severer inductions of

science, and so have its own realisations of the possible
and the probable to compare with those assumed actual
anthropomorphic beings of a remote past with which
man is now affirmed to have such intimate genealogical
relations, the result would be one to be welcomed by
every lover of truth. We should then be·able to place
alongside of such creations of a well-regulated fancy, the
wholly independent deductions of scientific speculation
and research : whereas now the fancy of the evolutionist is subject to all the dictations of a preconceived
theory; and he realises for himself, as an undoubted link
in the pedigree of humanity, such a being as seems
wholly inconceivable to another class of cultivated
minds. To the one, this imaginary being, 'the progenitor of man,' seems as monstrous as the centaurs with
which the art of Phidias enriched the metopes of the
Parthenon ; to the other, every doubt, not merely of its
possible, but of its actual existence, appears the mere
offspring of prejudice.

Happily for the impartial inquirer, such an unbiassed
conception of the intermediate being, lower than man, as
man is 'a little lower than the angels,' is no vain dream
of modern doubt. The not wholly irrational brute, the
animal approximating in form and attributes as nearly
to man as the lower animal may be supposed to do
while still remaining a brute, has actually been conceived for us with all the perfection of an art more real
and suggestive than that of the chisel of Phidias, in one
of the most original creations of the Shakespearean
drama.

The world has known no age of bolder inquiry, or
freer liberty of thought, than the sixteenth century.
The men of that grand era knew both how to question
and how to believe, and were able to give a reason for

the faith that was in them. This manly faith, no less
than the vigorous freedom of intellect of that age, is
reflected in the pages of Spenser and Shakespeare, even
more than in many of the theological writings of the
time. With the seventeenth century a change began.
Two of the most independent thinkers that have appeared in modern Europe, Bacon and Hobbes, entered
on their labours, and gave a new bias to thought and
reasoning. The one undertook an analytical classification of human knowledge, and aimed at supplementing
the ancient or Aristotelian logic in such a way as to
check the reasoner from making undue deductions from
the premises before him. The Baconian method may
not suffice as a fitting instrument for all the ample demands of modern science; but it never was more needful than now to require with strictest severity that the
inferences we magnify into demonstrations shall be fully
sustained by the premises on which they are founded.
The other, Hobbes, with close and consistent reasoning,
took up the department of mental philosophy, and,
amid many ethical theories only too consistent with
modern ideas of the evolution of mind, furnished con-
tributions to the science of mental philosophy, the full
value of which was not perceived by his own age. But
he was an incomplete moralist. His utilitarian theories
were based on a standard far below that of the Elizabethan age. He belonged unmistakably, in his whole
reasonings as a moralist, to the era of decline. His
writings, as well as those of Bacon, abound with reflex
characteristics of that elder time; but they no less
clearly indicate that its earnestness had passed away.
Yet its influence long survived, and it is even more
curious to recognise the same faith and Puritan theology
of the sixteenth century reflected in the satires of

Dryden, than in the ethics of Hobbes, or the quaint musings of Sir Thomas Browne.

' That we are the breath and similitude of God,' writes the author of ' Religio Medici,' 'it is indisputable, and upon record of Holy Scripture; but to call ourselves a microcosm, or little world, I thought it only a pleasant trope of rhetoric, till my near judgment and second thoughts told me there was a real truth therein. For first, we are a rude mass, and in the rank of creatures which only are, and have a dull kind of being not yet privileged with life, or preferred to sense or reason ; next we live the life of plants, the life of animals, the life of men, and at last the life of spirits, running on in one mysterious nature those five kind of existences, which comprehend the creatures not only of the world, but of the universe.' Here we have unmistakable glimmerings of Lamarckian and other theories of metamorphosis, evolution, and progression.

But long before the author of the ' Religio Medici ' had penned his ingenious musings on the development of the human microcosm, Shakespeare had presented, in the clear mirror of his matchless realisations alike of the natural and supernatural, the vivid conception of 'that amphibious piece between corporal and spiritual essence,' by which, according to modern hypothesis, the human mind is conjoined in nature and origin with the very lowest forms of vital organism. The greatest of poets, who seems to grow ever more wise and more true as growing wisdom helps new generations to appreciate his worth, has thus left for us materials not without their value in discussing, even prosaically and literally, the imaginary perfectibility of the irrational brute; the imaginable degradation of rational man. Since Shake-speare's day a school of didactic poets has merged into a philosophical and metaphysical one; and the most objective poet of this metaphysical school has, in his 'Caliban upon Setebos; or, Natural Theology in the Island,' dealt with a new ideal of the same intermediate being, shaped according to the beliefs and fancies of later generations.

Those realisations of the same rational brute, in its aboriginal habitat, in contact with the informing intelligence of a higher nature, and in conflict with the doubts which appear as the natural twin of new-born reason : present us with conceptions, by two widely differing minds, responding to the influences of eras no less dissimilar. The object aimed at in the following chapters is to place the conceptions of modern science in relation to the assumed brute progenitor of man, alongside of those imaginative picturings, and of the whole world of fancy and superstition pertaining to that elder time; while also, the literary excellences, and the textual difficulties of the two dramas of Shakespeare chiefly appealed to in illustration of the scientific element of inquiry, are made the subjects of careful study.

CHAPTER II.

THE CALIBAN OF EVOLUTION.

> ' What seest thou else
> In the dark backward and abysm of time?
> If thou remember st aught ere thou camest here,
> How thou camest here thou mayst.'—*The Tempest.*

IT is a pleasant fancy, due to the poet Campbell, that
' The Tempest' of Shakespeare, which stands first in
the earliest collected edition of his dramas, has a special
sacredness, as in reality the last of the great magician's
works ; and that in the sage Prospero, holding nature in
all her most mysterious attributes subject to his will,
yet on the very eve of yielding up this sway, the poet
unconsciously pictured himself. In the plenitude of
his power, with all his wondrous genius at command, he
wrought this exquisite work of art ; and that done, the
wizard staff was broken, and silence displaced the
heavenly music it had wrought. It is not of moment
for our purposed criticism that this should be proved.
It suffices that the work in question is universally acknowledged as one peculiarly inspired with the poetry
of nature and the creative power of genius. The scene
of this remarkable drama is laid on a nameless island ;
the actors are beings of air and of earth ; but pre-
eminently for us, the island has a being of its own,
native-born, its sole aboriginal inhabitant :—

> ' Then was this island—
> Save for the son that she did litter here,
> A freckled whelp, hag-born,—not honour'd with
> A human shape.'

The poor monster—sole lord of his nameless island in an unknown sea,—has excited mingled feelings of wonder, admiration, and disgust. But the latter feeling must be transient with all but the superficial student. With truer appreciation, Franz Horn has said : ' In spite of his imperfect, brutish, half-human nature, Caliban is something marvellously exciting, and as pretender to the sovereignty of the island ridiculously sublime. He is inimitable as a creation of the most powerful poetic fancy ; and the longer the character is studied the more marvellous does it appear.' It is by reason of this imperfect, brutish, half-human nature, that Caliban anew invites our study, in relation to disclosures of science undreamt of in that age which witnessed his marvellous birth.

The idea of beings, monstrous and brutal in every physical characteristic, and yet in some not clearly defined sense human, as the inhabitants of strange lands, was familiar not only in Shakespeare's day but long before. Medieval chroniclers describe the Huns who ravaged Germany, Italy, and France in the ninth and tenth centuries, as hideous, boar-tusked, child-devouring ogres ; and after somewhat the same type, Marco Polo represents the Andaman Islanders as ' a most brutish, savage race, having heads, eyes, and teeth resembling those of the canine species : ' cruel cannibals who ate human flesh raw, and devoured every one on whom they could lay their hands. Yet after all, much of this was only an exaggeration of the actual savage, such as he is to be met with even in our own day.

An older English writer, the famous traveller, Sir John Mandeville, who commenced his wanderings in 1322, tells how he had ' ben long tyme over the see, and seyn and gon thorgh manye dyverse londes, and many provynces and kyngdomes and iles: where dwellen many dyverse folk, and of dyverse maneres and lawes, and of dyverse schappes of men ; of whiche I shalle speke more pleynly hereafter.' And so he accordingly does: telling, for example, of 'the land of Bacharie, where be full evil folk and full cruel. In that country been many Ipotaynes, that dwell sometimes in the water and sometimes on the land : half-man and half-horse, and they eat men when they may take them.' Besides these, he also describes the griffons of the same country, half-eagle, half-lion, but so large that they carry off a horse or couple of oxen to their nest ; in proof of which Mandeville tells us, the griffon's talons are as big as great oxen's horns, 'so that men maken cuppes of hem to drynken of.' No doubt Milton had Mandeville's griffon in view when he compared the fiend to this monster, as he laboriously winged his way up from the nethermost abyss of Hell.

Of the like travellers' tales of more modern date, there will be occasion to speak by and by. The classification of men by the naturalists of Mandeville's and Marco Polo's days, was into Christians and infidels ; and it seemed then not only natural, but most logical, to conceive of the latter as of betusked ogres, hippocentaurs, or any other monstrous half-brutish and wholly devilish humanity. But a different ideal of imperfect transitional human beings originated at a later date in the very natural exaggerations of gorilla, chimpanzee, or orang, as first seen or reported of in their native haunts.

If 'The Tempest' was indeed the latest production of Shakespeare's pen, then the date of that most amusing old book of travels, 'Purchas his Pilgrimage,' closely corresponds in point of time with its appearance on the

English stage. Published in 1613, that is within less
than three years before Shakespeare's death, its author
embodies among its miscellaneous contents, the story
of his friend, Andrew Battle, who while a serjeant in the
service of the Portugese, in the kingdom of Congo, on
quarrelling with his masters fled to the woods, where he
lived eight or nine months; and there he saw 'a kinde
of great apes, if they might be so termed, of the height
of a man, but twice as bigge in feature of their limmes,
with strength proportionable, hairie all over, otherwise
altogether like men and women in their whole bodily
shape.' At a later date Purchas described more
minutely the pongo, a huge brute-man, sleeping in the
trees, building a roof to shelter himself from the rain,
and living wholly on fruits and nuts. 'They cannot
speake,' he says, 'and have no understanding more than
a beast. The people of the countrie, when they travail
in the woods, make fires where they sleepe in the night;
and in the morning, when they are gone, the pongoes
will come and sit about the fire till it goeth out; for
they have no understanding to lay the wood together.'

This may suffice to illustrate the 'wild men' who,
with greater or less exaggeration, figure in the traveller's
tales of the seventeenth and eighteenth centuries. They
attract us now with a fresh interest, when we are being
taught by novel inductions of science to look, in recent
or tertiary life, for some such link between the lowest
type of savage man and the highest of the anthropomorpha. In truth we have the best scientific authority
for affirming that the differences between man and the
chimpanzee, according to all recognised physical tests,
are much less than those which separate that anthropoid
ape from lower quadrumana. So much less indeed are
they, that, compared limb with limb and brain with

brain, the result may well raise a doubt as to the fitness of a test which admits of such close affinities physically, and such enormous diversities morally and intellectually. If, however, man is but this ' quintessence of dust,' 'the paragon of animals,' estimable in utmost requisite comprehensibility by the test of physical structure, then it is well that all should learn to

> ' Admire such wisdom in an earthly shape,
> And show a Newton as we show an ape.'

Linnæus indeed, with intuitive foresight anticipating modern naturalists, long hesitated whether to rank the chimpanzee as a second species of the genus *Homo*, or as first among apes. But the Swedish naturalist could not speak from personal observation; and indeed placed too implicit faith in the exaggerated, if not wholly fabulous accounts of a female animal of human proportions and pleasing features, but covered with hair, the *Orang outang, sive Homo Sylvestris*, as furnished by Bontius and later writers. But there is a long step between the classificatory idea of Linnæus and the modern doctrine of the Descent of Man. To recognise that man and the ape are both animals, and so to determine their classification in the same animal kingdom solely by means of physical tests on which the whole system is based, is one thing; to assume that man is but the latest phase of development in a progressive scale of evolution, of which the ape is an earlier stage, is the other and more startling affirmation which is permeating the minds of the present generation of thinkers, and revolutionising the science of the nineteenth century.

With cautious reticence, the author of 'The Origin of Species by means of Natural Selection' continued to

C

accumulate evidence as to the origin or descent of man, while freely communicating to the world all other proofs leading up, as he conceives, to that end. He not only hesitated to startle and prejudice his readers against the novel system as a whole, by publishing what nevertheless seemed to him the inevitable deduction from his general views, but he had determined to withhold that crowning result of his research. Yet as he had indicated in no obscure fashion, in his earlier work, that man must be included with all other beings in the new theory of the origin of species : no wonder that his disciples hastened to break through prudential restraints, and proclaim in undisguised simplicity the doctrine of affinities and genealogy, by which we are taught to conceive of a remote marine group of hermaphrodites diverging into two great branches, the one in retrograde descent producing the present class of Ascidians, hardly recognisable as animals ; the other giving birth to the vertebrata, and so to man himself.

Of the latest ramifications in this genealogical tree, its discoverer tells us, 'there can hardly be a doubt that man is an offshoot from the old-world simian stem ; and that, under a genealogical point of view, he must be classed with the catarhine division,' or old-world monkeys, with their more human-like nostrils, dentition, and other minor characteristics. 'If,' continues Mr. Darwin, 'the anthropomorphous apes be admitted to form a natural sub-group, then as man agrees with them, not only in all those characters which he possesses in common with the whole catarhine group, but in other peculiar characters, such as the absence of a tail, and of callosities, and in general appearance, we may infer that some ancient member of the anthropomorphous sub-group gave birth to man.' And he adds

thus further : 'No doubt man, in comparison with most
of his allies, has undergone an extraordinary amount of
modification, chiefly in consequence of his greatly-
developed brain and erect position : nevertheless, we
should bear in mind that he is but one of several exceptional forms of primates.'

The extremely remote progenitor of man was thus a
catarhine monkey, probably dwelling in those African
regions which were formerly inhabited by extinct apes
closely allied to the gorilla and chimpanzee. As, however, the Dryopithecus of Lartet, an ape nearly as large
as a man, and closely allied to the anthropomorphous
Hylobates, existed in Europe during the Upper Miocene
period, when oceans of the present time were solid land,
and continents of our present globe were buried below
long-extinct oceans, we can very vaguely surmise as to
the locality which, under the assumed process of evolution, gave birth to our progenitor.

But while the wanderings of the world's gray fathers
in such inconceivably remote and dark ages are hard to
trace, their forms reveal themselves with no vague
uncertainty to the scientific seer. 'The early progenitors of man,' says Mr. Darwin, 'were *no doubt* once
covered with hair, both sexes having beards : their ears
were pointed and capable of movement, and their bodies
were provided with a tail having the proper muscles.'
They had numerous other characteristics normally
present in living quadrumana, but now not ordinarily to
be looked for in man. But of this also Mr. Darwin
speaks as beyond doubt, that our progenitors were
arboreal in their habits, frequenting some warm, forest-
clad land ; and the males provided with great canine
teeth, which served as formidable weapons for assault
and defence.

The being which thus rises in clear vision to the mind's eye as the product of this theory of evolution, is not man, but only man's progenitor. He is still irrational and dumb, or at best only entering on the threshold of that transitional stage of anthropomorphism which is to transform him into the rational being endowed with speech. To the author of 'The Descent of Man,' however, it does not appear altogether incredible that some unusually wise ape-like animal should have thought of imitating the growl of a beast of prey, so as to indicate to his fellow-monkeys the nature of the expected danger; and so, with forethought and reasoning thus fairly at work, and even perhaps a benevolent regard for the interests of his weaker and less-experienced fellow-monkeys,—which would indicate something of a moral sense already present,—the first step is taken in the formation of a language for the coming man.

To all appearance, the further process in the assumed descent—or, as we might more fitly call it here, the ascent,—of man from the purely animal to the rational and intellectual stage, is but a question of brain development; and this cerebral growth is the assigned source of the manward progress : not a result of any functional harmonising of mind and brain. Man as compared with the anthropomorphous apes has 'undergone an extraordinary amount of modification, *chiefly in consequence of his greatly developed brain.*' It is difficult to dissociate from such an idea the further conclusion, that reason and mind are no more than the action of the enlarged brain ; yet this is not necessarily implied. The mind must communicate with the outer world by the senses; and within those gateways of knowledge must lie a brain of adequate compass to receive and turn to account the impressions conveyed to it. The brain is certainly the organ of reasoning, the vital instrument through which the mind acts ; but it need not therefore be assumed that brain and mind are one. The microcephalic idiot may have dormant mental powers only requiring an adequate organisation for rational activity. The imprisoned soul may be only awaiting the emancipation of death to enter upon its true life.

In the deductions based on comparative anatomy, cerebral bulk and structure have necessarily played an important part. The more carefully the human brain has been compared with those of the anthropomorpha, the tendency has been to diminish the distinctive features, apart from absolute size. The brain of man, in a healthy, normal state, ranges from one hundred and fifteen to fifty-five cubic inches. The lowest of these numbers is, therefore, the point of comparison with the most highly developed brute. Midway between it and the highest cerebral development of the latter, lies the intermediate, hypothetical 'man's progenitor,' the Caliban of Science. In the gorilla, according to the trustworthy authority of Professor Huxley, the volume of brain rises to nearly thirty-five cubic inches; the human brain at its lowest is fifty-five. Twenty cubic inches, therefore, is the whole interval to be bridged over. Yet narrow as it seems, on one side of this gulf is the irrational ape, on the other side is man.

This brain-test has been made the subject of much controversy and of very conflicting opinions. Professor Owen sought to make it the basis of a system of classification, in which, by means of cerebral characteristics, he assigned to the genus *Homo* not merely a distinct order, but a sub-class of the mammalia, to which he gave the name *Archencephala*. But the assumed differences, otherwise than in actual volume, have been nearly all rejected by some of the highest authorities in comparative anatomy. As to mere bulk, the volume of brain, of the gorilla, for example, must be regarded relatively to the size of the animal ; but in all most notable characteristics we have the authority of Professor Huxley for asserting that 'the brain of man differs far less from that of the chimpanzee than that of the latter does from the pig's brain.'

The essential difference between man and the ape, then, as tested by the brain, chiefly rests on superiority in relative size; and the process of transition in this respect is mainly, if not entirely, one of growth. But the most ancient human crania hitherto recovered, such as that from the Engis Cave, near Liége, and the most degraded types, approximating in any considerable degree to an ape-like form, as the Neanderthal skull, betray no corresponding diminution of cerebral mass. The latter is described by Mr. Busk as 'the most brutal of all known human skulls, resembling those of the apes not only in the prodigious development of the superciliary prominences, and the forward extension of the orbits, but still more in the depressed form of the brain-case, in the straightness of the squamosal suture, and in the complete retreat of the occiput forward and upward, from the superior occipital ridges.' This skull, however, has no such antiquity as can give it any legitimate claim to rank as the transitional brute-man ; while its cerebral capacity is estimated at seventy-five cubic inches. So far, therefore, as the mass of brain is concerned, it exceeds that of many living savages, and of not a few Europeans. The fossil remains of man hitherto recovered are assigned to no older deposits than those of the Later Tertiary, or the Quaternary period,

or contemporary with animals of the post-glacial epoch.
Remote as those are, according to all ordinary esti-
mates of the antiquity of man, their disclosures are acknowledged to lend little countenance to the doctrine
of progressive development from lower simian forms ;
and the evolutionist now relegates his hypothetical
evidence of man's brute progenitor to geological ages
even more removed from the glacial epoch than that
is from our own. Sir Charles Lyell has expressed his
belief in the probable recovery of human remains in
the Pliocene strata ; but there he pauses. In the Miocene
period, he conceives, ' had some other rational being
representing man then flourished, some signs of his existence could hardly have escaped unnoticed, in the shape of
implements of stone and metal, more frequent and more
durable than the osseous remains of any of the mammalia.' But Sir John Lubbock will by no means allow
the line to be so drawn. ' If,' he says, ' man constitutes
a separate family of mammalia, as he does in the opinion
of the highest authorities, then, according to all palæon-
tological analogies, he must have had representatives in
Miocene times. We need not, however, expect to find
the proofs in Europe ; our nearest relatives in the
animal kingdom are confined to hot, almost tropical
climates, and it is in such countries that we must look
for the earliest traces of the human race.' There, accordingly, the expectant palæontologist anticipates the discovery of the Caliban of evolution, whose fossil skeleton,
of strange unperfected humanity, with intermediate
cerebral development between ape and man, may yet
displace the Guadeloupe slab, and claim the place of
honour among the choicest treasures of the British
Museum.

But the brain, to which we as definitely assign the

work of thinking and reasoning, as to the eye that of seeing, and to the ear that of hearing—or, more strictly, of conveying the impressions of sight and hearing to the brain, and so to the mind,—seems to fail us as any guide or key to an evolutionary classification. When we turn to the variations in the lower forms of animal life, the relative volume of brain furnishes no index of the enormous contrast ultimately ascribed to its full development. The brain of the orang and chimpanzee is about twenty-six inches in volume, or half the minimum size assigned to the normal human brain. That of the gibbon and baboon is still less; while, on the other hand, in the gorilla, as already shown, the volume of brain rises to nearly thirty-five cubic inches ; or, in other words, between the brain of the orang or chimpanzee and that of the gorilla there is nearly half the difference by which, according to this cerebral test, the latter is separated from man. The capacity of fifty-five cubic inches as the lowest normal human brain is that assigned by Professor Huxley, while thirty-five cubic inches is the volume of brain in the gorilla. In cranial characteristics, as well as in dentition, and in the proportional size of the arms, the chimpanzee is liker man than the gorilla ; and in certain special cerebral details, and especially in the form of the cerebral hemispheres, as well as in other less important elements of structure, the orang still more nearly resembles man. But in point of cerebral volume, the gorilla approaches him by nearly half the difference between the two, as compared with that which distinguishes it from the chimpanzee or orang. Man thus stands in relation to the gorilla as fifty-five to thirty-five. Between the brain of the gorilla and that of the chimpanzee or orang there is nearly half this difference in its favour : thirty-five to twenty-six cubic inches. Yet we look in vain for corresponding traces of augmented intelligence or approximation to reason. But, as water at two hundred and twelve degrees suddenly passes beyond the boiling point into vapour: so at some undetermined degree in this cerebral scale, between thirty-five and fifty-five, the point is reached at which the irrational brute flashes into the living soul.

If the premises can be accepted, the results follow by very simple evolution. Given the requisite brain-development; and, if mental power, reason, moral sense, language, and all else that makes man man, are but products of the larger brain : then the process by which the ape grew 'unusually wise,' and the next step, and all subsequent steps by which it passed into the so-called 'progenitor of man,' and so onward to man himself, are conceivable. The mere fact indeed of being hairy, having ears pointed and capable of motion, or even being provided with a tail and every caudal muscle, need no more conflict with the idea of a reasoning reflecting being endowed with speech, than the flattened nose, prognathous jaws, oblique pelvis, or any other known approximation to types of degradation.

It is pleasant to associate the noble presence of Shakespeare with his matchless drama ; yet physical beauty is no needful complement of intellectual power. Socrates was none the less fitted to be the master of Plato, though his ungainly features and disproportioned body suggested the ideal satyr, and made him the butt of Aristophanes on the Athenian comic stage. But the hairy covering, the prognathous jaws and formidable canine teeth, with all else that pertain to the true brute, are no deformities so long as they are the indices of functions essential to the well-being of the animal. What we do recognise is, on the one hand,

the irrational creature naturally provided with clothing,
—hairy, woolly, feathery, or the like,—armed and furnished in its own structure with every needful tool;
and endowed with the requisite weaving, cell-making,
mining, nest-building instincts, independent of all instruction, experience, or accumulated knowledge. On
the other hand is Man, naked, unarmed, unprovided
with tools, naturally the most helpless, defenceless of
animals; but, by means of his reason, clothing, arming,
housing himself, and assuming the mastery over the
whole irrational creation, as well as over inanimate
nature. With the aid of fire he can adapt not only
the products but the climates of the most widely
severed latitudes to his requirements. He cooks, and
the ample range of animal and vegetable life in every
climate yields him wholesome nutriment. Wood, bone,
flint, shells, stone, and at length the native and wrought
metals, arm him, furnish him with tools,—with steam-
ships, railroads, telegraphic cables. He is lord of all
this nether world.

Is this being really no more than the latest development of the other? Is there not still a missing
link, forged though it has seemed to be by the
creative fancy of the scientific speculator? It is not
merely that intermediate transitional forms are wanting:
the far greater difficulty remains, by any legitimate
process of induction to realise that evolution which
consistently links by natural gradation the brute in
absolute subjection to the laws of matter, and the
rational being ruling over animate and inanimate
nature by force of intellect. Very true it may be, as
Mr. Darwin says, that 'if man had not been his own
classifier, he would never have thought of founding a
separate order for his own reception.' That is to say,

the irrational classifier would necessarily have excluded
the unknown element of reason as a basis of classification. But does this not amount to the very fact
that man does stand apart, as the only reasoning,
intelligent, classifying animal ? He is conscious of an
element peculiar to himself, distinguishing him, not
in degree, but radically, from the very wisest of apes.
The reasoning faculty—whether it be the mere large
brain-power, or something as essentially distinct as that
which 'smiles at the drawn dagger and defies its
point,'—lies beyond the ken of any such anthropoid
classifier. Yet reason may, on that very account, be
a more distinctive element than hand, foot, pelvis,
vertebræ, brain, or any other structural characteristic.

As the metaphysician appears at times to become
sceptical as to the very existence of matter, so a too
exclusive devotion to physical science is apt even more
to remove the metaphysical and psychical beyond all
practical recognition in the reasonings of the physicist.
Hence the spiritual element in man seems to dwindle
into insignificance in the argument of the evolutionists. There is an unconscious evasion of the real
difficulty in their conception of a transitional half-
brute, half-man ; an illusive literalness, like the fancy
of Milton, when from the Earth's fertile womb

> 'Now half appeared
> The tawny lion, pawing to get free
> His hinder parts.'

The difficulty is not to conceive of the transitional
form, but of the transitional mind. After all has been
most strongly dwelt upon which seems to degrade the
brutified Australian Bushman, Andaman Islander, or
other lowest type of human savage, he is still human.
It can with no propriety be said of him that he

has only doubtfully attained to the rank of manhood. The ape, caught young, may be taught some very notable tricks. The young savage, whenever he has been subjected to adequate training, has shown a fair capacity, at the least, for such intellectual culture as is familiar to the English peasant. The savage is in no transitional stage. The mental faculties are dormant, not undeveloped. The active energies of his mind are expended in dealing with the exigencies of life. Take the Patagonian, the Red Indian, or the Esquimaux : his whole energies are exhausted in providing the means of existence. If his exertions are remitted he pays the forfeit with his life. So is it with the Australian. Intellect is the means with which he fights the battle of life. The ingenuity shown in all needful arts is great : in his bags, baskets, nets for fishing and bird-catching, his spear and boomerang. Nor is even his æsthetic faculty to be despised. The ornamentation of his weapons is tasteful and elaborate, while the carvings on rocks, of animate and inanimate forms in considerable detail, are far from contemptible. Moreover these latter are by no means mere products of idle pastime. Like the corresponding gravings of the American savage, they embody the rudiments of written language, the first stage of that ideography through which the hieroglyphics of Egypt passed into the true phonetics of Phœnician and Greek, Roman and English alphabets.

After all the minuteness of modern research, then, into the degradation of the savage, he is still no less man than ourselves. We are struck with wonder at any manifestation of half-reasoning sagacity or inherited instinctive ingenuity in the dog, the horse, the elephant, or the ape, because we judge of it from the standard of an irrational brute. But the infant, even of the savage, ere it has completed its third year, does daily and hourly, without attracting notice, what surpasses every marvel of the 'half-reasoning' elephant or dog. In truth, the difference between the Australian savage and a Shakespeare or a Newton is trifling, compared with the unbridged gulf which separates him from the very wisest of dogs or apes.

So far then it would seem, that not one but many links are missing between man and his nearest anthropoid fellow-creature. Moreover, the deduction is by no means settled beyond all question which assumes the Australian Bushman, or other savage, as the lowest, and therefore the earliest existing type in an ascending scale of humanity; still less is it an indisputable assumption that they furnish in any sense illustrations of man in a state of nature. The gorilla or other wild animal in his native arboreal retreat is thoroughly natural and at home. He is there the perfect gorilla. His long, black, glossy fur is in beautiful condition. His whole physical state is one of cleanly, healthful consistency with all the natural functions of his being. He is incapable of moral wrong; and in every relationship that binds him to his species he fulfils the duties of life unerringly. 'Our early semi-human progenitors,' says Darwin, 'would not have practised infanticide, for the instincts of the lower animals are never so perverted as to lead them regularly to destroy their own offspring.' Are we not then guilty of gross injustice when we speak of the savage as brutish? His is a degraded and abject humanity the farthest removed from the brutes. Man is most like the healthy well-conditioned wild animal, when seen in a state of civilisation: well-housed, cleanly, and in all virtuous obedience to the laws of nature, alike personally and in every social relation. It is not more reasonable to speak of those savages of civilisation, the city Arab or Bohemian, as in a state of nature, than of the filthy, unnaturally licentious, morally abject savage. If that is the state of nature for the brute in which it is found perfect in form, in fur, or plumage, fulfilling the ends of life in healthful accordance with every natural instinct, then savage man, regarded as an animal, is in no such state. On the contrary, he exhibits just such an abnormal deterioration from his true condition as is consistent with the perverted free-will of the rational free agent that he is. He is controlled by motives and impulses radically diverse from any brute instinct. This very capacity for moral degradation is one of the distinctions which separate man, by a no less impassable barrier than his latent aptitude for highest intellectual development, from all other living creatures. 'A beast, that wants discourse of reason,' is Shakespeare's idea of the inferior animal, when in his ' Hamlet ' he would contrast it with the unnatural conduct of rational man.

If this view of the perfectly developed brute in a state of nature, and of man in conditions which seem no less natural to him as a being so diversely endowed, be correct, then we start with a fallacy when we compare degraded man with the matured lower animal. The points of seeming resemblance have no relation as links of a common descent. On the contrary, they have converged from opposite directions, and deceive us : just as the idiot, who is unquestionably a product of degradation, might be mistaken for the manward stage of progression of the ape. We have first to determine what is the nature of man before we can say what is a state of nature for him. But is it not an assumption of the major premiss to assert that he is but a developed brute, and therefore that which is a state of nature for the one must be so for the other?

On any theory of evolution which assumes the savage to be the lowest surviving type of man as a link in the progressive stages of development of the brute into a rational being, the first manifestations of reason, while they blunt the pure instincts, would seem to result in a perverted moral sense, antagonistic to all the healthful instincts of its nature. Instinct is a safe guide to the brute, reason supplants it to the advantage of man; but how to conceive of a survival of the fittest among those 'semi-human progenitors' in the hybrid condition, with passions emancipated from the restraint of half-obliterated instincts, and uncontrolled by the glimmering reason, is the difficult problem of the new science. We must look elsewhere than in the kraal or lair of the Australian or Borneo savage, if we would forge anew the missing link between man and his nearest fellow-creatures: that intermediate brute-man which, on any theory of evolution, must have actually existed in some early stage of the world. We have to conceive, if we can, of a being superior to the very wisest of our simian fellow-creatures in every reasoning power short of rationality; but inferior to the most anthropoid ape in all those natural provisions for covering, defence, and subsistence, which are the substitutes for that reasoning foresight and inherited knowledge on which the naked defenceless savage relies. Why, on any theory of survival of the fittest, of natural, or of sexual selection, we should find the Fuegian or the Esquimaux naked descendants of progenitors naturally clothed with fur, becomes all the more incomprehensible if any significance is to be attached to the observation of Agassiz, that the boundaries of distinct species and genera of mammals on the earth's surface coincide with the natural range of distinct types of man. If so, we should expect to find arctic man not less amply provided than the polar bear with a natural covering so indispensable to his native habitat.

But, though the difficulty here suggested is one which must have occurred to many minds, it is not the half-human form of man's brute progenitor that puzzles the imagination. Fancy has long familiarised itself with sylvan fauns and satyrs, as with centaurs, mermaids, werwolves, and the like intermediate beings. It is the half-human intellect which is most difficult to realise : not the dormant reasoning faculties of the savage, but the undeveloped or partially developed rationality of a being that has ceased to be a brute, but has yet to become a man. Mr. Darwin, with that candour which has won for him the confidence of many a reluctant student, remarks that the difference of man in respect to his mental power, from all other animals ' is enormous, even if we compare the mind of one of the lowest savages, who has no words to express any number higher than four, and who uses no abstract terms for the commonest objects or affections, with that of the most highly organised ape. The difference would, no doubt, still remain immense, even if one of the higher apes had been improved or civilised as much as a dog has been in comparison with its parent form, the wolf or jackal. The Fuegians rank among the lowest barbarians ; but I was continually struck with surprise how closely the three natives on board of H.M.S. "Beagle," who had lived some years in England, and could talk a little English, resembled us in disposition, and in most of our mental faculties.' The same idea impressed myself when camping out on the north shore of Lake Superior with Red Indian guides, who had come from beyond the Saskatchewan to trade their furs. The mental faculties of the Red Indian savage are dormant, not absent. He manifests, after some brief intercourse, a wonderful aptitude for conforming in many ways to his civilised associates ; and much of the silent impassive stoicism of the Indian disappears,—turns out, indeed, to be no ethnical characteristic or native instinct, but an acquired habit. He is, in truth, as inquisitive as a child.

Starting, then, from the assumed brute-progenitor of man, we are to suppose, it may be presumed, that the brain went on growing, and with it the various mental faculties forming, until the transitional being acquired craft enough to outmatch all the mere physical force or instinctive wiles of its inferior fellow-creatures. But simultaneously with this approximation to man in cerebral development, we are also to assume that the huge jaws and great canine teeth became reduced in size, and all other brute-like attributes and powers declined. The arboreal haunts of the frugivorous or carnivorous anthropoid were forsaken. The prehensile powers of the foot were exchanged for the firmer tread by means of which the weighty brain-mass is thenceforth to rest on the summit of the upright spinal column. He has learned to walk erect. His hands are thenceforth free for all ingenious and artistic manipulation which the growing brain may suggest ; but with increasing delicacy of action and sense of touch, they lose in a corresponding degree an excess of mere muscular power. Reason is to be of more account than physical force. Nor is it to be assumed that the evolution is even now complete, or that man has attained to finality as such; and so may hold himself ready for that next stage, or

D

fifth order of existence, which, according to the author of the ' Religio Medici,' is to make him superhuman : a creature not of the world, but of the universe. Evolution is progressive as ever, though it moves in a new direction. The brain is now to be brought into ever-increasing activity, with corresponding developments, until Shakespeares and Newtons shall be, not the exceptions, but the rule. This evolutionary being has thus, in a distant future, still higher destinies awaiting him, as the summit of the organic scale ; yet he is to bear to the last in his bodily frame the indelible stamp of his lowly origin.

But in this process of exchanging native instincts and weapons, strength of muscle and natural clothing, for the compensating intellect, the transmuted brute must have reached a stage in which it was inferior in intellect to the very lowest existing savages, and in brute force to the lower animals. This is the being most difficult to realise, or to find an Eden for him, where, under any favouring circumstances, he could survive the latest stages of his marvellous transformation. That gulf bridged over by the sheltering aid of some mild insulated region and every favouring circumstance for the maturing and survival of a being dependent on such novel conditions, we have man's progenitor fairly started on his anthropomorphous course. With progressive cerebral growth, and a corresponding development of mental activity, a· brain-power results capable of carrying on continuous trains of thought, and so tracing results to their causes. Hence experience, selfish caution, prudential motives, sympathetic feelings : until at length there results the moral sense, a recognition of the distinction between right and wrong, a possibility of conceiving of moral responsibility, and so of God. The brute has become man.

To realise for ourselves this strangely-evolved being, we have to think of something with greatly more of the healthy natural instincts of animal life than pertain to the degraded savage. Nevertheless the supreme difficulties lie in the earlier stages, which, on this hypothesis, are already past. Nature could now proceed freely with that last stage, in which the transformed brute dispensed with any remaining traces of natural clothing, nails or claws, teeth, and other offensive or defensive weapons : and so leave him to the novel resources, by means of which he is to become the tool-making, fire-using, cooking, clothing animal ; to make for himself houses, boats, implements, weapons ; to wander abroad with new capacities for adapting himself to all climates ; until, from being the most helpless and limited in range of the higher animals, he assumes his rightful dominion over all : the one cosmopolitan to whom every living thing is subject.

Had such an hypothesis of evolution been entertained in the sixteenth or the seventeenth century, it would have been vain to presume that the being, transitional alike in form and mind, which it presupposes, might not then exist in some unexplored region of the world. Now, however, such an idea cannot be entertained. On the contrary the advocates of the theory acknowledge the existence of an enormous and indeed ever-widening break in the organic chain between man and his nearest allies, which cannot be relinked by any living or extinct species.

The most brutish of human savages holds out no acknowledgment of near affinity to the most anthropoid of apes ; and imagination is left to work its will in realising the intermediate being, midway between the two, in which the brute came to an end and man began.

To the evolutionist, the whole process by which such a change is assumed to have resulted seems so easy that he slights, if he does not wholly pass over, this final transitional stage, unconscious of the difficulties pressing on minds not less earnestly awakened to the reception of novel truths. To the inquirer who still acknowledges a natural repugnance to the acceptance of a law of progress which makes man no more than a highly developed ape, it is difficult to give the imagination fair play in whatever share it should take in the solution of the problem. Yet imagination has its legitimate work to perform. In the grand discoveries of science, the conceiving imagination, which 'darts the soul into the dawning plan,' and realises beforehand what is to be proved by severest induction, plays a part no less important than in the work of the poet. But happily at this stage we are enabled to summon to our aid the most original and creative fancy to realise for us the large-brained, half-reasoning brute, with some capacity for continuous thought and the accumulations of experience, but as yet devoid of moral sense, and so actuated solely by animal cravings and passions.

Such a creature, it is admitted by the evolutionist, required very peculiar and exceptional circumstances to allow of its perpetuation. On any theory of the survival of the fittest it is difficult to deal with a being inferior in intellect, and probably in social disposition, to the lowest existing savages; and at the same time inferior in brute-like powers, in the offensive or defensive weapons of nature, in the prehensile aptitude for climbing trees, in natural clothing, in all means of escape from danger or violence incident to its condition. But the peculiar circumstances which can alone give it the chance of survival are hypothetically found for it in an imaginary island of the cainozoic world, warm and genial in climate, furnished with abundance of suitable food, and free from all special dangers. If Plato may have freest scope with his Atlantis, More with his Utopia, and Swift with his Laputa, it would be hard to stint our modern philosophers in the furnishing of their more ancient island with all needful requisites for a commonwealth on which the very existence of every subsequent one is believed by them to depend.

The genial protection of an island-home may well suggest itself to the race which owes so much to the protective insulation of Britain. In far-off palæolithic ages, when its manufacturing energies were exhausted on the flint and bone implements of the Drift-Folk, it was a bit of the neighbouring continent, and had its troubles accordingly, with cave-tigers, cave-bears, and other devouring monsters, such as must have been wholly unknown to that happy island-home of the ape-progenitor of man, when in his latest evolutionary stage. Britain was made and unmade, so far as its insular autonomy is concerned, during the post-Pliocene period. It had been reunited to the continent, after a lengthened period of insulation, when man coexisted with the mammoth, and the Thames is believed to have been a tributary of the Rhine. But happily its tributary eras lie far off and obscure ; and through all its latest and best stages of ethnical and historical evolution its occupants may well

> ' Thank Him who isled us here, and roughly set
> His Saxon in blown seas and storming showers.'

Here, in one of England's pleasantest vales, in the year 1564, and in an age in which the moral and intellectual energies of the human race were manifesting themselves with peculiar force throughout the civilised world,

Shakespeare was born ; and he, before the close of his too brief career, dealt with the very conception which now seems so difficult to realise, and, untrammelled alike by Darwinian theories or anti-Darwinian prejudices, gave the 'airy nothing a local habitation and a name.'

CHAPTER III.

CALIBAN'S ISLAND.

'Antonio. What impossible matter will he make easy next?
Sebastian. I think he will carry this island home in his pocket, and give it his son for an apple.
Antonio. And sowing the kernels of it in the sea, bring forth more islands.'—*The Tempest.*

THE idea of an island-world lying in some unexplored ocean, beyond the influences that affect humanity at large, with its native beings, institutions, its civilisation, and a history of its own, has been the dream of very diverse ages, and the fancy of very dissimilar minds. It seems far from improbable, that in early unrecorded centuries, when, nevertheless, voyagers of the Mediterranean claimed to have circumnavigated the coasts of Africa, the world beyond the western ocean was not unknown to them. Vague intimations, derived seemingly from Egypt, encouraged the belief in a submerged island or continent, once the seat of arts and learning, far on the Atlantic main. The most definite narrative of this lost continent is that recorded in the 'Timæus' of Plato, on the authority of an older account which Solon is affirmed to have received from an Egyptian priest. The narrative is not without an air of truthfulness, when read in the light of modern geographical and geological disclosures. The priest of the Nile claims for the temple-records of Egypt a vast antiquity, and tells the Athenian lawgiver that his people are mere children, their histories but nursery tales. In fables and vague traditions of the Greeks, faint memories had survived of deluges and convulsions by which the earth had been revolutionised in ages long prior to their historical records. In one of those the vast island of Atlantis—a continent larger than Lybia and Asia conjoined,—had been ingulfed in the ocean which bears its name.

Whether the idea was a mere fancy of the first Egyptian narrator, or an allusion to transatlantic islands and continents with which communication had been held in some earlier age, it pleased the poets and philosophers of antiquity ; and frequent references occur in Greek and Roman authors to the lost Atlantis. But above all, this oceanic world of fancy or tradition has a special interest as the seat of Plato's imaginary commonwealth ; while it acquired a new significance when Columbus revealed what actually lay beyond that mysterious ocean in which the Hesperides and other mythological islands of antiquity had been placed by the poets.

When the geologist in our own day proceeds to define the physical geography of Europe in that strange glacial period when the British Islands were conjoined to a continent which then existed in a condition analogous to the Arctic wastes of Greenland at the present time, he deals with revelations of science which outvie the legends of the old Nile, and restores a lost Atlantis to us, peopled with its extinct fauna, and on which man also appears, furnished with strange weapons and primeval arts. In the sober literalness of scientific induction, the chorographer far outrivals the fables of antique mythology, and undertakes to furnish, from well-accredited data, an ideal restoration of continents and islands as they existed when the *Elephas Meridionalis*, or huge pachyderm, older than the mammoth, roamed in their forests ; or of that island which was neither

Ireland nor England, though it included much of both, over which the *Megaceros*, or gigantic deer of the Irish bogs, wandered at will ; and the human cave-dwellers of centuries undreamt of in historical chronology, played their unheeded part in the primeval dawn. Remoter, however, than that submerged and renewed island-world of prehistoric ages is the birthplace or scene of latest evolution of man's progenitor. It has to be located as yet with the Atlantis of Plato and the Utopia of More, in some unexplored ocean of unimaginably remote eras. But who shall venture to say that it lies beyond the compass of science in the triumphs of the coming time?

Already the first steps have been indicated whereby the explorer is to pursue his way towards that undetermined birthplace of man, at that stage of the pedigree where our progenitors diverged from that selected catarhine division of the Simiadæ, the determination of which robs the western world of all claim to the primeval Atlantis. The fact that the Simian progenitors of man belonged to this stock clearly shows, according to its demonstrator, that they inhabited the old world ; but, Mr. Darwin adds, 'not Australia, nor any oceanic island, as we may infer from the laws of geographical distribution. In each great region of the world the living mammals are closely related to the extinct species of the same region. It is therefore probable that Africa was formerly inhabited by extinct apes closely allied to the gorilla and chimpanzee; and as these two species are now man's nearest allies, it is somewhat more probable that our early progenitors lived on the African continent than elsewhere.' When, however, Mr. Darwin is speculating on the immediate Simian ancestry of man, he reflects on the deficiency in the social element of the huge, powerful, ferocious gorilla: whereby the development of such peculiarly human qualities as sympathy, and the love of his fellow-creatures, would be impeded in an improved descendant; and hence he conceives that it may have been no unimportant element in the ampler humanity of the final evolution, that man sprung rather from some comparatively small and weak species like the chimpanzee, but growing ultimately larger and stronger, even while losing such offensive and defensive appliances as pertained to his brute-original. The social element which leads man to give and receive aid, when combined with his tool-making aptitude, more than counterbalances any inferiority in strength to the wild beasts he may have to encounter. The puny Bushman of Africa holds his ground against the fiercest animals of that continent, and the stunted Esquimaux is equally successful in resisting alike the physical hardships and the ravenous monsters of arctic snows. Still Mr. Darwin recognises the peculiar dangers incident to that last semi-human transitional stage. 'The early progenitors of man,' he remarks, 'were, no doubt, inferior in intellect, and probably in social disposition, to the lowest existing savages; but it is quite conceivable that they might have existed, or even flourished, if while they gradually lost their brute-like powers, such as climbing trees, &c., they at the same time advanced in intellect. But granting that the progenitors of man were far more helpless and defenceless than any existing savages, if they had inhabited some warm continent, or large island, such as Australia, or New Guinea, or Borneo, they would not have been exposed to any special danger.'

So says Mr. Darwin, when in search of an earthly

paradise for the brute-progenitor of man. In such an imagined island, with all other conditions favouring, he sees no further impediment to the final elevation of this transitional being to a perfected humanity, 'through the survival of the fittest, combined with the inherited effects of habit.' But such a process, under the most favourable conditions, must be conceived of as one multiplied through countless generations, during which that irrational animal rose by imperceptible degrees into the novel condition of a rational intelligent being.

Though Borneo—still tenanted by the orang,—is selected by Mr. Darwin as an island presenting many such requirements as the early progenitors of man stood in need of, its area is insufficient for some of the necessities of a being so widely diffused within the remotest ascertainable period of his existence. He points rather to an insular Africa as the seat of the catarhine Eden, where the final step in anthropomorphic evolution was effected; yet in this he owns that speculation is striving after what probably lies beyond its reach. The continents of that imagined era, whatever their fauna may have included, lie for the most part among the ruins of an elder geological world, submerged it may be by oceans that have long since upheaved their beds into new land; and the data by means of which the obliterated map may be retraced, have yet to be sought for in their buried strata. But in the map of that other world of fancy over which the genius of Shakespeare reigns supreme, an island may still be found, such as the speculator on man's evolution and long descent craves for his last transitional stage. There the dramatist, for purposes of his own, has anticipated the enormous lapse of time needful for evolving intellect out of such irrational germs, by bringing the rude, speechless, 'freckled whelp,' with its brute-like powers and instincts, into direct contact with intellect in its very highest activity. Humanity is represented as endowed with extraordinary, or even what may for our present purpose be styled miraculous powers; and so the transmutation, for which under any conceivable normal process its originators would deem centuries inadequate, is exhibited as it were under a forcing process, whereby we can study some of its most important gradations as they presented themselves to the most original and objective mind.

The sixteenth century, to which this latter evolutionist belongs, was an age of earnest faith, nor altogether devoid of credulity. To the men of Shakespeare's day, the strange approximations to humanity which we are now called on, in reliance upon severest scientific induction, to realise for ourselves, by no means seemed so improbable as they now do. The new worlds of which Columbus, Amerigo Vespucci, the apocryphal Raphael Hythloday, Gomara, Lane, Harriott and Raleigh wrote, seemed more fitly occupied by Calibans than any ordinary type of humanity. The grotesque tales of monsters, giants, and the like supernatural extravagances, with which Mandeville and other early travellers garnished their narratives, were suited to the expectations, no less than to the taste of much more enlightened ages than theirs. The most incredible news that a Columbus or a Raleigh could have brought back from the New World, would have been the reported existence of men and women, in person, customs, arts, and all else, exactly like themselves. It was in all honesty that Othello entertained Desdemona with the story of his life,—

'Of moving accidents by flood and field,
And of the cannibals that each other eat,
The anthropophagi, and men whose heads
Do grow beneath their shoulders.'

And in like ingenuous simplicity to hear this 'would
Desdemona seriously incline;' for Shakespeare had the
very best authority for such quaint anthropophagi. In
his account of Guiana, Raleigh tells of a nation of
people on the Caoro 'whose heads appear not above
their shoulders, which, though it may be thought a
mere fable, yet,' says the astute Raleigh, 'I am resolved it is true, because every child in the provinces
of Arromaia and Canuri affirms the same. They are
called Ewaipanoma; they are reported to have their
eyes in their shoulders, and their mouths in the middle
of their breasts.' Though all the exertions of Raleigh
to get sight of those marvellous Ewaipanoma, the true
type of antipodes, proved vain, yet he evidently
credited the story. He reverts to it anew in another
place, as a thing in which he fully believed; and when
enumerating the various tribes by which the region is
occupied, he states, as though it were a fact no less
thoroughly authenticated than all else he has to write
about, 'To the west of Caroli are divers nations of
cannibals, and of those Ewaipanoma without heads.'

Mr. Joseph Hunter fancies Prospero's enchanted
island to have been in the Mediterranean; and indeed
the foremost point to be established by his 'Disquisition on Shakespeare's Tempest' is that the island of
Lampedusa, lying midway between Malta and the
African coast, is the veritable Prospero's island. 'It
is precisely in the situation which the circumstances
of every part of the story require. Sailors from
Algiers land Sycorax on its shores; Prospero, sailing
from an Italian port, and beating about at the mercy

of the waves, is found at last with his lovely charge,
at Lampedusa ; Alonzo, sailing from Tunis, and steer-
ing his course for Naples, is driven by a storm a little
out of his track, and lights on Lampedusa.' So writes
Mr. Hunter, with even less doubt about his enchanted
island than Sir Walter Raleigh entertained regarding
the headless Ewaipanoma on the Caoro river of 'the
beautiful empire of Guiana.' It only remains to trace
out Ariel's course to the same island, and then all its
occupants will be accounted for. Nor is this wholly
neglected, for Mr. Hunter gravely notes that 'Lampedusa is in seas where the beautiful phenomenon is
often seen, called by sailors the Querpo Santo, or the
Fires of Saint Helmo. The commentators have told
us that these fires are the fires of Ariel. But the
very name of the island itself, *Lampedusa*, may seem
to be derived, as Fazellus says it is, from flames such
as Ariel's.' The island measures in circuit thirteen
miles and a half, is situated in a stormy sea, abounds
with troglodytic caves, and 'writers worthy of confidence assert that no one can reside in it, on account
of the phantasms, spectres, and horrible visions that
appear in the night : repose and quiet being banished
by the formidable apparitions and frightful dreams
that fatally afflict with deathlike terrors whoever does
remain there so much as one night.' Were it worth
while marshalling evidence to refute all this, the
first witness to be summoned is Caliban himself, who
gives it all the flattest contradiction so far as his
island is concerned. 'Come, swear to that ; kiss the
book,' says Stephano, when he tells him that his mistress, the old witch Sycorax, had shown him the man
in the moon, with his dog and brush. But he tells
him without prompting, that—

'The isle is full of noises,
Sounds and sweet airs that give delight and hurt not;'

and so far from night being made horrible by frightful apparitions, the poor monster found his dreams so
delightful that when he waked he cried to dream
again. Ferdinand, again, might very properly be
called on to explain how it was that, if Lampedusa, a
Mediterranean island, within easy sail of the neighbouring Italian coast, was the actual Prospero's isle,
it should have struck him as so marvellous a thing to
meet a maiden there whose speech was Italian, that
he exclaims in utter astonishment, 'My language!
heavens!' Mr. Hunter does indeed proceed with
other coincidences, to him absolutely extraordinary.
There is on Lampedusa an actual hermit's cell, and
'this cell is surely the origin of the cell of Prospero.'
Again, 'there is a coincidence which would be very
extraordinary if it were merely accidental, between
the chief occupation of Caliban and the labour im-
posed upon Ferdinand, on the one hand, and something which we find belonging to Lampedusa on the
other. Caliban's employment is collecting firewood.
It may be but for the use of Prospero. But Ferdinand
is employed in piling up thousands of logs of wood.'
It only requires, in order to complete the coincidence,
to assume that Duke Prospero drove a brisk trade in
firewood with the Algerine and other sailors; for he
could not possibly want all this huge pile for himself. In reality the task of piling logs, to which
Ferdinand is compelled by Prospero, as a test of
his devotion to Miranda, is just the very work
of which the English adventurers who accompanied
Captain Smith to Virginia, are found making in-
dignant complaint, and adds one more indication to

point us beyond the Atlantic in search of the magic isle.

Chalmers and Malone have concurred in asserting, that the title of the play, as well as the circumstances of its opening scene, were suggested by a dreadful hurricane which dispersed the fleet of Sir George Somers, in July, 1609, when on the way to the infant colony of Virginia with a large supply of men and provisions. The ship, called 'The Admiral,' with Sir George Somers and Sir Thomas Gates on board, was separated from the rest of the fleet, and wrecked on the island of Bermuda. Of this an account was published by Jourdan the following year, entitled 'A Discovery of the Bermudas, otherwise called the Isle of Devils;' and it is by no means improbable that from this pamphlet Shakespeare derived the first hint of the incidents on which the plot of 'The Tempest' is constructed. But as Ariel is despatched for dew to 'the still-vexed Bermoothes,' that at least is not the scene of Prospero's enchantments; nor was it in any degree requisite that the dramatist should give precise longitude and latitude to the 'uninhabited island,' where the scenes of his 'Tempest' are laid. The poets had in various ways an interest in the strange worlds that were then being revealed beyond the Atlantic. Spenser had as his special friend and wise critic, Sir Walter Raleigh, 'The Shepheard of the Ocean,' who 'said he came far from the main-sea deep.' Sir Philip Sidney's correspondence is replete with evidence of the interest he took in the voyages of Gilbert, Frobisher, and others, 'for the finding of a passage to Cathaya;' and to him is dedicated the first publication of Hakluyt, 'touching the discoveries of America and the islands adjacent unto the same.' The Earl of Southampton, the noble godfather to Shakespeare's 'Venus and Adonis,' the 'first heir of his invention,' was an active co-operator in the Virginia Company. Ralph Lane, whose letters, written on the island of Roanoke in 1585, have an interest as the oldest extant English writings from the New World, sailed under Raleigh's patronage ; and Thomas Harriott, who was in his family, not only pursued on the same island the algebraic experiments to which the solution of equations was due, but carried out some of those astronomical observations which, among other distinctions, now mark him for special note as the first observer of the spots on the sun. Have we not, in this Thomas Harriott—discoverer of the complele system of modern algebra, rival of Galileo in the first observations on the satellites of Jupiter, author of the 'Brief and True Report of the New Found Land of Virginia,' and reputed bearer of the gift of 'divine tobacco' to the English nation,—the true type of Prospero, who, with the aid of his magical books and his potent wand, could boast that he had bedimmed the noontide sun ?

That Shakespeare had in view the strange new lands of the western ocean we can discern very clearly ; for Gonzalo comforts his companions in their affright at some of the monstrous 'people of the island' very much in Raleigh's own words :

> ' Faith, sir, you need not fear. When we were boys,
> Who would believe that there were mountaineers
> Dew-lapp'd like bulls, whose throats had hanging at 'em
> Wallets of flesh? or that there were such men
> Whose heads stood in their breasts? which now we find
> Each putter-out of five for one will bring us
> Good warrant of.'

The 'putters-out of five for one' were the merchant adventurers, who risked their money, and not unfre

E

quently their lives, in the search for new worlds, and
came back laden with travellers' tales, if with no other
riches.

It is vain to search on the map for Prospero's island.
Malone and Chalmers, indeed, entertained no doubt
that Shakespeare had Bermuda in view.   Mr. Joseph
Hunter, among other notices of Shakespeare's own
time, quotes a curious account, from 'The Silver Watch
Bell' of Thomas Tymme, of the Bermudas, or Isle of
Devils, where 'to such as approach near the same, there
do not only appear fearful sights of devils and evil
spirits, but also mighty tempests with most terrible and
continual thunder and lightning, and the noise of
horrible cries, with screeching,' &c., which are reported
to make all glad to fly with utmost speed from the
horrible place.   This is supposed to have suggested to
Shakespeare the scene of his opening tempest, and the
island whereon Sycorax preceded his enchantments
with her terrible sorceries.   Moore, in his 'Epistle from
the Bermudas,' accordingly says, 'We cannot forget that
it is the scene of Shakespeare's *Tempest;* and that here
he conjured up the delicate Ariel, who alone is worth
the whole heaven of ancient mythology.'   Mr. Hunter
has felt it incumbent on him to enter on a course of
very elaborate argument to overthrow these Bermudan
claims, before his own grand Lampedusan discovery
could have any chance of popular favour.   But the
whole argument was very needless.   Wherever Prospero's isle may have been, the poet was careful to tell
us that it was not Bermuda ; otherwise how could Ariel
have been called up at midnight to do his master's
errand, and 'fetch dew from the still-vexed Bermoothes'?
In truth, the island belongs to the poet's sole domain ;
and having done its work in the realm of fancy, we may

be content to leave it till modern science rediscover it and
its true lord, the missing Caliban of fancy or of fact.
Otherwise ' deeper than did ever plummet sound,' it lies
with Prospero's magic books.

From Milan the banished duke and his infant daughter
were indeed borne only some leagues to sea, before they
were abandoned in

> ' A rotten carcass of a boat, not rigg'd,
> Nor tackle, sail, nor mast : the very rats
> Instinctively had quit it.'

But then the noble Gonzalo had not only furnished
his old master with rich garments and provisions of all
sorts, but out of the ducal library had culled the
precious volumes of science and of magic which he
prized above his dukedom ; and so, with these and his
wizard staff, he was as well provisioned for an ocean
voyage as the witch in ' Macbeth,' when she set sail for
Aleppo in a sieve : able no less to dispense with helm
or oar than ' a rat without a tail.' When the scene
opens with the tempest, which gives name to this
charming drama, we learn indeed that the rest of the
fleet which had escorted the usurping duke in his
unpropitious voyage, after being storm-tossed and dispersed by Ariel's wiles,

> ' All have met again,
> And are upon the Mediterranean flote,
> Bound sadly home for Naples.'

But the ocean tides rise and fall upon the yellow sands
of Prospero's island as they never did to Virgil's sea-
nymphs ; and when he would

> ' Betwixt the green sea and the azur'd vault
> Set roaring war.'

he can call at will, not only the

> ' Elves of hills, brooks, standing lakes, and groves;
> But those that on the sands with printless feet
> Do chase the ebbing Neptune, and do fly him
> When he comes back.'

Prospero is, indeed, full of the idea of the tide's ebb and
flow, as if to remove his enchanted island beyond all
question into regions remotest from Mediterranean
tideless shores. When, at the last, he has all charmed
within his enchanted circle, he exclaims, in mingled
metaphor and allusion—

> ' Their understanding
> Begins to swell; and the approaching tide
> Will shortly fill the reasonable shore
> That now lies foul and muddy.'

There is one anciently described island of the New
World, very familiar to the men of Shakespeare's day,
and which it is obvious enough that the poet himself had
in view, when he lets the gentle Gonzalo picture to us
what would be, had he the plantation of this new-found
isle. He is fresh from the study of Montaigne's philosophy ; and as to the island-scene of his communistic
idealism, it is the veritable Utopia of which Sir Thomas
More had already learned so much from the Raphael
Hythloday of his philosophic fiction. Gonzalo, we must
remember, philosophises in playful banter, dealing in such
wise fooling as may suit his fickle auditors : ' Gentlemen
of brave mettle, who would lift the moon out of her sphere,
if she would continue in it five weeks without changing!'
It is thus he deals with the Platonic fiction :—

> ' *Gon.* I' the commonwealth, I would by contraries
> Execute all things; for no kind of traffic
> Would I admit; no name of magistrate;
> Letters should not be known: riches, poverty,

And use of service, none; contract, succession,
Bourn, bound of land, tilth, vineyard, none:
No use of metal, corn, or wine, or oil:
No occupation; all men idle, all;
And women too; but innocent and pure:
No sovereignty;—
 Seb.   Yet he would be king on 't.
 Ant. The latter end of his commonwealth forgets the beginning.
 Gon. All things in common nature should produce
Without sweat or endeavour: treason, felony,
Sword, pike, knife, gun, or need of any engine,
Would I not have; but nature should bring forth,
Of its own kind, all foison, all abundance,
To feed my innocent people.
 Seb. No marrying 'mong his subjects?
 Ant. None, man; all idle; whores and knaves.
 Gon. I would with such perfection govern, sir,
To excel the golden age.
 Seb.   Save his majesty!
 Ant. Long live Gonzalo!
 Gon.   And,—do you mark me, sir?
 Alon. Prithee, no more: thou dost talk nothing to me.
 Gon. I do well believe your highness; and did it to minister
occasion to these gentlemen, who are of such sensible and nimble
lungs that they always use to laugh at nothing.'

But when we have identified Prospero's island with the
Utopia of Hythloday, we are still far as ever from fixed
longitudes and latitudes ; for it is but the ουτοπος, the
nowhere, of More's imaginary commonwealth : nowhere,
yet nevertheless the discovery of a reputed fellow-
voyager of Amerigo Vespucci. With this latter help to
such geographical research, the mythology of the island
agrees : for Setebos, the god of the witch Sycorax, is
a Patagonian deity, mentioned by Richard Eden in his
' History of Travayle in the West and East Indies, and
other countreys lying eyther way towards the fruitfull
and ryche Moluccaes.' There it may be presumed
Shakespeare picked up the name, and what else he
needed for the ' uninhabited island'—uninhabited, that
is, so far as human beings are concerned, before Pros-

pero's arrival,—which he has peopled for us so well.
There, as Ariel tells his master in the second act—

> 'Safely in harbour
> Is the king's ship; in the deep nook, where once
> Thou call'd'st me up at midnight to fetch dew
> From the still-vex'd Bermoothes.'

The island, therefore, is not farther, at any rate, from
the Bermudas, than from Naples or Milan ; and though
the dispersed fleet is once more safely afloat on the
Mediterranean, and—all but the king's ship,—already
bound for Naples, before Prospero restores his Ariel to
the elements, that tricksy spirit has one more duty to
perform ; and so the Duke is able to promise to all

> 'Calm seas, auspicious gales,
> And sail so expeditious, that shall catch
> The royal fleet far off,'

and so be in Naples as soon as them. It is vain, then,
to apply any ordinary reckoning to such voyagers' log,
or to seek by longitude or latitude to fix the locality
of Caliban's island-home : any more than to map out
on a geographical chart of modern centuries that prehistoric Borneo, New Guinea, or other anthropomorphic
Eden, where the half-brute progenitor of man, when in a
state considerably in advance of the chimpanzee, orang,
or gorilla, in all intellectual attributes, but far more helpless and defenceless than any existing savage, found
those favouring conditions which admitted of the slow
process of evolution resulting in MAN.

CHAPTER IV.

THE TEMPEST.

> ' *Sebastian.* A living drollery. Now I will believe
> That there are unicorns; that in Arabia
> There is one tree, the phœnix' throne; one phœnix
> At this hour reigning there.'—*The Tempest.*

THE grave comedy which supplies to us Shakespeare's realisation of the half-human beings which in the sixteenth century were supposed to inhabit the new-found lands of the deep-sea main, is in other respects rich in some of the choicest imaginings of his genius. In ' The Tempest,' as in the lighter comedy of ' A Midsummer Night's Dream,' his fancy revels in the embodiment of the supernatural creed of his own day. In both the homely and grotesque intermingle with the super-human elements of the drama with such seeming naturalness and simplicity, that it becomes no more improbable than the marvels of night's wonderland appear to the dreamer. But it is with a graver purpose and more earnest meaning that Shakespeare has wrought the scenes of the later drama into such artful consistency ; and interwoven with the unsophisticated tenderness of Miranda's love, the philosophy of Gonzalo, and Duke Prospero's sage reflections on this fleeting shadow of mortality.

The Caliban of ' The Tempest,' cannot be rightly estimated, unless viewed in the rich setting in which Shakespeare has placed his rude disproportioned shape. It is, as a whole, an assay piece of his art. He sports there with its difficulties, as the Prospero of his own creation does with the spirits of the elements; and seems to have set himself what shall task and prove the ample compass of his power. He endows Prospero with superhuman wisdom, and arms him with all the forbidden mastery of the magician's art; yet preserves to him the generous attributes of a noble nature, giving absolute power, where it is employed without abuse under the restraints of virtue. In Miranda he aims at realising what a pure guileless woman would become, trained from infancy apart from all intercourse with her own sex, nurtured in every refinement of intellectual culture, yet the inmate of a rude cell, ignorant of all the conventionalities which society breeds, and having never from infancy seen any human being but her own father. In her, accordingly, Shakespeare embodies all that is pure and lovely in true womanhood, apart from the conventional proprieties of artificial life; and having thus made her

> 'So perfect and so peerless; one created
> Of every creature's best,'

yet not perfected into aught that is superhuman, he places alongside of her two other beings begot by the same prolific fancy, the one above and the other below the rank of humanity. Of these the superhuman is an ethereal spirit, incapable of human passions, and only withheld from the elements, in which it longs to mingle, by the constraining power of Prospero's magical art; the other is the rude, earth-born animal which so strikingly realises for us the highest conceivable development of brute-nature. They stand alongside of each other, yet have nothing in common, hold no intercourse, exchange no words : the representative embodiments, as it were, of two incompatible elements brought into compulsory apposition by the mediate humanity of Prospero. The scenes in which such widely diverse characters enact their parts, constitute as a whole one of the most original, as it is one of the most beautiful, of all that special department of the Shakespearean drama in which the world of ideal fancy mingles without constraint with the realities of every-day life.

In the list of characters, or 'Names of the Actors,' as it is styled, appended to the first edition of the play, Caliban is described as 'a salvage and deformed slave,' and has a rank assigned to him between the noble followers of the'King of Naples and Trinculo the jester, Stephano, a drunken butler, and the rude sailors; while Miranda intervenes between the latter and Ariel, 'an ayerie spirit,' with the other spirits who play their part as actors in the masque.

In the folio of 1623, 'The Tempest' ranks foremost in place, and appeared there for the first time seven years after its author's death. The supposition that it is the very last of all the creations of his genius has already been referred to. It is a poet's fancy, and cannot now admit of proof. But the play is printed with so few imperfections, that it may be assumed to have been derived directly from the author's manuscript. It may indeed have been this manuscript—then fresh from Shakespeare's pen, the final triumph of his magic art,—that his editors had specially in view, when in the preface to the collected edition of his dramas, they say, in loving remembrance of the genius of their deceased friend : 'Who as he was a happy imitator of Nature, was a most gentle expresser of it. His mind and hand went together, and what he thought, he uttered with that easiness that we have scarce received from him a blot in his papers.'

The last days of the poet had been pleasantly passed

in the haunts of his boyhood ; and among his pastimes it is not to be doubted had been the painsful pleasure of revising and completing some of his marvellous dramas, and preparing the whole for the press.   To his brother actors and literary executors—'my fellows,' as he styles them,—John Heminge and Henry Condell, he bequeathed ' twenty-six shillings and eightpence apiece, to buy them rings;' and to them were transferred the revised quartos and original MSS. which were the source of the famous 1623 folio.   'We have scarce received from him a blot in his papers,' the admiring editors declare.   It were to be wished that they had done their editorial work with like pains and care.   And yet had they done so the world might not altogether have been the gainer.   In that case, for example, Pope had never produced his superb critical edition of Shakespeare, in which he laboured so assiduously to constrain the Elizabethan poet's ' native wood-notes wild ' to a conformity with the artificial standards of that year of grace A.D. 1725 ; and then Theobald, 'poor piddling Tibbald,' would have had no cause to write his ' Shakespeare Restored : or, a Specimen of the Many Errors, as well committed as unamended, in Pope's edition of this Poet ;' and so the irascible little bard of Twickenham would have missed the chief incentive which begot his ' Dunciad,' with Theobald for its hero : —

> 'Where hapless Shakespeare, yet of Tibbald sore,
> Wished he had blotted for himself before.'

The process of evolution thus originating in the ' errors as well committed as unamended ' in the famous first folio, has gone on in prolific multiplication of blots and blotters, till Shakespearean commentaries and illustrative criticisms have grown into a library ample enough to task the reading of a lifetime. But 'The Tempest' is exceptional in the correctness of its text, as in much else; though Dryden did league with D'Avenant to show how utterly a noble work of art could be desecrated in adapting it to the tastes of a mean age; and Pope, in trimming it to those of an artificial one, resyllabled its heroic numbers, attuned to his own ear, if not counted on his fingers; and made other alterations which neither the hero of the 'Dunciad' nor any other sound critic could accept as improvements.

To the refined reader of this exquisite comedy, the central charm unquestionably must be that rare concep- tion of purest womanly grace and instinctive delicacy, Miranda. Womanly we call her, though she is but fifteen, and as unsophisticated in her sweet simplicity as when

'In the dark backward and abysm of time,'

'not out three years old,' she, with her banished father, was hurried on board the leaky 'rotten carcass of a boat' which bore them to their island solitude. When, at length, 'bountiful Fortune' brought thither Prospero's enemies, and placed them at his mercy : the same fortune brought with these Ferdinand, the young heir to the crown of Naples, to own that, though full many a lady he had 'eyed with best regard,' and found in each some special virtue to distinguish her, never till now did he look on one that had not some defect. But the guileless Miranda has no such experiences to tell of; and when her father would restrain the too ready response of his daughter to this noble lover, it is thus he schools her :—

'Thou think'st there is no more such shapes as he,
Having seen but him and Caliban; foolish wench!
To the most of men this is a Caliban,
And they to him are angels.'

But she only replies—

> ' My affections
> Are then most humble; I have no ambition
> To see a goodlier man.'

She gives her whole heart, in utter unconsciousness of
the prudent fears which trouble her father, lest ' too light
winning make the prize light.' Her innocency is still as
untutored as when the scarce three-years-old child parted
with the last of those woman-tendants whose memory
haunted her rather like a dream than an assurance of
which memory gave any warrant. She tells her lover:

> ' I do not know
> One of my sex; no woman's face remember,
> Save, from my glass, mine own: nor have I seen
> More that I may call men than you, good friend,
> And my dear father: how features are abroad,
> I am skilless of; but, by my modesty,
> The jewel in my dower, I would not wish
> Any companion in the world but you:
> Nor can imagination form a shape,
> Besides yourself, to like of.'

And so this ' fair encounter of two most rare affections'
proceeds in ' plain and holy innocence': the realisation
of a child of nature, unrestrained by all mere conventional
proprieties, but guided by the unerring instincts of
native modesty and purity.

The setting of this exquisite creation of Shakespeare's
genius has been designed with rare art to display by
contrast the peculiar graces of perfect womanhood. The
refined, ethereal, dainty Ariel, most delicate of sprites,
incapable of affections that can become tender, and yet,
though ' but of air,' having a touch, a feeling of human
affections, hovers around Miranda, fulfilling her father's
commands, but otherwise no more familiar with her
than the zephyrs which lift her hair and fan her cheek.

He is a sylph-like, spiritual essence, suited for fancy's lightest behests; a being born as it were of the sweet breeze and the butterfly, as incapable of human love as of human hate or sin. But while this embodiment of the zephyr floats airily about Miranda in her mortal loveliness, by the cunning art of the dramatist she is brought into more immediate contact with the other extreme. Caliban is her fellow-creature, in a way that Ariel could never be, and provokes comparisons such as the other in no way suggests. For his is the palpable grossness of a lower nature, a creature of earth, not unredeemed by its own fitting attributes nor untrue to itself, but altogether below the level of humanity.

Of the estimate formed of this unique creation of genius by the men of Shakespeare's own day, we have very slight means of judging. But the evidence of an utter incapacity for appreciating his genius by the Restoration court and age is nowhere more manifest than in the impure vulgar buffoonery with which the greatest of the poets of that new era helped to travesty the wild and savage nature of Caliban. 'The Tempest; or, The Enchanted Island,' takes its place among the collected works of John Dryden, though it might perhaps more fitly rank with the forgotten dramas, masques, and other productions of Davenant's pen. Referring to their joint labours in vulgarising and polluting Shakespeare's comedy, Dryden says: 'It was originally Shakespeare's, a poet for whom he had a particularly high veneration, and whom he taught me first to admire.' The mode adopted by teacher and pupil for giving expression to their admiring veneration is sufficiently equivocal. The play itself, as Dryden tells us, had formerly been acted with success in the Blackfriars; and its aptness for scenic effect and showy spectacle—far more, it is to be presumed, than any appreciation of its higher excellences,—tempted Fletcher, Suckling, D'Avenant, and Dryden himself, to tamper with its delicate refinement, and debase it by means of spurious adaptations to the taste of a corrupt age. As to Fletcher's ' Sea Voyage,' he has rather borrowed the idea than tampered with the text of Shakespeare's ' Tempest '; and as the supernatural elements are wholly omitted, it need not detain us. ' The Desert Islands ' of Fletcher are the scene of a gyneocracy or commonwealth of women : a Utopian paradise, which ' yields not fawns, nor satyrs, or most lustful men ; ' and he only borrows remotely the one idea of women trained from infancy on a desert island, without knowledge of the other sex. The Clarinda of Fletcher is mainly his own creation, and scarcely provokes the comparison with Shakespeare's Miranda which it is so little fitted to stand. But D'Avenant and Dryden deal with the latter even more coarsely than with Caliban, in their efforts to adapt the chaste elder drama to the lascivious revels of the Restoration court.

Sir William D'Avenant, cavalier and poet-laureat, with whom Dryden was associated in the travesty of ' The Tempest,' was the son of an Oxford innkeeper, at whose hostle Shakespeare is said to have been a frequent guest. The cavalier poet-laureat had been balked in his purposed exploration of the new-found lands of the Western world, exchanging for this only too ample opportunities to yearn for the imaginary commonwealth in which Gonzalo and many another philosophic dreamer had purposed to excel the golden age. He was made prisoner by a man-of-war in the service of England's newly realised commonwealth, in 1651, when on his way to Virginia, to plant a royalist colony there ; and so exchanged the cavalier Utopia he was in search of, for a long captivity in the Tower. But better days were in store for him. After the Restoration he became manager of the Duke of York's players, and did his best to indemnify the dramatic muse for recent Puritan restraints by every conceivable liberty that could be found in the opposite extreme of licence. In the preface to their joint labours, Dryden describes his fellow-worker as 'a man of quick and piercing imagination,' and ' of so quick a fancy that nothing was proposed to him on which he could not suddenly produce a thought extremely pleasant and surprising; and as his fancy was quick, so likewise were the products of it remote and new. He borrowed not of any other ; and his imaginations were such as could not easily enter into any other man.' The commendations of his original and pregnant genius read strangely out of place appended to such a specimen of his art. His quick fancy and piercing imagination are there shown by superadding to Shakespeare's Caliban a twin-sister, Sycorax, of whom her brother tells Trinculo, she is ' beautiful and bright as the full moon. I left her clambering up a hollow oak, and plucking thence the dropping honeycombs.' As to this beauty, it is intended to be judged of by Caliban's own standard; for she no sooner appears than Trinculo addresses her as ' my dear blubber-lips !' But there is nothing to tempt us to linger on Dryden's ' enchanted island,' unless it be the marvel that within an interval so brief the taste of a whole nation should have become so depraved as to tolerate this gross caricature of an exquisite work of genius.

The strange being which invites our notice as the native-born occupant of Shakespeare's nameless island, and forms the counterpart to Ariel in the dramatic setting by which Miranda is displayed with such rare art, can only be properly estimated by the careful student. At a first glance the brutish Caliban appears to occupy a very subordinate place among the creations of Shakespeare; and, compared with the ethereal minister of Prospero's wizard spells, he is apt to be regarded as a mere passive agent in the byplay of the comedy. Placed, moreover, as he is, in direct contrast to Miranda, 'so perfect and so peerless,' the half-human monster appears all the more deformed. But, in Dryden's vulgar travesty, he becomes, with his mother's legacy of 'great roaring devils,' the actual 'hag's seed' and 'born devil' of Prospero's mere wrathful hyperbole ; and, worthless as this contemptible rifacciamento is in all other respects, it has perhaps the one merit of showing how far removed the original Caliban is from the vulgar twin-monsters of the Restoration stage.

So far from being either superficial or repulsive, Caliban is a character which admits of the minutest study, and is wrought to the perfection of a consistent ideal not less harmoniously, and even beautifully, than Ariel himself. Both are supernatural beings, called into existence by the creative fancy of the poet ; but the grosser nature is the more original of the two : more thoroughly imaged forth without the aid of current fancies of elves, and sprites, and all the airy denizens of Fairyland, which made the Puck of Shakespeare homely to all, and his Ariel, exquisite as it is, conceivable enough. For Dryden truly says of the poet in the prologue to his remodelled 'Tempest,' that 'he wrote as people then believed ;' while Dryden himself unhappily stooped to write as people of his later day desired. But, if he was indeed first taught by Davenant to admire Shakespeare, it is the less wonder that he should so very partially appreciate the elements

of his wondrous originality. In the same prologue
he says :—

> ' So from old Shakespeare's honoured dust, this day
> Springs up and buds a new-reviving play:
> Shakespeare who, taught by none, did first impart
> To Fletcher wit, to labouring Jonson art;
> He, monarch-like, gave those his subjects law,
> And is that Nature which they paint and draw.'

But it is in a very peculiar and exceptional sense that
we can appeal to Nature in testing such impersonations
of contemporary belief as either Ariel or Caliban. They
are creations conceived by the most original genius,
though fashioned in perfect harmony with the beliefs of
his age. To this they owe their peculiar charm. In
them, as in others of his rare imaginings, his supernatural
seems so natural, that we only realise to how large an·
extent it is the work of his own fancy, when we test it
by comparison with that of his most gifted contemporaries.

It is the triumph of the poet thus to mirror the
thoughts of his age. He does not startle it with what
is strange, but with what seems most familiar to it. Yet
with all the seeming familiarity of those exquisite embodiments of popular belief, and their consistency with
the folk-lore of the time, they are as purely fancy-
wrought as the visions that haunt unbidden the gay
romance of dreams. They were Shakespeare's own
creations, but they seemed so thoroughly to realise
what already commanded universal credence, that the
charmed onlooker regarded them as no more than the
mirroring of his own vaguest fancies. The imaginative
power thus displayed in giving corporeal seeming and a
consistent individuality to such 'airy nothings' will be
best appreciated by the reader who has already familiarised himself with the supernatural beings that figure in

the verse of Marlow, Jonson, Fletcher, and even of
Milton. They are no less Shakespeare's own creations
than his Othello, or Hamlet, his Portia, Imogen, Ophelia,
or Lady Macbeth. He wrought indeed with the current
thought of his age, but of none of them can it be said,
that he merely produces the portraiture of what was
already familiar to it ; and least of all could this be
affirmed of Caliban. He is in a peculiar sense a supernatural character, lying as much beyond the bounds of
human experience as any fairy, ghost, or spirit of the
creed of superstition, either in that age or our own :
earth-born, and fashioned on the ideal of the brute,
yet so distinct from anything hitherto seen or known
on earth, that only now, two centuries and a half after
its production on the English stage, has it entered into
the mind of the scientific naturalist to conceive of such
a being as possible.

CHAPTER V.

THE MONSTER CALIBAN.

' Arise, and fly
The reeling Faun, the sensual feast;
Move upward, working out the beast,
And let the ape and tiger die.'
In Memoriam.

THE innate and seemingly instinctive aptitude of
the human mind to conceive of the supernatural
is so universal, and so intimately interwoven with that
other conception of a spiritual life, the successor of this
present corporeal existence,—which, far more than any
supposed belief in a Supreme Being, seems the universal
attribute of man,—that Shakespeare's whole conception
of the supernatural may fitly come under review as a
sequel to the more limited subject specially occupying
our consideration. But it is sufficient for the present
to bear in mind the originality and prolific powers
revealed in his supernatural imaginings, in order the
more clearly to appreciate the one portraiture of a
being which, though in no sense spiritual, is so far as
all experience goes, thoroughly supra-natural.

''Tis strange, my Theseus,' says Hippolyta to her
ducal lover, as the fifth act of ' A Midsummer Night's
Dream' opens in a hall of his palace at Athens,
where they hold discourse on the themes that lovers
speak of. The previous scenes have been ripe with
the sportive creations of the poet's fancy, with his
Oberon, Titania, and all their fairy train ; and now, in

true dramatic fashion, he claims the shadowy beings as his own. 'More strange than true,' Theseus
replies :—

> ' I never may believe
> These antique fables, nor these fairy toys.
> Lovers and madmen have such seething brains,
> Such shaping fantasies, that apprehend
> More than cool reason ever comprehends;'

and then, after quaintly coupling the lover and the
lunatic as beings 'of imagination all compact,' he adds
this other picture of the poet's fantasies :—

> ' The poet's eye, in a fine frenzy rolling,
> Doth glance from heaven to earth, from earth to heaven;
> And as imagination bodies foith
> The forms of things unknown, the poet's pen
> Turns them to shapes, and gives to airy nothing
> A local habitation and a name.
> Such tricks hath strong imagination.'

As to the actual belief in the beings so dealt with,
among the men of that generation, it was vague and
indeterminate as themselves. When, indeed, the poet
glanced to earth, and called up on the blasted heath,
near by the scene of Macbeth's great victory over the
Norweyan host, those wild and withered hags, that
'looked not like the inhabitants o' the earth, and yet
were on't,' he idealised a very harsh and deep-rooted
belief of his age. When again he glanced from earth,
not to heaven, but to that intermediate spirit-world,
with all the ghostly or airy habitants with which fancy
or superstition had favoured it, he wrought with materials that had fashioned the creed of many generations.
He had, himself, believed in fairies; and doubtless still
regarded ghosts with becoming awe. They had held
mastery over his youthful imagination ; constituted the

fancies and the terror of his childhood; and were in his maturer years translated into those supernatural beings which have proved so substantial to other generations.

But the poet's own age had been familiarised with ideal beings of a wholly different kind, the reality of which seemed scarcely to admit of question. Of the new world of the West which Columbus had revealed, there was, at any rate, no room for doubt; and yet when, nearly a century after its discovery, Spenser refers, in his 'Faerie Queen,' not only to the Indian Peru and the Amazon, but to that 'fruitfullest Virginia' of which his friend Raleigh had told him many a wondrous tale, it is obvious that to his fancy America was still almost as much a world apart as if his 'Shepherd of the Ocean' had sailed up the blue vault of heaven, and told of the dwellers in another planet on which it had been his fortune to alight. He is defending the verisimilitude of that Fairyland in which Una and the Red Cross Knight, Duessa, Belphœbe, Orgoglio, Malecastaes and so many more fanciful impersonations disport themselves, with King Arthur and the Faerie Queen herself: and he argues that since Peru, Virginia, and all the wonders of that new-found hemisphere prove to be real, what marvel if this Fairyland of his fancy be no less substantial a verity. For even now, of the world the least part is known to us; and daily through hardy enterprise new regions are discovered, as unheard-of as were the huge Amazon, the Indian Peru, or other strange lands now found true :—

> 'Yet all these were, when no man did them know,
> Yet have from wisest ages hidden been;
> And later times things more unknown shall show:
> Why then should witless man so much misween,

That nothing is but that which he hath seen?
What if, within the moon's fair shining sphere,
What if, in every other star unseen
Of other worlds he happily should hear?
He wonder would much more; yet such to some appear '

For voyagers to return from that new world with stories
of its being peopled with human beings like themselves,
was a kind of blasphemy intolerable to all honest
Christians. The council of clerical sages which as-
sembled in the Dominican Convent of St. Stephen, at
Salamanca, in 1486, to take into consideration the theory
of Columbus as to a Cathaya, or other world of humanity lying beyond the Atlantic, after bringing all
the science and philosophy of the age to bear on the
subject, pronounced the idea of the earth's spherical
form heterodox, and a belief in antipodes incompatible
with the historical traditions of our faith : since to assert
that there were inhabited lands on the opposite side of
the globe, would be to maintain that there were nations
not descended from Adam, it being impossible for them
to have passed the intervening ocean. This would
be, therefore, to discredit the Bible, which expressly
declares that all men are descendants of one common
pair.

It is amusing, but also instructive, thus to find an
ethnological problem of our own day adduced by the
orthodox sages of Salamanca in the fifteenth century
to prove that America could not exist. It is obvious
enough, that with such Dominican philosophers in
the councils of science, it was safer for their orthodoxy
as well as their credibility, for travellers to tell of
' anthropophagi, and men whose heads do grow beneath
their shoulders,' than to hint of a race of ordinary men
and women. This kind of union of scepticism and
credulity belongs exclusively to no special epoch. A

story is told of a Scottish sailor returning to his old
mother, and greeting her with an account of the wonders
he had seen in far-away lands and seas. But his most
guarded narrations conflicted so entirely with her personal experience that they were repelled as wholly
incredible. 'Weel, mother,' said the baffled traveller,
'what will ye say when I tell you that, in sailing up
the Red Sea, on pulling up our anchor, we fand ane
o' Pharaoh's chariot-wheels on the fluke?' 'Ay, ay!
Sandy, that I can weel believe,' responded the old
dame; 'there's Scripture for that!' It was in a like
critical spirit that the men of the fifteenth and sixteenth
centuries refused all belief in the humanity of the
antipodes, while they welcomed the most monstrous
exaggerations for the very air of truthfulness they bore,
when tried by their own canons of credibility.

The reasoning of that age arranged itself in a very
simple syllogism. All men were descended from Adam;
the beings inhabiting the worlds beyond the ocean could
not possibly be descended from Adam; therefore they
were not human beings. Yet as truth slowly dawned
through a whole century, it became more and more
obvious that, whatever their pedigree might be, they
had many points in common with humanity. They had
a kind of speech of their own; and could be taught
with no great difficulty that of their discoverers. They
had arts, arms, architecture and sculpture, and even
religious rites, though of a very horrible kind. So the
Spanish Dominicans pronounced them to be devils; and
yet did not wholly abandon the hope of converting
them, and making them Christians after a sort. The
English adventurers, having no love for the Spaniards
of the New World, and a very special aversion to their
priests, were the less likely to be guided by their

estimation of the Carib or Mexican ; and hence there
grew up a vague idea of inhabitants of the strange
islands reported from time to time by returned voyagers,
who, though they could not possibly be of the race of
Adam, had yet a far nearer resemblance, in many ways,
to our perfected humanity than any ape, baboon, or
other anthropomorphous being with which older travellers had made them familiar.

On this ideal Shakespeare unquestionably wrought in
the creation of that 'freckled whelp,' as disproportioned
in manners as in shape, whom Prospero found sole
habitant of the lonely island on which he and Miranda
were cast. As to Caliban's maternity, the theories of
man's descent, and the consequent transitional stages
of an unperfected humanity, with which we are now
familiar, are of very modern date, and did not at all
lie in Shakespeare's vein, whatever Bacon might have
said of them. Unless the poet had contented himself
with simply letting Prospero find the strange monster
on the island, he had, like more modern philosophers,
to account in some way for his being; and so he vaguely
hints at supernatural conception, known to Prospero
only at second-hand. For the witch Sycorax had died,
and Ariel had writhed and groaned for years, imprisoned
in the rifted pine where she had left him, till Prospero
arrived and set him free. 'As thou report'st thyself,'
is accordingly the form in which Prospero alludes to
Sycorax and all else that pertained to those prehistoric
island-times before he set foot there. Sufficient for us,
therefore, is it, that the Duke of Milan found on that
strange island just such a monstrous being as travellers'
tales had already made familiar to all men as natives
of such regions. The terms Carib and Cannibal were
synonymous. The edicts of Isabella·expressly excluded

the Carribeans from all the ordinary rights of humanity on this very ground. They therefore were the anthropophagi of travellers' tales; and Caliban is but an anagram of the significant name.

'Do you put tricks upon us with savages and men of Ind?' says Stephano; while the drunken Trinculo, puzzling, in his besotted fashion, over Caliban, who has fallen flat at his approach in the hope of escaping notice, exclaims: 'What have we here? a man or a fish? A strange fish! Were I in England now, as once I was, and had but this fish painted, not a holiday fool there but would give a piece of silver; there would this monster make a man; any strange beast there makes a man; when they will not give a doit to relieve a lame beggar, they will lay out ten to see a dead Indian. Legged like a man! and his fins like arms! Warm, o' my troth! I do now let loose my opinion; hold it no longer: this is no fish, but an islander, that hath lately suffered by a thunderbolt.' It would be curious to recover an exact delineation of the Caliban of the Elizabethan stage. 'This is a strange thing as e'er I looked on,' is the exclamation of the King of Naples, when Caliban is driven in, along with the revellers who have been plotting who should 'be king o' the isle;' and on his brother, Sebastian, asking, 'What things are these, my Lord Antonio?' he replies: 'One of them is a plain fish, and no doubt marketable.' There was obviously something marine, or fish-like, in the aspect of the island monster. 'In the dim obscurity of the past,' says Darwin, 'we can see that the early progenitor of all the vertebræ must have been an aquatic animal;' in its earliest stages 'more like the larvæ of our existing marine Ascidians than any other known form,' but destined in process of time,

through lancelot, ganoid, and other kindred tran-
sitions, to —

> 'Suffer a sea change
> Into something rich and strange.'

In Caliban there was undesignedly embodied, seemingly,
an ideal of the latest stages of such an evolution.   Mr.
Joseph Hunter in dealing with this, as with other details,
in his 'Disquisition on Shakespeare's Tempest,' lets his
learning come into needless conflict with the idealisation of the poet.   He will by no means admit of so
simple a solution of the name of Caliban as the mere
metathesis of *cannibal*, but goes in search for it among
the many names by which Gaspar, Melchior, and Bal-
thazar, the three magi, were known throughout medieval
Europe.   In like fashion he finds his form to be of
Hebraistic origin, and not at all 'a pure creation of
Shakespeare's own mind.'   He accordingly proceeds to
'compare him with the fish-idol of Ashdod, the Dagon
of the Philistines :—

> "Sea-monster ! upward man,
> And downward fish."—P. L., Bk. i.

'Here we have also a figure half-fish, half-man;' and
so the learned commentator proceeds to questions of
Rabbinical literature; discusses how the two elements
of fish and man coalesced in the form of Dagon; quotes
Abarbinel and Kimchi; and finally arrives at this conclusion: 'The true form of Dagon was a figure shaped
like a fish, only with feet and hands like a man.   Now
this is precisely the form of Shakespeare's Caliban, "a
fish legged like a man, and his fins like arms."   Nothing
can be more precise than the resemblance.   The two
are in fact one, as to form.   Caliban is therefore a kind
of tortoise, the paddles expanding in arms and hands,
legs and feet.   And accordingly, before he appears upon

the stage, the audience are prepared for the strange figure by the words of Prospero :—

" Come forth, thou tortoise ! "

' How he became changed into a monkey, while the play is full of allusions to his fish-like form,' the learned critic leaves to others to explain.

There is an amusing literalness in this application alike of the confused ideas of the drunken Trinculo, and of the invective of Prospero. The wrathful magician calls to the creature whom Miranda has been denouncing as a villain,—'What ho! slave! Caliban! Thou earth, thou!' and as he still lingers, muttering his refusal, Prospero shouts, 'Come forth, I say; come, thou tortoise! when?' In a milder mood he might have said, 'Come, thou snail!' expressing thereby the same idea of tardy reluctant obedience, with equally little reference to his form.

In reality, though by some scaly or fin-like appendages, the idea of a fish, or sea-monster, is suggested to all, the form of Caliban is, nevertheless, essentially human. In a fashion more characteristic of Milton's than of Shakespeare's wonted figure of speech, this is affirmed in language that no doubt purposely suggests the opposite idea to the mind, where Prospero says :—

' Then was this island—
Save for the son that she did litter here,
A freckled whelp, hag-born,—not honoured with
A human shape.'

The double bearing of this is singularly expressive :—save for this son of Sycorax, the island was not honoured with a human shape. And, having thus indicated that his shape was human, by the use of the terms 'whelp' and 'littered' the brutish ideal is strongly impressed on

the mind.   But his strictly anthropomorphic character
is delicately suggested in other ways.   When Miranda
says of Ferdinand—

> ' This
> Is the third man that e'er I saw, the first
> That e'er I sigh'd for,'

she can only refer to her father and Caliban.   In this the
poet purposely glances at the simplicity of the inex-
perienced maiden, to whom the repulsive monster had
hitherto been the sole ideal of manhood presented to her
mind, apart from the venerable Prospero.   How far he
falls short of all manly perfections is indicated immediately afterwards in the contrast instituted between him
and Ferdinand :—

> ' Thou think'st there are no more such shapes as he,
> Having seen but him and Caliban.   Foolish wench !
> To the most of men this is a Caliban,
> And they to him are angels.'

This is, of course, the purposed exaggeration of Prospero,
in his fear 'lest too light winning make the prize light.'
But so soon as Miranda has become thoroughly impressed with the image of her new-found lover, with ' no
ambition to see a goodlier man,' she ceases to think of
Caliban as a being to be associated with him in common
manhood.   When, accordingly, she responds to Ferdinand's admiring exclamation—

> ' But you, O you,
> So perfect and so peerless, are created
> Of every creature's best,'

it is by a declaration which wholly ignores Caliban's
claims to rank in the same order of beings with those
among whom she had so recently classed him.

> ' I do not know
> One of my sex ; no woman's face remember,

> Save, from my glass, mine own; nor have I seen
> More that 1 may call men, than you, good friend,
> And my dear father.'

In this way the gradual expansion of the ideas of this innocent maiden are traced by the most delicate indications; until at length, when Alonzo and his company are introduced into Prospero's cell, where Ferdinand and Miranda are seated, playing at chess, she exclaims—

> 'Oh! wonder!
> How many goodly creatures are there here!
> How beauteous mankind is! O brave new world
> That has such people in't!'

The development being thus completed, and the perfection of true manhood fairly presented to her eye and mind, Caliban is then introduced, with the awe-struck exclamation—

> 'O Setebos, these be brave spirits indeed!'

and immediately thereafter we have the remark of Antonio—'One of them is a plain fish, and no doubt marketable.' He is a 'thing of darkness,' as Prospero calls him; a being 'as disproportioned in his manners as in his shape;' yet nevertheless so closely approximating, in the main, to ordinary humanity, that Miranda had associated him in her own mind, along with her father, as 'honoured with a human shape.'

Again, we are furnished with a tolerably definite clue to the age which Caliban has attained at the date of his introduction to our notice. Littered on the island soon after the reputed arrival of Sycorax, we learn that that malignant hag, unable to subdue the delicate Ariel to the execution of her abhorred commands, imprisoned him in the cloven pine, where he groaned out twelve wretched years, till relieved from his torments by the art of Prospero. Next, it appears from the discourse of her father to Miranda that she has grown up on that lonely island for a like period. 'Twelve years since, Miranda, thy father was the Duke of Milan, and a prince of power.' But she was not then three years old, and so the memory of that former state, and of the maidens who tended her in her father's palace, has faded away, 'far off, and like a dream;' while the banished Duke, 'rapt in secret studies,' his library 'a dukedom large enough,' had more and more perfected himself in occult science, until he learns by its aid that now the very crisis of their fates has come. Caliban is, therefore, to all appearance in his twenty-fifth year, as we catch a first glimpse of this pre-Darwinian realisation of the intermediate link between brute and man. It seems moreover to be implied that he has already passed his maturity. At an earlier age than that at which man is capable of self-support, the creature had been abandoned to the solitude of his island-home, and learned with his long claws to dig for pig-nuts; and now, says Prospero, 'as with age his body uglier grows, so his mind cankers.' We may conceive of the huge canine teeth and prognathous jaws which in old age assume such prominence in the higher quadrumana. Darwin. claims for the bonnet-monkey 'the forehead which gives to man his noble and intellectual appearance;' and it is obvious that it was not wanting in Caliban: for when he discovers the true quality of the drunken fools he has mistaken for gods, his remonstrance is, 'we shall all be turned to apes with foreheads villainous low.' Here then is the highest developement of 'the beast that wants discourse of reason.' He has attained to all the maturity his nature admits of, and so is perfect as the study of a living creature distinct from, yet next in order below the level of humanity.

The being thus called into existence for the purposes
of dramatic art is a creation well meriting the thoughtful study of the modern philosopher, whatever deductions he may have based on the hypotheses of recent
speculation. Caliban's is not a brutalised, but a natural
brute mind. He is a being in whom the moral instincts of man have no part ; but also in whom the
degradation of savage humanity is equally wanting.
He is a novel anthropoid of a high type—such as on
the hypothesis of evolution must have existed inter-
mediately between the ape and man,—in whom some
spark of rational intelligence has been enkindled, under
the tutorship of one who has already mastered the
secrets of nature. We must not be betrayed into a too
literal interpretation of the hyperboles of the wrathful
Duke of Milan. He is truly enough the 'freckled
whelp' whom Prospero has subdued to useful services, as
he might break in a wild colt, or rear a young wolf to
do his bidding, though in token of higher capacity he
has specially trained him to menial duties peculiar to
man. For not only does he 'fetch in our wood,' as
Prospero reminds his daughter, 'and serves in offices
that profit us,' but 'he does make our fire.'

No incident attending the discovery of the New World
is more significant than that of Columbus stationed on
the poop of the Santa Maria, his eye ranging along the
darkened horizon, when the sun had once more gone
down on the disappointed hopes of the voyagers.
Suddenly a light glimmered in the distance, once and
again reappeared to the eyes of Pedro Gutierrez and
others whom the great admiral summoned to catch this
gleam of realised hopes ; and then darkness and doubt
resumed their reign. But to Columbus all was light.
That feeble ray had told of the presence of the fire-

maker, man. The natural habits of Caliban, however,
are those of the denizen of the woods. We may conceive
of him like the pongoes of Mayombe, described by
Purchas, who would come and sit by the travellers'
deserted camp-fire, but had not sense enough to re-
plenish it with fuel. We have no reason to think of him
as naturally a cooking or fire-using animal; though,
under the training of Prospero, he proves to be so far in
advance of the most highly developed anthropoid as to
be capable of learning the art of fire-making.

'We'll visit Caliban, my slave, who never yields us
kind answers,' Duke Prospero says to his daughter in the
second scene of 'The Tempest,' where they first appear,
and Caliban is introduced; but the gentle Miranda
recalls with shuddering revulsion the brutal violence of
their strange servitor, and exclaims with unwonted
vehemence: ''Tis a villain, sir, I do not love to look on.'
But repulsive as he is, his services cannot be dispensed
with. 'As 'tis, we cannot miss him,' is Prospero's reply;
and then, irritated alike by the sense of his obnoxious
instincts and reluctant service, he heaps opprobrious epithets upon him: 'What, ho! slave! Caliban! thou earth,
thou! Come forth, I say, thou tortoise!' and at length,
as he still lingers, muttering in his den, Prospero breaks
out in wrath—'Thou poisonous slave, got by the devil
himself upon thy wicked dam, come forth!' Schlegel
and Hazlitt accordingly speak in nearly the same terms
of 'the savage Caliban, half brute, half demon;' while
Gervinus—although elsewhere characterising him with
more appreciative acumen as 'an embryonic being defiled as it were by his earthly origin from the womb of
savage nature,'—does, with prosaic literalness, assume
that his mother was the witch Sycorax, and the devil
his father. Shakespeare assuredly aimed at the depiction

of no such foul ideal. It is the recluse student of nature's mysteries, and not the poor island monster that is characteristically revealed in such harsh vituperations. Prospero habitually accomplishes his projects through the agency of enforced service. He has usurped a power over the spirits of air, as well as over this earth-born slave ; and both are constrained to unwilling obedience. Hence he has learned to exact and compel service to the utmost ; to count only on the agency of enslaved power : until an imperious habit disguises the promptings of a generous and kindly nature. With all his tenderness towards the daughter whose presence alone has made life endurable to him, he flashes up in sudden ire at the slightest interference with his plans for her ; as when she interposes on behalf of Ferdinand, he exclaims —' Silence ! One word more shall make me chide thee, if not hate thee.' He is indeed acting an assumed part, 'lest too light winning' should make the lover undervalue his prize ; but it is done in the imperious tone with which habit has taught him to respond to the slightest thwarting of his commands. This is still more apparent in his dealings with the gentle Ariel, who owes to him delivery from cruellest bondage. The relations subsisting between them are indicated with rare art, and are as tender as is compatible with beings of different elements. The sylph is generally addressed in kindly admiring terms, as 'my brave spirit,' 'my tricksy spirit,' 'my delicate, my dainty Ariel.' Yet on the slightest questioning of Prospero's orders, he is told : 'Thou liest, malignant thing !' and on the mere show of murmuring is threatened with durance more terrible than that from which he has been set free.

In all this the characteristics of the magician are consistently wrought out. According to the ideas of an age

G

which still believed in magic, he has usurped the lordship of nature, and subdued to his will the spirits of the elements, by presumptuous, if not altogether sinful arts. They are retained in subjection by the constant exercise of this supernatural power, and yield him only the reluctant obedience of slaves. This has to be borne in remembrance, if we would not misinterpret the ebullitions of imperious harshness on the part of Prospero towards beings who can only be retained in subjection by such enforced mastery. That Caliban regards him with as malignant a hatred as the caged and muzzled bear may be supposed to entertain towards his keeper, is set forth with clear consistency. Nor is it without abundant reason. He is dealt with not merely as a 'lying slave, whom stripes may move, not kindness;' but by his master's magical art, the most familiar objects of nature are made instruments of torture. They pinch, affright him, pitch him into the mire, as deceptive fire-brands mislead him in the dark, grind his joints with convulsions, contort his sinews with cramp, and, as he says,

> 'For every trifle are they set upon me ·
> Sometimes like apes, that mow and chatter at me,
> And after bite me: then like hedgehogs, which
> Lie tumbling in my barefoot way, and mount
> Their pricks at my footfall; sometimes am I
> All wound with adders, who with cloven tongues
> Do hiss me into madness.'

To reconcile such harsh violence with the merciful forgiving character of Prospero in his dealings with those who, after having done him the cruellest wrongs, are placed in his power, we have to conceive of the outcast father and child compelled in their island solitude to subdue a gorilla, or other brute menial, to their service; and, after in vain trying kindness, driven in self-defence to protect themselves from its

brutal violence. The provocation which had roused the
unappeasable wrath of Miranda's father was indeed great;
but recognising the 'most poor credulous monster' as the
mere brute that he is, it involved no moral delinquency:
and therefore he is not to be regarded as devilish in
origin and inclinations, because he tells Stephano what
is literally true—'I am subject to a tyrant, a sorcerer,
that by his cunning hath cheated me of the island.' He
accordingly invites the drunken butler to be his sup-
planter :—

> ' If thy greatness will
> Revenge it on him,—for I know thou darest,—
> Thou shalt be lord of it, and I'll serve thee.'

He gloats on the idea of braining the tyrant, just as an
abused human slave might, and indeed many a time has
done.

> ' Why, as I told thee, 'tis a custom with him
> I' the afternoon to sleep : there thou mayst brain him,
> Having first seized his books ; or with a log
> Batter his skull, or paunch him with a stake,
> Or cut his weazand with thy knife. Remember
> First to possess his books; for without them
> He's but a sot, as I am, nor hath not
> One spirit to command : they all do hate him
> As rootedly as I.'

All this would be hateful enough in a human being ; but
before we pronounce Caliban a 'demi-devil,' we must
place alongside of him the butler Stephano, who, with
no other provocation than that of a base nature, and
with no wrongs whatever to avenge, is ready with
the response—'Monster, I will kill this man ; his
daughter and I will be king and queen, and Trinculo
and thyself shall be viceroys ; ' and so the poor servant
monster already fancies his slavery at an end, and exclaims, ' Freedom, hey-day ! hey-day, freedom ! '

He who undertakes to subdue the wild nature of ape,

leopard, wolf, or tiger, must not charge it with moral delinquency when it yields to its native instincts. It may be, as modern science would teach us, that our most human characteristics are but developed instincts of the brute ; for the churl

> 'Will let his coltish nature break
> At seasons through the gilded pale.'

The savage, though familiarised with habits of civilisation, reverts with easy recoil to his barbarian licence ; and the highest happiness which the tamed monster of the island could conceive of, was once more to range in unrestrained liberty, digging up the pig-nuts with his long nails, or following the jay and the nimble marmoset over rock and tree. But there is nothing malignant in this ; and that nothing essentially repulsive is to be assumed as natural to him is apparent from the very invectives of Prospero :—

> 'Thou most lying slave,
> Whom stripes may move, not kindness : I have used thee,
> Filth as thou art, with human care ; and lodged thee
> In mine own cell, till thou didst seek to violate
> The honour of my child.'

Leaving aside, then, the exaggerations of the incensed Prospero, which have their legitimate place in the development of the drama, let us study, as far as may be, the actual characteristics of the strange islander. His story is told, briefly indeed, yet with adequate minuteness. Prospero retorts on him the recapitulation of kindnesses which had been repaid with outrage never to be forgiven :—

> 'Abhorred slave,
> Which any print of goodness will not take,
> Being capable of all ill! I pitied thee,
> Took pains to make thee speak, taught thee each hour
> One thing or other: when thou didst not, savage,
> Know thine own meaning, but wouldst gabble like

> A thing most brutish, I endowed thy purposes
> With words that made them known. But thy vile race,
> Though thou didst learn, had that in't which good natures
> Could not abide to be with.'

In other words, he proved to be simply an animal, actuated by the ordinary unrestrained passions and desires which in the brute involve no moral evil, and but for the presence of Miranda would have attracted no special notice. Situated as he actually is, he is not to be judged of wholly from the invectives of his master. With brute instincts which have brought on him the condign punishment of Prospero, and a savage nature which watches, like any wild creature under harsh restraint, for escape and revenge, his feelings are nevertheless rather those of the captive bear than of 'one who treasures up a wrong.' There is in him still a dog-like aptitude for attachment, a craving even for the mastership of some higher nature, and an appreciation of kindness not unlike that of the domesticated dog, though conjoined with faculties of intelligent enjoyment more nearly approximating to humanity. When compelled reluctantly to emerge from his den, he enters muttering curses; yet even they have a smack of nature in them. They are in no ways devilish, but such as the wild creature exposed to the elements may be supposed to recognise as the blight and mildew with which Nature gratifies her ill-will. He imprecates on his enslaver—

> 'As wicked dew as e'er my mother brushed
> With raven's feather from unwholesome fen
> Drop on you both ! A south-west blow on ye
> And blister you all o'er !'

Prospero threatens him with cramps, side-stitches that shall pen his breath up, urchins to prick him, and pinching pains more stinging than the bees; but his

answer has no smack of fiendishness, though he does
retort with bootless imprecations. He stolidly replies—

> ' I must eat my dinner.
> This island's mine, by Sycorax my mother,
> Which thou takest from me. When thou camest first,
> Thou strokedst me, and madest much of me ; wouldst give me
> Water with berries in't ; and teach me how
> To name the bigger light, and how the less,
> That burn by day and night ; and then I loved thee,
> And shew'd thee all the qualities o' the isle,
> The fresh springs, brine-pits, barren place and fertile ;
> Cursed be I that did so ! All the charms
> Of Sycorax, toads, beetles, bats, light on you !
> For I am all the subjects that you have,
> Which first was mine own king ; and here you sty me
> In this hard rock, whiles you do keep from me
> The rest o' the island.'

Prospero replies to him as a creature ' whom stripes may
move, not kindness,' who had been treated companion-
ably, with human care, till his brute instincts compelled
the subjection of him to such restraint. He describes
the pity with which he at first regarded the poor monster,
whose brutish gabble he had trained to the intelligent
speech which is now used for curses. In all this do we
not realise the ideal anthropoid in the highest stage of
Simian evolution, stroked and made much of like a
favourite dog, fed with dainties, and at length taught to
frame his brute cries into words by which his wishes
could find intelligible utterance. The bigger and the
lesser light receive names, and are even traced, as we
may presume, to their origin. But the intellectual development compasses, at the utmost, a very narrow
range ; and when the drunken Stephano plies him with
his bottle of sack, the dialogue runs in this characteristic
fashion :—

> ' *Steph.* How now, moon-calf ? how does thine ague ?
> *Cal.* Hast thou not dropt from heaven ?

Steph. Out o' the moon, I do assure thee: I was the man in the moon, when time was.

Cal. I have seen thee in her, and I do adore thee. My mistress shewed me thee, and thy dog, and thy bush.

Steph. Come, swear to that; kiss the book: I will furnish it anon with new contents: swear.

Trin. By this good light, this is a very shallow monster! I am afeard of him! A very weak monster! The man i' the moon! A most poor credulous monster! Well drawn, monster, in good sooth!

Cal. I'll shew thee every fertile inch o' the island; And I will kiss thy foot: 1 pr'ythee, be my god.'

But we presently see Caliban in another and wholly different aspect. Like the domesticated animal, which he really is, he has certain artificial habits and tastes superinduced in him; but whenever his natural instincts reveal themselves we see neither a born devil, nor a being bearing any likeness to degraded savage humanity. He is an animal at home among the sounds and scenes of living nature. 'Pray you, tread softly, that the blind mole may not hear a footfall,' is his exhortation to his drunken companions as they approach the entrance of Prospero's cell. When Trinculo frets him, his threatened revenge is, 'He shall drink nought but brine; for I'll not show him where the quick freshes are;' and he encourages his equally rude companion with the assurance—

'Be not afeard; the isle is full of noises,
Sounds, and sweet airs, that give delight and hurt not.
Sometimes a thousand twangling instruments
Will hum about mine ears; and sometimes voices,
That, if I then had waked after long sleep,
Will make me sleep again: and then, in dreaming,
The clouds, methought, would open, and shew riches
Ready to drop upon me; that, when I waked,
I cried to dream again.'

To the drunken butler and his comrade, Caliban is 'a most poor credulous monster! a puppy-headed, scurvy,

abominable monster! a most ridiculous monster!' and
when, by their aid, he has drowned his tongue in sack,
he is no more to them than a debauched fish. But
Shakespeare has purposely placed the true anthropo-
morphoid alongside of these types of degraded humanity,
to shew the contrast between them. He is careful to
draw a wide and strongly-marked distinction between
the coarse prosaic brutality of debased human nature,
and the inferior, but in no ways degraded, brute nature
of Caliban. ' He is,' says Prospero, ' as disproportioned
in his manners as in his shape.' He had associated for
years in friendly dependence, lodged with Prospero in
his own cell; for we have to remember that Miranda
was but three years old when her father took in hand
the taming of the poor monster, and used him with
human care, until compelled to drive him forth to his
rocky prison. His narrow faculties have thus been
forced into strange development; but though the
wrathful Prospero pronounces him a creature 'which any
print of goodness will not take, being capable of all ill,'
that is by no means the impression which the poet
designs to convey. Man, by reason of his higher nature
which invites him to aspire, and his moral sense which
clearly presents to him the choice between good and
evil, is capable of a degradation beyond reach of the
brute. The very criminality which has so hardened
Prospero's heart against his poor slave, involves to himself no sense of moral wrong. 'O ho! O ho! would it had
been done!' is his retort to Prospero; 'thou didst
prevent me; I had peopled else this isle with Calibans.'
    The distinction between the coarse sensuality of
degraded humanity, and this most original creation of
poetic fancy, with its gross brute-mind, its limited
faculties, its purely animal cravings and impulses, is

maintained throughout. The first scene opens with the sailors, released from all ordinary deference and restraint by the perils of the storm, shouting and blaspheming in reckless desperation ; and no sooner are they ashore than Caliban is brought into closest relations with the still more worthless topers who win his admiration, till experience teaches him—

> ' What a thrice-double ass
> Was I, to take this drunkard for a god,
> And worship this dull fool ! '

The dog-like attachment which had drawn him to Prospero, till harsh treatment and restraint eradicated this feeling, and utterly alienated him from his first master, is transferred to the next being who treats him with any appearance of kindness. ' I'll shew thee every fertile inch o' the island,' is the first form in which his gratitude finds utterance ;

> ' I'll shew thee the best springs; I'll pluck thee berries;
> I'll fish for thee, and get thee wood enough.
> A plague upon the tyrant that I serve!
> I'll bear him no more sticks, but follow thee,
> Thou wondrous man.'

The drunken butler, with his bottle of sack, seems to the poor monster to have dropped from heaven, or rather from the moon, where once his mistress showed him that favourite myth of old popular folk-lore, the man-in-the-moon, with his dog and bush : and so he fawns on him as a dog might on an old acquaintance. ' A most ridiculous monster,' thinks Trinculo, ' to make a wonder of a poor drunkard ; ' but Caliban is ready to lavish all his dog-like fidelity on his new-found master.

> ' I prithee, let me bring thee where crabs grow;
> And I, with my long nails, will dig thee pig-nuts;
> Shew thee a jay's nest, and instruct thee how
> To snare the nimble marmoset; I'll bring thee

> To clustering filberts; and sometimes I'll get thee
> Young scamels from the rock. Wilt thou go with me?'

If we can conceive of a baboon endowed with speech, and moved by gratitude, have we not here the very ideas to which its nature would prompt it. It is a creature native to the rocks and the woods, at home in the haunts of the jay and marmoset : a fellow-creature of like nature and sympathies with themselves. The talk of the ship's crew is not only coarse, but even what it is customary to call brutal ; while that of Stephano and Trinculo accords with their debased and besotted humanity. Their language never assumes a rhythmical structure, or rises to poetic thought. But Caliban is in perfect harmony with the rhythm of the breezes and the tides. His thoughts are essentially poetical, within the range of his lower nature; and so his speech is, for the most part, in verse. He has that poetry of the senses which seems natural to his companionship with the creatures of the forest and the seashore. Even his growl, as he retorts impotent curses on the power that has enslaved him, is rhythmical. Bogs, fens, and the infectious exhalations that the sun sucks up, embody his ideas of evil ; and his acute senses are chiefly at home with the dew, and the fresh springs, the clustering filberts, the jay in his leafy nest, or the blind mole in its burrow.

No being of all that people the Shakespearean drama more thoroughly suggests the idea of a pure creation of the poetic fancy than Caliban. He has a nature of his own essentially distinct from the human beings with whom he is brought in contact. He seems indeed the half-human link between the brute and man ; and realises, as no degraded Bushman or Australian savage can do, a conceivable intermediate stage of the anthropomorphous existence, as far above the most highly organised ape as it falls short of rational humanity. He excites a sympathy such as no degraded savage could. We feel for the poor monster, so helplessly in the power of the stern Prospero, as for some caged wild beast pining in cruel captivity, and rejoice to think of him at last free to range in harmless mastery over his island solitude. He provokes no more jealousy as the inheritor of Prospero's usurped lordship over his island home than the caged bird which has escaped to the free forest again. His is a type of development essentially non-human,—though, for the purposes of the drama, endued to an extent altogether beyond the highest attainments of the civilised, domesticated animal, with the exercise of reason and the use of language;—a conceivable civilisation such as would, to a certain extent, run parallel to that of man, but could never converge to a common centre.

CHAPTER VI.

CALIBAN, THE METAPHYSICIAN.

'Titled with many a name, almighty lord of immortals,
Zeus, thou crown of creation, whose sway by law is directed,
Hail! It is right and just for mortals thus to approach thee:
We are thy offspring. We alone, of thy varied dependents
Living and moving on earth, are gifted with speech to address thee.'

Hymn of Cleanthes to Zeus.

A PROPOSITION of no slight significance in the argument for man's evolution from the brute is that there is no evidence of his having been 'aboriginally endowed with the ennobling belief in the existence of an omnipotent God.' It seems more than doubtful, in the process of developed ideas and beliefs assigned to him, whether there is any room at a later stage for his receiving such belief as an ' endowment' or a revelation. If, as the whole line of argument assumes, the characteristics of humanity are no more than the developed instincts of the brute, and all that is highest in our nature is but an evolution from the very lowest and meanest phenomena of mere vitality, the absence of any such ennobling belief in all the stages of life but the latest, is inevitable. The growing difficulty, indeed, is not so much to find man's place in nature, as to find any place left for mind: either that of the Supreme Omnipotence, or the immortal entity which it has been habitual to conceive of as the body's guest.

It is not merely the pedigree of this highest vertebrate animal, Man, which is undoubtingly traced back to one of the lowest classes in the sub-kingdom of the mollusca. His intellect, his conscience, and his religious beliefs are but the latest ramifications of that primitive Ascidian germ which clung to the rocks on the shores of inconceivably ancient seas. Nor, indeed, must we think of the Ascidian as of the primeval seed-vessel of animal life, with all the possibilities of evolution embodied in it in embryo. The pedigree has indeed been carried back wondrous lengths ; but having got so far, why stop there? The distinctions between the moluscoid on its tidal rock and the vegetable lichens beyond reach of the waves, is trifling compared with later feats of evolution. Life is present in both ; and if conscience, religion, the apprehension of truth, the belief in God and immortality, are all no more than developed or transformed animal sensations ; and intellect is only the latest elaboration of the perceptions of the senses : it need not surprise us that inquiry has already been extended in search of relations between the inorganic and the organic. On this new hypothesis of evolution 'what a piece of work is man!' and as for God, it is hard to see what is left for Him to do in the universe.

But if we are limited to the conception of our physical organisation as the product of evolution, while the living soul is still allowed its divine origin, then, so far as creation is concerned, it matters little whether we are assumed to be literally made of the dust of the ground, or to have originated in Ascidian germs, and been at latest evolved from apes. The one transformation seems to be no less supernatural than the other. In so far as it is strictly a physiological and anatomical question, let physical science have untrammelled scope in deciding it ; but when it becomes a psychical question, it is not as a mere matter of sentiment that the mind revolts at a theory of evolution which professes to recognise its own emanation as no more than the accumulation of impressions and sensations of the nervous organisation gathered in the slow lapse of ages, until at last it has culminated in a moral sense. Our belief in a great First Cause is inextricably bound up with our belief in the human soul: mind first, then matter. It is an instinct of our being which arms us with patience against a thousand ills which the brute escapes from, because he 'wants discourse of reason,' and neither 'looks before nor after.' Hence it is that we now turn with an altogether novel interest to Shakespeare's unprejudiced realisation of what is conceivable as the product of highest evolution in the brute.

But a living poet, of rare objective power, yet not un-influenced by the spirit of his age, has aimed at carrying us a step further in the comprehension of the ideal brute-precursor, if not the progenitor, of man. Shakespeare fashioned for us the 'beast Caliban' in the sullenness of his harsh enslavement, hankering after the fresh springs and brine-pits; or pining for the music of the winds as he goes a-nesting, or the long wash of the billows while he gathers the scamels from the rock, and chases the nimble crabs when tides are low. The isle is full of noises; and though he has no linnet-note of his own, nor any such powers as those by which, according to Audubon, that *Orpheus polyglottus*, the American mock-ing-bird, puts to silence the Virginia nightingale and other mortified songsters of the woods, yet the sounds of nature hum welcomely about his ears, and soothe him to sleep.

But it is not Caliban who sleeps, but Prospero and Miranda:—slumbering in full confidence that he drudges at their task;—while our other poet, Robert Browning, pictures the poor monster, constrained by the very luxury of leisure snatched from toil, to give such reasoning powers as are developed in him a wider sweep, while he lets the rank tongue blossom into speech. The opening picture is one of sheer animal enjoyment :—

> ' Will sprawl, now that the heat of day is best,
> Flat on his belly, in the pit's much mire,
> With elbows wide, fists clenched to prop his chin ;
> And while he kicks both feet in the cool slush,
> And feels about his spine small eft-things course,
> Run in and out each arm, and make him laugh ;
> And while above his head a pompion-plant,
> Coating the cave-top as a brow its eye,
> Creeps down to touch and tickle hair and beard,
> And now a flower drops with a bee inside,
> And now a fruit to snap at, catch, and crunch :
> He looks out o'er yon sea which sunbeams cross
> And recross till they weave a spider-web,
> (Meshes of fire, some great fish breaks at times,)
> And talks to his own self, howe'er he please,
> Touching that other, whom his dam called God.'

In the traditions of that prehistoric island-time, before Caliban had been endowed with speech, or Duke Prospero had come to rule with supernatural authority over the elemental powers, there had been impressed on that dim mind some perception of a power called divine. The modern students of man's place in nature have been much perplexed on the question of religion as an assumed attribute of man. Any doctrine of final causes is not to be tolerated ; and yet that out of nothing something has come, with all the evolutions, physical and and moral, of that entity, is a kind of positivism against which reason rebels. It is legitimate, therefore, to inquire whether the idea of God is innate in the human mind ; or if it be true, as has undoubtedly been affirmed by travellers, missionaries, and scientific observers, that there are races of men altogether devoid of religion. ' If,' says Sir John Lubbock, ' the mere sensation of fear, and the recognition that there are probably other beings

more powerful than man, are sufficient alone to constitute a religion, then we must, I think, admit that religion
is general to the human race.' But, in reality, he sees in
it no more than a child's dread of the darkness, which no
one regards as a token of religious belief; or if it be,
then the proof of the general existence of religion
founded on this sensation of fear, will no longer limit it
among the things peculiar to man. The feelings with
which a dog regards its master partake of the like
mingling of awe and dependent regard, as that which
constitutes much of human religious feeling; and as for
rites and religious services, Sir John considers the baying
of a dog to the moon as much an act of worship as some
ceremonies which travellers have described as religious.

If it could be shown that there is actually present in
the savage mind such a mingled sense of awe and dependence on an unseen power as the dog recognises in relation to his master, there would remain no further room
for doubt as to the existence of religion in the case.
The late Dr. John Duncan, of New College, Edinburgh,
or Rabbi Duncan as he is more generally styled, when
bringing his acute metaphysical turn of speculation to
bear on his own favourite dog, came to a conclusion that
may seem wonderfully acceptable to the modern evolutionist. He recognised in little Topsy, not only what
seemed to him many undeveloped elements of human
nature, but something resembling a conscience toward
man; and he was wont to quote with favour the dictum
of an old Puritan divine, that 'Man is a little god unto
the lower animals; their waiting eyes are fixed upon
him, and he giveth them their meat in due season.' As
to the state of mind of the dog when he bays the moon,
or its precise ideas in relation to that 'lesser light,' we
must await the revelations of some 'unusually wise'

canine philosopher. This, however, appears for our present purpose, according to the revelations of the poets, that there had been impressed on the dull brain of Caliban some idea of a supernatural, though by no means omnipotent power. Judging of supernal powers, and the Divine attributes, solely by his own experiences, the conclusions he arrives at are confused enough. He has far-off remembrances of Sycorax, terrible in her sorceries, unmitigable in her rage ; one so strong that she could control the moon, and command the ebb and flow of the tides : but yet altogether beneficent in her dealings with him. Very different are his perceptions of another overruling power, the tyrant Prospero, who, as he says, 'by sorcery got this isle, from me he got it,' and who continues to the present hour to manifest his omnipotence in very terrible judgments for every trifle. So far as Caliban's experiences went, this abhorred hag, the worker of sorceries too terrible for human utterance, was, according to his crude Manichean creed, the representative of beneficent superhuman power ; while the sage Prospero—who with his nobler reason against his fury takes part, and recognises a choicer action in virtue than in vengeance,—appeared to him a malignant and wholly evil power.

But besides those two potencies, of both of which Caliban has had actual sight and experience, there is that dam's god, Setebos. Prospero was not only a superhuman power, but to him was all powerful. To resist his will was impossible.

> ' His art is of such power,
> It would control my dam's god, Setebos,
> And make a vassal of him.'

Yet that is a power not wholly mysterious. Caliban has learned to refer it, not to him, but to his art ; and

H

believes that, without his books he would not have one
spirit to command : ' They all do hate him as rootedly
as I.'   But these books are the symbols, as well as the
instruments of moral supremacy.   So long as he holds
these, the spirits may hate, but, like himself, they must
tremble and obey ; for his power is such that it can control even the divine Setebos,—a very puzzling state of
things for such a mind to ponder over.   In early days,
when Prospero stroked and made much of his poor slave,
Caliban yielded him a dog-like fidelity, and showed him
all the qualities of the island.   Now that their relations
have so wholly changed, he hates him according to the
hate of ' a thing most brutish,' and feels neither awe nor
compunction, but only pleasure, at the idea that Stephano
should   ' With a log

> Batter his skull, or paunch him with a stake,
> Or cut his weazand with his knife.'

Setebos is a wholly different being from this : an invisible and very vague divinity, on whom no such attempts
are possible, inferior though he is in some sense to the
artful Prospero.   Nevertheless it is inevitable that when
Caliban takes to thinking of that other whom his dam
called God, he should, like metaphysicians of more
matured powers and higher advantages, realise little
more than a being ' altogether such an one as himself.'
And yet his ideas are confused and obscure, as is inevitable
in the best attempts at reasoning on such supra-physical
matters.   Prospero's power is a very tangible reality to
him : a power that admitted of no thought of resistance
by its most unwilling slave ; and so he doubted not it
could make a vassal of Setebos as well as of his poor
self.   But in these puzzlings of his, which the poet
Browning records for us, over the origin of his little
island-world, and the bigger and the less light that burn

by day and night for its special benefit, the vague unseen Setebos seems fitter creator than the magician;
though as for the stars, they may be 'the poetry of
heaven;' but in his present prosaic mood they do not
seem much to concern him or his island, and so he
fancies they may have come otherwise, it not being
needful for the poor puzzled philosopher to say how.

> 'Setebos, Setebos, and Setebos!
> Thinketh He dwelleth i' the cold o' the moon.
> Thinketh He made it, with the sun to match,
> But not the stars; the stars came otherwise;
> Only made clouds, winds, meteors, such as that:
> Also this isle, what lives and grows thereon,
> And snaky sea which rounds and ends the same.'

If Setebos does indeed dwell in the cold moon, then
Caliban, to whom cold is very unwelcome, can conceive of how such creation might come of the very
restlessness of being ill at ease. The cold o' the moon
is his dwelling-place. He cannot change his cold, nor
cure its ache; and so, in an uneasy way, he betakes
himself to making clouds, meteors, the sun itself, to
match his moon. For has not Caliban, as he sprawled
in the heat of the day, on the breezy rocks that overlook the strand,

> 'Spied an icy fish
> That longed to 'scape the rock-stream where she lived,
> And thaw herself within the lukewarm brine
> O' the lazy sea her stream thrusts far amid,
> A crystal spike 'twixt two warm walls of wave;
> Only she ever sickened, found repulse
> At the other kind of water, not her life,
> (Green-dense and dim-delicious, bred o' the sun,)
> Flounced back from bliss she was not born to breathe,
> And in her old bounds buried her despair,
> Hating and loving warmth alike.'

And so, judging accordingly—and like more learned
philosophers sometimes mistaking deduction for induc-

tion,—Caliban surmises that he, in some such mood, made the sun, this isle, and so much else : fowl, beast, and creeping thing :—

> 'Yon otter, sleek-wet, black, lithe as a leech;
> Yon auk, one fire-eye in a ball of foam,
> That floats and feeds; a certain badger brown
> He hath watched hunt with that slant white-wedge eye
> By moonlight; and the pie with the long tongue
> That pricks deep into oakwarts for a worm,
> And says a plain word when she finds her prize,
> But will not eat the ants; the ants themselves
> That build a wall of seeds and settled stalks
> About their hole—He made all these and more,
> Made all we see, and us, in spite: how else?'

But our modern poet has other purposes than merely to ingraft some island-details on that pure creative conception in which the genius of Shakespeare has revealed its mastery. If not metaphysical, like poor Caliban, he at any rate has Bridgewater philosophers, metaphysical realists, theologians—Calvinistic and anti-Calvinistic,—all in view. Setebos, the divine power in the island mythology—great First Cause, if not infinite originator,—is being comprehended by this very finite metaphysician. For instead of contentedly enjoying his comfortable sprawl in the mire, now that the heat of the day is at its best : Caliban suddenly finds himself involved in all the subtleties of the Ego and Non-ego, and much else of a like kind, with results very much akin to the experiences of those whom Milton describes as retiring apart from their fellows who sang the songs of a lost heaven, and there they

> 'Reasoned high
> Of providence, foreknowledge, will, and fate;
> Fix'd fate, free will, foreknowledge absolute;
> And found no end, in wandering mazes lost.
> Of good and evil much they argued then.'

The reasoning, though pronounced 'vain wisdom all, and

false philosophy,' may have suited metaphysical devils ; but it must be owned that Caliban, as the representative missing link—no 'born devil,' in spite of Prospero's imprecations, but only a poor half-witted brute,—gets terribly out of his depth. The modern searchers into the origin of man, and of his civilisation, marshal an imposing array of witnesses to the existence of tribes of men wholly destitute of any trace of religion. Some of their evidence is more than doubtful. We have only to remember one memorable example, to understand how men apply their own standards of religion to test its existence amongst others.

In 1617, Dr. Laud, then Archdeacon of Huntingdon, paid his first visit to Presbyterian Scotland, as chaplain to King James ; and finding there no such forms, ceremonies, or artistically-devised ritual as constituted to his mind the very essence of worship, he pronounced with grief of heart that there was ' no religion at all, that he could see !' We will pit Dr. Laud against the most reliable witnesses of the Evolutionists, as a trained expert in the discernment of visible religions ; and yet other very trustworthy authorities seem to indicate that, in Scotland in that year, 1617, and in subsequent years, the Scots really had some sort of thing deserving the name of religion, though Dr. Land could not see it.

Among savages religion is not a thing to be talked of. Gods, manitous, spirits, the dead, are not to be named, save under the extremest urgency. The mere wayfaring traveller's report is valueless. The missionary has repeatedly found that he has not only used in his teaching, but given a place in his native version of the Scriptures, to religious terms that he has wholly misapplied. The ideas themselves are undefined, and are apt to elude the questioner altogether, when he insists on a definition. We have ourselves tried, in converse with the Indians of North America, to get at their ideas on much simpler things than God, creation, free-will, or the belief in a future life; and found it no easy matter to get them to entertain questions foreign to their ordinary current of thought. We were told by a Christian missionary who had laboured for years among the Chippeway Indians, preaching to them at first with the aid of a native interpreter, that he was shocked, when at a later date he listened to similar renderings of a young missionary's address into the language now familiar. to him, to discover that nearly all the ideas most essential to the doctrines they sought to inculcate were lost in the process. The interpreter translated them into the pagan notions of the tribe, and so the Christian element was well-nigh eliminated, while the preacher complacently waited for the fruits of the seed he fancied to have been sown.

It is necessary to know what shape the ideas of the supernatural have assumed to the savage mind, before it can be appealed to in any intelligible language. The difficulty indeed may be tested by trying to obtain an intelligent definition of an over-ruling providence from the ordinary untutored mind. Put, for example, to the English peasant, unaccustomed to abstract thought, some of the questions on election, effectual calling, and the like points of Calvinistic theology, contained in " The Shorter Catechism" prepared by the Westminster divines for the use of children. You are speaking his own language, and have a good many ideas in common; yet the answers will be vague and intangible enough. They may, however, help us to understand how the savage mind may be interrogated in reference to its ideas of God, religion, a future state, creation, life, death, and much else, with results exceedingly misleading and deceptive.

But however we may estimate the bearings of the evidence adduced, there is something very touching in the first narrative quoted by Sir John Lubbock in proof of the total absence of religious belief in the earlier savage stage. M. Bik is the authority; and his subject is the Arafura of one of the islands lying between New Guinea and North Australia. 'It is evident,' says the narrator, 'that the Arafuras of Vorkay possess no religion whatever. Of the immortality of the soul they have not the least conception. To all my inquiries on this subject they answered, 'No Arafura has ever returned to us after death, therefore we know nothing of a future state; and this is the first time we have heard of it.' The questioner was a passing voyager of the Dourga, speaking through an interpreter, and as ignorant of the Arafura ideas of the soul, the future state, and other matters referred to, as if some German Kant were to demand of an English peasant concerning his belief in the empirical reality and transcendental ideality of space and time; or required from him a definition of his ideas of *a priori* intuition. His answer would be very much after the fashion of the Arafura, when desired to state his notions as to the creation of the world. 'None of us are aware of this; we have never heard anything about it, and therefore do not know who has done it all.' The German philosopher might report very truly that he could not discover in the English peasant any notion of space or time, or indeed any innate ideas at all; and yet he would convey a very false impression of the peasant's

actual notions and beliefs. But M. Bik thus proceeds :
'To convince myself more fully respecting their want of
knowledge of a Supreme Being, I demanded of them
on what they called for help in their need, when, far
from their homes, engaged in the trepang fishery, their
vessels were overtaken by violent tempests, and no
human power could save them, their wives and children, from destruction. The eldest among them, after
having consulted the others, answered that they knew
not on whom they could call for assistance, but begged
me, if I knew, to be so good as to inform them.'

This is very tender and touching in its childlike
simplicity ; but the mode adopted by the voyager to
convince himself of the point aimed at was exceedingly deceptive. They no more prayed to God, or any
unseen power, after his fashion, than the Presbyterians
of Scotland did after the high Anglican fashion of
Laud. But this by no means proves that they had
no faith in the supernatural, no altar, like that of the
Athenians, to the unknown God. As to the poor
Arafuras' idea of a divine refuge in their hour of need,
the savage mind is slow indeed to realise the idea of
beneficent power. In truth the strongest argument
against the evolution of the Christian religion from
our own sensations and perceptions, is that it so utterly
transcends the purest aspirations of the human soul,
as to make it vain to imagine they could ever beget
a 'Sermon on the Mount.' 'An eye for an eye, and
a tooth for a tooth,' seems thoroughly human ; but
'Blessed are the merciful,' 'the pure in heart,' and all
the maxims of the Great Teacher, partake not of the
humanity either of the first or of this nineteenth century.

An Indian chief on Lake Superior explained to myself the difference between the white man's God and

his own Manitou, in this simple way: 'When the lake rises in a storm, and the north-west wind howls through the trees, and lightnings kindle them, we know that is the great Manitou, and we are afraid, and hide ourselves, We offer him much tobacco; we try to avert his anger; and are at peace again when he is gone. As for you white men, you call on your God, and want him to come to you. Are you not afraid of him?' The idea of the All-powerful being also the All-loving pertains alone to Christianity. The savage's conception of divine power in any sense is necessarily associated with the only moral qualities actively present in himself; and as the strong savage tyrannises over the weak, and is very indifferent to his privations, his sufferings, or wrongs, he finds it hard to realise any idea of omnipotence dissociated from the disposition to abuse such power. The moral sense is weak, the passions are strong; and love, generosity, or any golden rule of charity and beneficence is apt to appear to him an evidence of weakness rather than an expression of power. 'The mighty God, even the Lord hath spoken, and called the earth from the rising of the sun unto the going down thereof. Out of Zion, the perfection of beauty, God hath shined.' So says the inspired Hebrew poet. But when, as with the poor Arafura savage, 'God hath not spoken a single word;' and he has been left to his own heart's devices, to turn his strength to cruelty, then the utter-ance might follow from the same song of praise, 'These things hast thou done, and I kept silence. Thou thoughtest that I was altogether such an one as thyself.'

Another French traveller, M. Arbrousset, gives a very different account of the searching of Sekesa, an intelligent Kaffir, to find out God, while he still dwelt a lonely savage among the wilds of southern Africa. 'Your tidings,' he said, 'are what I want; and I was seeking before I knew you, as you shall hear. Twelve years ago, I went to feed my flocks. The weather was hazy. I sat down upon a rock and asked myself sorrowful questions : yes, sorrowful, because I was unable to answer them. "Who has touched the stars with his hands? on what pillars do they rest?" I asked myself. "The waters are never weary; they know no other law than to flow without ceasing from morning till night, and from night till morning : but where do they stop, and who makes them flow thus? The clouds also come and go, and burst in water over the earth. Whence come they? Who sends them? The diviners certainly do not give us rain; for how could they do it? And why do I not see them with my own eyes when they go up to heaven to fetch it?"' And so the Kaffir details his vain questionings, until he says, 'Then I buried my face in my hands.' Sir John Lubbock says of this : it is an exceptional case. In reality the question rises to our mind in relation to it, as to many similar reports of savage utterances : How much of this is, however undesignedly, due to the questioner? Our own experience with the American savage is that it is only by slow and careful observation of his spontaneous utterances that any conception of his real beliefs can be arrived at. By means of leading questions you may get any answers you like. As a rule, the savage will reply in the way he thinks you desire, however wide of the truth. It is difficult to evade some suspicion that the thoughts which troubled Sekesa's mind have acquired some of their definiteness in transmission through that of the narrator.

The poet Browning, reasoning as his fashion is, as it were for the time being with the very brain and faculties of his subject, thus sets Caliban to work out his ideal of a Supreme Being, conceivable only as powerful, by no means as loving :—

> ' He made all these, and more,
> Made all we see, and us, in spite : how else?
> He could not, Himself, make a second self . . . . .
> But did in envy. listlessness, or sport,
> Make what Himself would fain, in a manner, be—
> Look now, I melt a gourd-fruit into mash,
> Add honeycomb and pods, I have perceived,
> Which bite like finches when they bill and kiss,—
> Then when froth rises bladdery, drink up all,
> Quick, quick, till maggots scamper through my brain ;
> And throw me on my back i' the seeded thyme,
> And wanton, wishing I were born a bird.
> Put case, unable to be what I wish,
> I yet could make a live bird out of clay;
> Would not I take clay, pinch my Caliban
> Able to fly?—for, there, see, he hath wings,
> And great comb like the hoopoe's to admire,
> And there a sting to do his foes offence,
> There, and I will that he begin to live,
> Fly to yon rock-top, nip me off the horns
> Of grigs high up that make the merry din,
> Saucy, through thin-veined wings, and mind me not.
> In which feat, if his leg snapped, brittle clay,
> And he lay stupid-like,—why, I should laugh ;
> And, if he, spying me, should fall to weep,
> Beseech me to be good, repair his wrong,
> Bid his poor leg smart less, or grow again—
> Well, as the chance were, this might take, or else
> Not take my fancy : I might hear his cry,
> And give the manikin three legs for his one,
> Or pluck the other off, leave him like an egg,
> And lessoned he was mine, and merely clay.
> Were this no pleasure, lying in the thyme,
> Drinking the mash, with brain become alive,
> Making and marring clay at will ? '

The later poet, it is obvious, has here lost sight of the ideal of man's brute progenitor,—of the dimly

reasoning chimpanzee or baboon,—and is rather be-
thinking himself of greatly more modern controver-
sialists. He is no longer with the Athenian free-
thinker on Mars' Hill; but among the proselytes of
Rome, to whose questionings Paul responds in inter-
rogatives, 'O man, who art thou that repliest against
God? Shall the thing formed say to him that formed
it, Why hast thou formed me thus? Hath not the
potter power over the clay, of the same lump to make
one vessel unto honour and another to dishonour?'
Caliban, having no conception of mercy, self-sacrificing
love, generosity, or other motives which exercise a
sway over human action, and dimly reflect the highest
attributes of God,

> 'Thinketh such shows nor right nor wrong in Him,
> Nor kind, nor cruel: He is strong, and Lord.
> 'Am strong myself compared to yonder crabs,
> That march now from the mountain to the sea;
> 'Let twenty pass, and stone the twenty-first,
> Loving not, hating not, just choosing so.
> 'Say the first straggler that boasts purple spots
> Shall join the pile, one pincer twisted off;
> 'Say, this bruised fellow shall receive a worm,
> And two worms he whose nippers end in red;
> As it likes me each time, I do: so He.'

But that Setebos, the Creator, is capable of jealousy,
envy of his own handiwork if it should seem to rival
himself, is altogether natural to the mind of Caliban, —
the metaphysical Caliban of the later poet. He has,
himself, got to the length of creating; is a tool-using
animal; and does not see why, since Prospero transformed
his own brutish gabble into speech, and 'endowed his
purposes with words that made them known,' it might not
be possible to render other noises tractable and respon-
sive to the volitions of the utterer: say, for example,

to make this pipe of his, made of the pithless elder-joint, prattle its own thoughts, instead of only screaming one note when it is blown through. ' Will you play on this pipe?' says the Prince of Denmark to Rosencrantz, when the courtier, as he perceives, is attempting to play on himself, though, as he owns, he knows not a touch of the little pipe. 'Why, look you now, how unworthy a thing you make of me! You would play upon me; you would seem to know my stops; you would pluck out the heart of my mystery; you would sound me from my lowest note to the top of my compass: and there is much music, excellent voice, in this little organ, yet cannot you make it speak. 'Sblood! do you think I am easier to be played on than a pipe?'

But then, Hamlet was no ordinary human pipe. The modern poet has given us a sort of anthropoid Hamlet, in his version of Caliban dealing with the natural theology of the island. Setebos, as the poor monster reasons to himself, may be good in the main;—goodness mainly meaning with him, as with the Indian savage, unharmfulness. He may be placable, if his mind and ways were guessed aright: but then, if he takes to creating, the works of his hands must not presume to do anything unless through him. Suppose this pipe of Caliban's own manufacture, with which he can imitate the scream of the jay, were to take to blowing itself, and to boasting of its blowing, and of all the results of its music, as wholly its own: why then Caliban could endure no such presumption, and would crush it under foot. And if I, then so He ;—so Setebos, the Creator, with his creatures. Thus reasons Caliban :—

> ' Hath cut a pipe of pithless elder-joint
> That, blown through, gives exact the scream o' the jay
> When from her wing you twitch the feathers blue;

Sound this, and little birds that hate the jay
Flock within stone's throw, glad their foe is hurt:
Put case such pipe could prattle and boast forsooth,
"I catch the birds, I am the crafty thing,
I make the cry my maker cannot make
With his great round mouth: he must blow through mine!"
Would not I smash it with my foot?'

The self-made god, if it be fancy-wrought, and not
carven of wood or stone, must take its pattern and
compass from the conceiving mind. Under a process
of evolution which begets religious reverence and worship out of developed perceptions and sensations, the
imagined deity will grow with the imagining devotee;
but it must derive all its attributes from him. The self-
conceived God of the Arafura or Kaffir savage, will
therefore be altogether such an one as himself, and can
no more get beyond the mental conception of its
originator than the quart can be contained in a pint
measure. It is unquestionable that the divine ideal of
the savage very frequently presents just such characteristics. It is hard indeed to recover any trace of an instinctive consciousness of God, or any clear realisation of
immortality; whatever we may make of his belief in an
hereafter. In reality it is scarcely possible to formulate
the dimly conceived ideas of the savage mind on such
subjects. With man far above the savage state the inspira-
tions of conscience and religious reverence are not easily
reducible to written terms. They are indeed apt, not
only to elude the formulist, but actually to disappear
with the effort: as the synthetic processes of the poet's
fancy are incompatible with the anatomisings of the
critic. But if there be a human soul, distinct from the
mere animal life; and if there be also, as we believe, a
wholly different God, for rudest savage as for civilised
man, revealing Himself in the lilies of the field, in the

fowls of the air, in the stars of night ; taking care of the sparrow, numbering the very hairs of our head; not very far from every one of us :—then it may be possible for man, even in a ruder state than the Kaffir Sekesa, dimly to conceive of that unknown God, whom Paul found the Athenians ignorantly worshipping : ' God that made the world and all things therein, the Lord of heaven and earth, who giveth to all life, and breath, and all things.'

The religion of the old Greek had unquestionably more to do with the æsthetic faculty than the moral sense. His worship, to a large extent, addressed the sensuous emotions, and deceived himself, as fine ritual and solemn harmonies are apt to do, by affecting the emotional sensibilities alone. But this, and much else by which morality and religion were kept apart, belong to the evolutions of late ages. The traces of an underlying current of belief in something greatly more spiritual than the Zeus of his poetical mythology, is apparent in many allusions ; though too frequently this supreme omnipresence seemed to the Greek only an omnipotent, unapproachable, inexorable fate : ruler over gods and men, destined survivor of Olympus even more than of earth ; or as Caliban, in the dim searchings after a great First Cause, which belong to his later metaphysical stage, defines it—' the something over Setebos.' For, as he reasons,—

> 'There may be something quiet o'er His head,
> Out of His reach, that feels nor joy nor grief,
> Since both derive from weakness in some way.
> I joy because the quails come; would not joy
> Could I bring quails here when I have a mind :
> This Quiet, all it hath a mind to, doth.
> 'Esteemeth stars the outposts of its couch.
> But never spends much thought nor care that way.
> It may look up, work up,—the worse for those
> It works on ! 'Careth but for Setebos

The many-handed as a cuttle-fish,
Who, making Himself feared through what He does,
Looks up, first, and perceives He cannot soar
To what is quiet and hath happy life;
Next looks down here, and out of very spite
Makes this a bauble-world to ape yon real,
These good things to match those as hips do grapes.
'Tis solace making baubles, ay, and sport.'

For Caliban himself lately peeping, eyed Prospero at his magic books; and, vexed at the sight, stitched himself a make-believe magic book of leaves, scrawled thereon meaningless characters, portentous enough according to his wish; peeled for himself a wand, robed himself in skin of spotted oncelot, and tried to fancy himself Prospero. He has his tamed sleek ounce, which he makes cower, crouch, and mind his eye; he keeps his Ariel too, a tall pouch-bill crane, which at his word will go wade for fish and straight disgorge; and, to complete this realisation of being himself a lordly Prospero, he has got

' Also a sea-beast, lumpish, which he snared,
Blinded the eyes of, and brought somewhat tame,
And split its toe-webs, and now pens the drudge
In a hole o' the rock, and calls him Caliban;
A bitter heart, that bides its time and bites.
'Plays thus at being Prosper in a way.'

In many respects he seems to see a likeness to his own ways in the doings of the invisible power Setebos, or the something over Setebos. But, alas! if He has any favouring leanings, they are not towards him.

' He is terrible: watch His feats in proof !
One hurricane will spoil six good months' hope.
He hath a spite against me, that I know,
Just as he favours Prosper, who knows why?
So it is, all the same, as well I find.
'Wove wattles half the winter, fenced them firm
With stone and stake, to stop she-tortoises
Crawling to lay their eggs here: well, one wave,

Feeling the foot of Him upon its neck,
Gaped as a snake does, lolled out its large tongue,
And licked the whole labour flat: so much for spite.
'Dug up a newt He may have envied once
And turned to stone, shut up inside a stone.
Please Him, and hinder this?—What Prosper does?
Aha, if He would tell me how! Not He!——'

So Caliban proceeds, reasoning in his obscure, confused way : not, however, as Shakespeare's, but wholly as Browning's Caliban. For he is no longer the intermediate, half-brute, missing link ' that wants discourse of reason,' but the human savage, grovelling before the Manitou of his own conception ; betaking himself even to burnt sacrifices to appease this unseen Setebos, and ward off His envy, hoping the while that, some day, that other than Setebos may conquer Him ; or, likelier still, that He may grow decrepit, doze, and die. But at this stage the clouds gather, the wind rises to a hurricane,

' Crickets stop hissing ; not a bird—or, yes,
There scuds His raven that hath told Him all!
It was fool's play, this prattling! Ha! The wind
Shoulders the pillared dust, death's house o' the move,
And fast invading fires begin! White blaze—
A tree's head snaps—and there, there, there, there, there,
His thunder follows! Fool, to gibe at Him.'

Like the old Indian of Lake Superior, he hears the voice of God only in the violence and the terrors of nature ; and, like the first conscious offenders, when they heard, not the tempest and the whirlwind, but the still small voice among the trees of the garden, he is afraid. The evolution is, in truth, altogether too complete. This is no partially-developed irrational anthropoid, but man as he is to be met with in many a stage of mental progression far above the rude savage.

I

CHAPTER VII.

CALIBAN, THE THEOLOGIAN.

> ' How perplext
> Grows belief!
> Well, this clay-cold clod
> Was man's heart.
> Crumble it—and what comes next?
> Is it God?'—*Browning*.

ONE more idea, very foreign to anything pertaining to the brute-mind, presents itself, in modified evolution, to the Caliban of the later poet. Shakespeare's Caliban has his conception of death in its purely destructive form ; but not greatly differing, except in its definiteness, from that of the ravening beast. When Trinculo mocks him, he proposes at once that Stephano shall 'bite him to death ;' and when, in answer to the question 'Wilt thou destroy him, then?' Stephano promises, on his honour, that the tyrant Prospero shall be brained, Caliban is transported with joy. But in all this death is no more to him than to the wolf or the tiger, when it wrathfully makes an end of its foe, though the desire for it has something of the human in its treasured craving for revenge.

A dog is very capable of just such hatred, under similar provocation ; and its revenge, if unchecked, will not stop short of death. But the metaphysical island-monster of the modern poet gets greatly nearer to civilised humanity in his reasonings on the mystery of death. He does not indeed clearly realise the universality of this inevitable fate. For, looking on Setebos as a being not only terrible, but malevolent ; as a favourer of Prospero, and having a spite at himself : he wistfully longs that it were possible to learn how to propitiate this implacable power, or get beyond his reach :—

> ' Discover how, or die !
> All need not die, for of the things o' the isle
> Some flee afar, some dive, some run up trees ;
> Those at His mercy,—why they please Him most
> When . . when . . well, never try the same way twice !
> Repeat what act has pleased, He may grow wroth,
> You must not know His ways, and play Him off,
> Sure of the issue. 'Doth the like himself :
> 'Spareth a squirrel that it nothing fears,
> But steals the nut from underneath my thumb,
> And when I threat, bites stoutly in defence ;
> 'Spareth an urchin that, contrariwise,
> Curls up into a ball, pretending death
> For fright at my approach : the two ways please.
> But what would move my choler more than this,
> That either creature counted on its life
> To-morrow and next day, and all days to come,
> Saying, forsooth, in the inmost of its heart,
> " Because he did so yesterday with me,
> And otherwise with such another brute,
> So must he do henceforth and always."—Ay ?
> 'Would teach the reasoning couple what " must " means !
> 'Doth as he likes, or wherefore Lord ? So He.'

Caliban is thus, in this little island-world—over which, but for Prospero, he would be absolute lord, possessed of dominion over every living thing, — the conscious embodiment of an omnipotence unchecked by any beneficent attribute ; and he realises accordingly how terrible such a God is, when he conceives of himself as subject to just such power, Setebos or other. He can himself crush out the life of the squirrel or urchin, whenever it pleases him to do so ; and it causes him no compunction that they ' are as water spilt upon the ground, which cannot be gathered up again.' He does according to his will with all beneath him, reckless and unsympathetic as a blind remorseless fate. But if it please him to spare, then he sees nothing to prevent perpetual life. Life, in fact, is less of a mystery than death, except when produced by violence: as at his own pleasure it often is. 'All need not die;' in fact, only a few are actually brought within his own reach. But it is himself, not them, he cares for; and for himself the outlook is gloomy enough, since the Setebos, his sole providence, is altogether such a one as himself—excepting only in this terrible absolutism of power: and so he

> 'Conceiveth all things will continue thus,
> And we shall have to live in fear of Him
> So long as He lives, keeps His strength: no change,
> If He have done His best, make no new world
> To please Him more, so leave off watching this,—
> If He surprise not even the Quiet's self
> Some strange day,—or, suppose, grow into it
> As grubs grow butterflies: else, here are we,
> And there is He, and nowhere help at all.'

Here it must be confessed that Caliban, as the mere anthropoid, the brute-progenitor of man, and therefore the inferior of the lowest savage, is terribly out of his depth; for, indeed, the poet-resuscitator has revivified him for wholly different purposes than his first creator had in view. There is something of the inconsequential simplicity that might be conceived of in the deductions of the irrational being in such reasoning as this:—

> 'All need not die, for of the things o' the isle
> Some flee afar, some dive, some run up trees;'

and so there may be some way for us, too, to escape out of reach of Setebos. Yet the reasoning is probably less simple than that of many a savage philosopher of modern Pacific islands. Get beyond reach of this terrible Setebos by such very simple processes as the urchin or the squirrel at times eludes himself, or as those of strongest wing flee afar, escaping altogether from that island-microcosm which is the only world he knows of outside of the moon : this — or else things as they are ; for so far as he can see, all things remain, and will continue so.

The parable of the poet is not of difficult inter-pretation. The island and its puzzled philosopher deal with a condition of things in which the latest products of evolution have a personal interest, and from which reasoners of strongest flight have failed to effect their escape. This little island-world of ours, between the two illimitable oceans of an unbeginning and unending time, seems very unchangeable to the view of its ephemeron. He can conceive of no apter figure of stability than the everlasting hills. 'Since our fathers fell asleep, all things continue as they were from the beginning :' so reasons he. But it lies in the nature of things that reasoning beings learn to accumulate experience, to add what our fathers observed before they 'fell asleep' to what we ourselves perceive : and we begin to realise the fact that the hills are no more everlasting than the clouds or the waves. At the bottom of the ocean lie the moun-tains of former ages ; on the summits of our Andes and Himalayas are the sands of ancient ocean-beds ; and the mummied Pharaohs that ruled over ichthian or saurian worlds, when the foundations of those pyramids were laid, lie sepulchred there in the rocky matrix, like the island-newt that Setebos envied once, and turned to stone. But all this necessarily lies out-side of Caliban's philosophy. He is no link in a

chain of accumulated knowledge and experience, whatever other link he may supply: and so he can but
reason from what he knows.

Time is the grand factor in all theories of progressive
change or evolution. The universe is but an aggre-
gate of elements assuming ever new forms, in endless
but not lawless change. But for the reign of law,
indeed, there would seem to some to be no con-
trolling or overruling power. And yet the idea of
law without lawgiver or administrator, is one of those
legal fictions requiring something vastly beyond the
rationality of a Caliban to conceive. This, however, is
certain, that the grand revolutions in physical geography which reveal themselves by such manifest
chroniclings of process and result, are, for the most
part, no more than the products of forces still at
work. This is the key-note of modern geology; and
not less so of the newer anthropology. Given a
cumulative change—depression or elevation, degradation or evolution,—no matter how slight, how slow,
how nearly imperceptible it may seem: if the one
element of time be unlimited, it will suffice to rebuild
a cosmos out of chaos, to stop the clock-work of the
universe, or reorganise the heavens under conditions
wholly new. But the change must be continuously
progressive. A mere pendulum-motion, an ever-com-
pensating ebb and flow, can lead to no gradual un-
folding or maturing, but only to stability as the product of ceaseless change. The geologist has his one
planet, ever changing, on which

> 'The giant ages heave the hill
> And break the shore, and evermore
> Make, and break, and work their will.'

To the naturalist, race is a unit, on which he was

long content to trace the influences of time and change. But now his aggressive philosophy would comprehend the whole living catena, from the protozoic dawn till yesterday, as one ever-lengthening but unbroken chain. The death of countless units is no more than the counterpart to the ceaseless displacements and replacements which result from the vital actions of our own organism, and which are for it, not death but life : an indispensable part of the process of vital evolution. That which is unsuitable or injurious must be eliminated. The survival of the fittest can only be accomplished by the eradication of the inferior, the defective, or retrogressive. This useful process is death's work. Of this progressive elimination and evolution, whereby the greatest things are shown as the product of the least, man is the latest result ; the highest modification of pre-existent forms as yet developed ; the summit of the organic scale. He has risen to this lofty station through all the intermediate grades, from the very lowest. The higher he traces his pedigree, the lower must he be content to descend in recognising his original ancestry.

But even if Caliban could have accomplished his very natural desire, and 'peopled the isle with Calibans,' his individual happiness, the experiences which were to constitute his own life, would assume preeminent importance to him. Man may possibly learn to feel some pride at the idea of having risen, by processes of sexual selection, development, and evolution, to the summit of all organic life, instead of having been originally created its supreme lord. He may even accept ungrudgingly the idea of that higher destiny of a distant future which will prove him to be no more than the transitional link in a process destined to beget

a being to which he shall be no more than the Caliban
of our human ideal. Yet still, when we shall have
learned to recognise that death and life, working . together, carry onwards the race to all highest conceivable
perfectibilities, our personal interests are all concentrated
in our own entity. That unit is all in all to us, however
insignificant it may be to nature. Death may play its
useful part, no less than life, in working out the grandest
ideal of an unending chain of being, over which the
Divine Mind is recognised brooding in calm supremacy,
and watching the evolution of the creative plan. But
the little link which constitutes our own life is worth to
us all the rest ; and philosophy cannot rob death of its
terrors, whatever religion may do.

> ' The sense of death is most in apprehension ;
> And the poor beetle that we tread upon,
> In corporal sufferance finds a pang as great
> As when a giant dies.'

One summer serves alike for the butterfly and the blade
of grass. The oak lives a thousand summers in its
term. Three score and ten years is the allotted life of
man. But sooner or later death comes to all. The
organic being perishes. It is resolved into its elements.
It has ceased to be. But man, alone of all living
creatures, anticipates, hopes, or fears death. All others
escape that worse death which lies in its apprehension.
Few things are more calculated to illustrate the contrast
between the seemingly unprogressive, unaccumulating
instincts of the lower animals, and that experience which
is the product of human reason, than the sight of the
herd or the sheep-flock driven to the shambles : vic-
tims of that cruel necessity of our nature which, more
than anything else, allies man to the brute. They go
unconsciously as to the pasture field ; and yet for six
thousand years,—or, according to some reckonings, pos-

sibly for sixty thousand years,—the ox has been driven
to the shambles, and the lamb led to the slaughtering,
with no more warning to the survivors than reaches
ourselves from 'the undiscovered country from whose
bourn no traveller returns.' When the Duke, in 'Measure
for Measure,' plays the monitor to Claudio, disguised
as a friar, he urges this plea for the vanity of life :—

> 'The best of rest is sleep,
> And that thou oft provokest ; yet grossly fear'st
> Thy death, which is no more. Thou art not thyself;
> For thou exist'st on many a thousand grains
> That issue out of dust. Happy thou art not ;
> For what thou hast not, still thou strivest to get,
> And what thou hast forget'st. Thou art not certain ;
> For thy complexion shifts to strange effects,
> After the moon. If thou art rich, thou'rt poor ;
> For, like an ass whose back with ingots bows,
> Thou bear'st thy heavy riches but a journey,
> And death unloads thee.'

But the puzzling thing is, that man, in every stage of
his evolution, dreads death ' that makes these odds all
even ;' and yet defies it with a faith in something that
lies beyond. The author of ' The Origin of Civilisation '
puts, indeed, the savage's view of it in this light : ' Far
from having realised to themselves the idea of a future
life, they have not even learnt that death is the natural
end of this. We find a very general conviction among
savages that there is no such thing as natural death.'
To die by a wound is an obvious and explicable ending
of life ; though even in this case death is by means
universally acquiesced in as a natural result, still less
as an ending in the sense of absolute annihilation. But
to die what we customarily term a natural death, seems
to the savage mind contrary alike to reason and to
nature. A violent death is comprehensible. It is as
though the crank of your steam-engine were smashed,

or a hole rent in its boiler by some Armstrong or Whitworth bolt : and so the machinery must needs stop, and the life die out of it. But that, with crank whole, furnace bright, and boiler sound, the engine should suddenly stop, and defy all efforts to set it going again, is something akin to the idea which the savage realises of death in its most ordinary forms. To die by such obvious causes as a cleft skull, or a vital spear-thrust, is to die a natural death. To die by disease is, according to savage reasoning, to die by magic, a victim to the sorceries of some malignant foe.

So far this is death, according to the savage idea of it. The light has been quenched which no alchemy of his can relume. And it is so easy to put out the light ! Caliban himself, in the mere wantonness of irresponsible power, sees

> ' Yonder two flies, with purple films and pink,
> Bask on the pompion-bell above : kills both.'

But, however effected, 'if 'twere done when 'tis done,' it would less matter. But the savage has no belief in annihilation. He buries his dead out of sight ; burns the body to ashes; turns it adrift on the ocean; scaffolds it on bier, or in canoe, till the bleached bones alone are left; even feasts on it, or in other strangest ways disposes of the body. But the essential individuality that animated that body has not perished. He realises, in whatever crude fashion, the unseen presence of something which has survived the body, yet retains all its old personality. He anticipates or dreads its activity, as of one still existing, though no longer cognisant to bodily sense under the changed conditions of its new life. Even Shakespeare, with all his marvellous objective and creative power, wrought his supernatural beings on models familiar to him in nature.

When Sir Humphrey Davy took to peopling the planets with ideal life, the creations of his fancy proved to be mere monstrosities of the naturalist. No wonder then that the idea which the savage realises of the world of spirits is crude and base. The details are of his own fashioning ; but not so the belief in a life beyond the grave. This appears to be an instinct of his moral nature.

The savage of North Australia will not go near the graves of the tribe at night or alone. So far the same might be said of the peasantry of the most civilised nations of Christendom. But when the Australian savage must needs pass the graves of the tribe, Keppel tells us that he carries a fire-stick ' to keep off the spirit of darkness.' It should rather, probably, be said, to keep off the spirits : for darkness is everywhere, and at all times, a bugbear to the child, as to the savage ; though the grave-yard gives to it an added horror.

This belief in the supernatural seems very natural to man. It requires no effort in the savage mind to dissociate the ideal ego from ' this muddy vesture of decay,' and to recognise the essential individuality as a thing apart. The materialistic creed belongs to a very different speculative stage of evolution. Belief in the supernatural, in any sense, seems to be the supreme difficulty in our own day, as it has been that of other eras of speculative research. But doubt is not necessarily ' devil-born.' There lives much faith in honest doubt : far more, indeed, than in mere unreasoning credulity. ' Let knowledge grow from more to more ' : true faith has nothing to fear from that. There is no more suggestive passage in all the ingenious thought and accumulated research embodied in Mr. Darwin's ' Descent of Man,' than that in which he reflects on such

perplexing problems as are involved in the relapsing
of dominant historic races; or, again, in such awakenings
as that of Europe from the Dark Ages. 'At this early
period almost all the men of a gentle nature, those given
to meditation or culture of the mind, had no refuge
except in the bosom of the Church, which demanded
celibacy ; and this could hardly fail to have had a de-
teriorating influence on each successive generation.
During this same period the Holy Inquisition selected
with extreme care the freest and boldest men in order
to burn or imprison them. In Spain alone some of the
best men, those who doubted and questioned — and
without doubting there can be no progress,— were
eliminated during three centuries at the rate of a
thousand a year. The evil which the Church thus
effected, though no doubt counterbalanced to a certain, perhaps large extent in other ways, is incal-
culable.'

Mr. Darwin has expressed very clearly the impression
forced on his mind as the result of close intercourse
with typical representatives of widely-different savage
races, of many traits of character showing how similar
their minds are to our own. He traces a community of
arts, implements, &c., not to traditions derived from any
common progenitor, but to similarity in mental faculties.
The same observation is applicable to various simple
beliefs and customs, to modes of burial and choice of
places of sepulture ; and as naturalists, when they ob-
serve a close agreement in habits, tastes, and dispositions,
between two or more domestic races, trace them to a
common progenitor similarly endowed, so, says Mr.
Darwin, 'the same argument may be applied with much
force to the races of man.' The way in which he does
apply it, is, of course, in harmony with his own hypo-

thesis of evolution and descent, and need not now tempt us to discussion. It is the unity of mind, linking the rude savage and the Christian philosopher in a faith in the supernatural, and the conviction of a life beyond the grave, to which reference is now made. It requires no effort on the part of the savage to believe this. Faith with him is not an act of the mind. It is a state of the mind, from which he cannot emancipate himself if he would. And so, wherever civilised Europeans have found their way for the first time to new continents or isolated island-worlds, the idea has manifested itself that they were visitors from the world of spirits ; if not the native dead returned anew from beyond the grave.

The belief that there is 'no resurrection, neither angel nor spirit,' is the work of the Sadducees of civilisation in its decline. It reappears from time to time, not merely as the evolution of scepticism, but as the natural concomitant and counterpart of feverish credulity, the hot and cold fits of the same unhealthy moral condition. Man, in the unsophisticated stages of savage life—whether that be one of degradation, or only the lowest round of the ascending ladder of human evolution,—seems to find a doctrine of annihilation among the hardest things to believe. The American Indian, like the prehistoric races of Britain's cairns and barrows, provides food and weapons for his dead, wherewith to begin the new life on which they are entering. He hears their spirits in the winds as they moan among the trees, and listens for their voices in all the sounds of nature. According to his obscure conceptions of the disembodied spirit, it long haunts its old life-scenes, lingering around them, reluctant to depart. In its very crudest form, this belief in a life distinct from bodily existence, is something utterly inconceivable in relation to the brute mind.

But there is another idea, very familiar to the human mind in widely diverse stages of civilisation, and that is a realisation, in some sort, of the emancipated spirit, as, by its deliverance from the bonds of the flesh, released from all absolute restrictions in relation to space, and consequently present to the object of its affections, however remote the scene of death and the place of the body's rest may be. This idea is curiously indicated in one of the scenes of ' The Tempest.' Ferdinand, in astonishment at hearing his own Italian tongue uttered by the fair vision of the island maiden, exclaims to Miranda—

> ' My language! heavens!—
> I am the best of them that speak this speech,
> Were I but where 'tis spoken.'

Whereupon Prospero interposes, with this challenge—

> ' How! the best?
> What wert thou, if the King of Naples heard thee?'

And Ferdinand, whose belief in the death, not only of his father, but of the whole passengers and crew, is absolute, replies—

> ' A single thing, as I am now, that wonders
> To hear thee speak of Naples. He does hear me;
> And that he does I weep: myself am Naples;
> Who with mine eyes, never since at ebb, beheld
> The king my father wreck'd.'

The fact that his father is drowned involves, as it were of necessity, that his spirit must be present and hear these utterances; unless we interpret him in matter-of-fact literalness, as meaning no more than that he, being now king, hears himself speak. It is an idea dwelt on, in its purest and most elevated form, in the ' In Memoriam' of Tennyson; as where he asks—

'Do we indeed desire the dead
Should still be near us, at our side?
Is there no baseness we would hide?
No inner vileness that we dread?

Shall he for whose applause I strove,
I had such reverence for his blame,
See with clear eyes some hidden shame,
And I be lessen'd in his love?

I wrong the grave with fears untrue:
Shall love be blamed for want of faith?
There must be wisdom with great Death;
The dead shall look me through and through.

Be near us when we climb or fall:
Ye watch, like God, the rolling hours
With larger, other eyes than ours,
To make allowance for us all.'

So the poet shapes into noblest forms fancies which are
no less present to the most prosaic minds; and then,
glancing at the seeming strife between God and Nature
in the modern expositions of science, he pauses over
Nature's fancied response :—

'I bring to life, I bring to death,
The spirit does but mean the breath;
I know no more!'

But it is only to turn anew to the sure hope, and wait
for answer and redress 'behind the veil.' In this way
the loftiest ideas of the imaginative poet only expand
the undefined conceptions of a spiritual life, the instinctive yearnings after immortality, of the rudest
savage mind. To the evolutionist, however, this is no
innate, much less a divinely-prompted instinct, peculiar
to man, as a being made in the Divine image and
endowed with a living soul: but only one of the latest
phases in that continuous progression from the very
lowest stages of mere vitality, which seems to him so
easy of demonstration. To him the long vista shines

with light, and the development of each successive step, from the first dawn of embryo life—if not, indeed, from inorganic matter,—is clear; and it may be well here to glance at the process, as it reveals itself to him. 'There is no evidence,' says Mr. Darwin, 'that man was aboriginally endowed with the ennobling belief in the existence of an omnipotent God. On the contrary, there is ample evidence, derived not from hasty travellers, but from men who have long resided with savages, that numerous races have existed, and still exist, who have no idea of one or more gods, and who have no words in their languages to express such an idea. The question is, of course, wholly distinct from that higher one, whether there exists a Creator and Ruler of the universe; and this has been answered in the affirmative by the highest intellects that have ever lived. If, however, we include under the name "religion" the belief in unseen or spiritual agencies, the case is wholly different; for this belief seems to be almost universal with the less civilised races.' But, on the hypothesis of evolution, there is no difficulty in comprehending how this arose. The faculties of imagination, wonder, and curiosity, along with the first germ of reason, are all successive results of development; and the rational stage at length reached, by whatever process, it is not unreasonable to assume that the being—now become man,—would naturally crave to understand what was passing around him, and speculate on his own existence. He would, in fact, prove himself to be man by looking before and after; by asking Whence? and Whither?

That dreams may have first suggested the idea of spirits to the savage mind, is the theory most favoured as accounting for this indisputable universality of a faith in the supernatural; and to this Mr. Herbert

Spencer inclines to trace the earliest conception by man of his own dual nature, as a being at once corporeal and spiritual. But if man be in reality such a double essence, it would be strange that he should be utterly unconscious of that spiritual part of himself by which such consciousness is tested and appreciated. As to the visions of the night, they have their own unsolved mysteries; and very different theories as to their origin will depend on our faith in an actual human soul, or in a mere vital brain-force as an evolution of the living organism, and our intellect as the brute instinct developed into the self-conscious stage. The shapings of man's waking beliefs seem, on the latter theory, to be little less the mere defining of shadowy fancies, than the subjective impressions of his sleep. We may surely ask for an indisputable theory, comprehensive enough for the whole phenomena of dreams, before accepting what is assumed to be no more than a misinterpretation of cerebral impressions and sensations, as the source of man's faith in the spiritual world, and so of his religion and belief in a God. Some at least of the mental phenomena which dreams reveal by no means militate against the long-cherished faith in the soul as the body's guest : not a mere impersonation of brain-work, but the living worker alike through hand and brain, and which shall continue its being, and attain to a higher life, when hand and brain have alike returned to the elements, or become transformed into other organisms.

In this, as in other relations, time has done its work on the Caliban of the poet's creation, as on other entities. The Caliban of that first stage of evolution which offers itself for our study in 'The Tempest,' had, indeed, his dreams begot of the island harmonies, that gave delight and harmed not; soothed to sweetest sleep, and opened up to him such wealth of wonderland that when he waked he cried to dream again. These, however, belong to the enchantments wrought by Ariel's pipe and tabor, and took their shape accordingly: though the natural and supernatural intermingle so harmoniously in Shakespeare's art, that nothing seems to us strange there, any more than in our own dreams. They play their part accordingly, as the most naturally-begotten dreams might do, in helping us to realise the transitional characteristics of the strange being wrought by the poet's fancy in that pregnant age.

According to the promptings of his own limited desires, the Caliban of Shakespeare had no higher thought than to follow, dog-like, a better master than Prospero; or, as most covetable of all conceivable realisations, to roam at large, himself sole lord of nature in his little island-world. But even if, as some have fancied, 'The Tempest' is the latest of all Shakespeare's works, the last 'heir of his invention'; some two and a half centuries have since transpired, and evolution has done its work on the strange islander of the poet's fancy. The Caliban of Browning is a very different being from Trinculo's 'very shallow monster.' As he lies there kicking his feet in the cool slush, as much at his ease as metaphysics will let him, and looks out across the sea, puzzling his brains about many things very incomprehensible to brains in such a merely transitional stage of development, he comes upon the inexplicable problem of life and death; for, unless, some strange day, Setebos, or that mysterious greater than Setebos, should change, he sees no chance of bettering. 'Conceiveth all things will continue thus,' and having latterly, in his experiences with Prospero, found life hard

enough, and the supernal powers only omnipotent,—by
no means beneficent,—he

> ' Believeth with the life the pain shall stop.
> His dam held different, that after death
> He both plagued enemies and feasted friends :
> Idly! He doeth His worst in this our life,
> Giving just respite lest we die through pain,
> Saving last pain for worst,—with which, an end.
> Meanwhile the best way to escape His ire
> Is not to seem too happy.'

All which, as reasoning, may be apt enough for the
later savage stage of evolution, with its apprehension of
a last pain and worst, and its traditions of an untenable
Sycorax-creed of future rewards and plagues ; but it
by no means pertains to the true missing-link : man's
assumed progenitor, in that transitional stage of evolution which Shakespeare so nearly realises for us. It
is a stage of being which must be supposed, on any
theory, to have endured for the briefest possible period,
for it seems to place the half transmuted being in a
condition of most unstable equilibrium,—too much of
the brute for reasoning to do its part effectually ; too
much of the being dependent on reason for the requisite
brute means of offence and defence, in that struggle for
the survival of the fittest, on the results of which the
calling of perfected humanity into existence was to
depend.

The great difficulty, as the originator of the whole
theory and system of evolution admits, which presents
itself to the recipients of it as a satisfactory answer to
questionings concerning the origin of man, ' is the high
standard of intellectual power and of moral disposition
which he has attained. But every one who admits the
general principle of evolution, must see that the mental
powers of the higher animals, which are the same in

K 2

kind with those of mankind, though so different in degree, are capable of advancement. Thus the interval between the mental powers of one of the higher apes and of a fish, or between those of an ant and a scale-insect, is immense.' It is here taken for granted as certain to be admitted by all who accept the general principle of evolution, that the difference between the intellectual characteristics of man and the ape is only one of degree, though few assumptions would seem to stand more in need of proof. But this being supposed to be granted, it is further noticeable that the mental faculties are variable in domesticated animals, and that the variations are inherited. The same transmission of inherited and progressive faculties through natural selection, is further assumed as conceivable in an ever-progressive scale ; and assuming, as before stated, that the difference between the intellectual powers of the do-mesticated animal and man is only one of degree, when at length they reached that stage which would constitute the endowments of what we ordinarily under-stand as a rational being, then the intellect must have been all-important to the animal, now become man, ' enabling him to use language, to invent and make weapons, tools, traps, &c. ; by which means, in combi-nation with his social habits, he long ago became the most dominant of all living creatures.' As to the moral sense, that element which deals with motives, appeals to a standard of right and wrong, conceives the idea of re-tributive justice, responsibility, the immortality of the soul, and all the relations which link the human to the divine : that follows ' firstly, from the enduring and always present nature of the social instincts, in which respect man agrees with the lower animals ; and secondly, from his mental faculties being highly active, and his impressions of past events extremely vivid, in which respects he differs from the lower animals.'

The assumed instinctive belief in God has been affirmed to be universal in man, and so has been adduced as an unmistakable and absolute distinction between him and the lower animals. The capacity for such belief might be advanced with more force; for it cannot be denied that the belief in the divine father-hood, which constitutes an essential element in the conception of God, apart from the beneficent teachings of Christianity, rarely has a place in the savage's theology. But a belief in the supernatural appears to be admittedly universal, however accounted for or explained away. In reality, however, if we must look for a special, innate and instinctive faculty in man, which may be advanced before all such distinctive attributes as tool-using, fire-making, cooking, reason, speech, and all else, I should select his belief in his own immortality : the ineradicable conviction of the existence of some essential element of being, which survives death and defies annihilation. It is an idea vaguely, crudely, childishly set forth in the beliefs of the rude Australian, Pacific islander, or Pata-gonian savage. But, account for it how we may, the rudest and most uncultured mind conceives of man as something more than a mere animated organisation ; realises the conception of the soul as distinct from, even while dwelling in that body, and capable of continued existence apart from it. It is indeed affirmed, in reply, that the barbarous races of man ' possess no clear belief in the immortality of the soul.' But slight reflection on the nature of the doctrine should suffice to indicate the natural distinction between any clear definition of such a faith, and the instinctive, ineradicable con-viction, in which is involved the belief that death does not annihilate the individual; that wholly apart from that dead body the individuality of the deceased is still perpetuated and continues a conscious existence.

As to clearly-defined beliefs on immortality, the nature and personality of God, or kindred subjects, outside of formulised creeds and rituals, how rare are they. The definition extorted from the uneducated man, as from the child, rarely mirrors, even in a remote degree, the belief it professes to embody. The mere attempt at definition dissipates the ideal, as the making of a graven image clouds the perception of an unseen God. Obtain, if you can, from ordinary intelligent civilised men, apart from the formulæ of creeds and catechisms, answers to such questions as, ' What is heaven, or the place of departed spirits ? Has it any relation to space ? Is it a locality ? What is the soul ?' In some way or other they have been thinking of such matters all their lives, and yet the probability is that some will be shocked, and all will be puzzled by the demand. Or give them for text St. Paul's Corinthian questionings and definings : ' How are the dead raised up, and with what body do they come ?'—with the exquisite analogies of the seed which can only quicken if it die. ' So also is the resurrection of the dead. It is sown in corruption, it is raised in incorruption ; it is sown in dishonour, it is raised in glory ; it is sown in weakness, it is raised in power ; it is sown a natural body, it is raised a spiritual body :'— words which have sounded to so many in all their mysterious beauty and power, as with tearful eyes they have looked their last on the loved ones of earth, and heard those other words, ' earth to earth, ashes to ashes, dust to dust.'

As we return from thoughts so elevated and so solemn, to survey once more the kingdom of living

nature, and question it anew in relation to the novel but
singularly suggestive problems which science is ad-
vancing, all that is required of us is to admit what is
thus assumed to be indisputable. We must see, as every
one who admits the general principle of evolution does,
'that the mental powers of the higher animals are the
same in kind with those of mankind, though so different
in degree.' We start in the course of reasoning which
leads to the acceptance of the general principle referred
to, with such an infinitesimal minimum of capacity as
pertains to the Ascidian moluscoid, a mere sack adhering
to the rocks of primeval seas. From this we trace, or
assume, the gradual evolution of sensation, instinct, and
all else, up to the mental powers of the highest irrational
animal ; and then—while still acknowledging that the
difference between the mind of the very lowest savage
and that of the highest animal is enormous,—we are
required to grant that this is a mere difference of degree.
But why must this be granted? It assuredly does not
seem a self-evident proposition. When I compare the
most wonderful evidence of canine intelligence with the
every-day operations of the savage or the child, they
seem to have such an essential difference between them,
that I cannot conceive of the one changing into the other.
They differ in kind : or if not, the proof is still wanting
which shows them to be the same ; and surely the
enormous difference acknowledged on all hands is not to
be dismissed, as though it were one mere missing link in
an otherwise continuous chain. At best there seems in
the highest animals but a scanty minimum of intellectual
power, and no adequate initiative for anything bearing
even a shadowy resemblance to the moral elements of
humanity, out of which to evolve the being only 'a
little lower than the angels.'

The transitional being vaguely dreamed of in the visions of elder travellers,—human after some imperfect fashion, yet not of the seed of Adam,—seems to task the genius of Shakespeare for its realisation; and when clearly presented to us with his wondrous objective power, it is still but the highest evolution of the brute, and yet not without elements surpassing those of man's hypothetical brute-progenitor. To the modern evolutionist, however, no clear boundary-line is supposed to have separated the evolutionary anthropoid from the perfectly-developed man. 'Whether,' says Darwin, 'primeval man, when he possessed very few arts of the rudest kind, and when his power of language was extremely imperfect, would have deserved to be called man, must depend on the definition we employ. In a series of forms graduating insensibly from some ape-like creature to man as he now exists, it would be impossible to fix on any definite points where the term "man" ought to be used. But this is a matter of very little importance.' Of very little importance! And yet it takes for granted the grand step resulting, not in a mere gradation of form, but in a change so enormous as the transition from the irrational brute to rational man ; or, at the least, it assumes it to be an insensible graduation, easy, natural, inevitable : a mere bursting into flower of the ripened bud.

Our modern poet, Robert Browning, undesignedly perhaps, but as becomes the true poet, mirroring the thought of his own age,—an age begot of the French and other revolutions ; by no means of the German reformation,—has carried his Caliban far beyond the irrational stage of being, into that of an advanced reasoning savage : if not, indeed, in some respects beyond the highest point of definite reasoning in savage minds. Shakespeare, on the contrary, presents the ideal of highest brutish evolution, artificially or supernaturally endowed with the means of giving expression to its thoughts ; yet neither a man, nor any link in the possible pedigree of manhood : a fellow-being of the jay and the marmoset, of the spotted oncelot, the blind mole, and the crane. It is a true creation of genius; wonderfully distinctive, consistent, and well-defined.

In so far as the creative genius of the greatest of poets has thus conceived for us the ideal of the anthropo-morphoid, as far above the very highest known simiadæ, as that falls short of man—'endued with intellectual sense and soul,'—he has supplied a link more consistent with any conceivable evolution of which the anthropo-morpha are susceptible, than any ideal based on assumed stages of lowest degradation of savage man. But the lines of evolution of the anthropoid and the savage, according to such ideal, are parallels. They may admit of endless development, but they will not coalesce.

Dryden grossly travestied the wonderful ideal, when he dared, with profane hands, to drag down the beauti-ful comedy of Shakespeare's mature genius to the impure standard of the Restoration stage ; yet even he was struck with wonder at the profound truthfulness of a creature of which nature furnished no type. Schlegel pronounces the conception to be one of inconceivable consistency and depth. Hazlitt, speaking of it as one of the wildest and most abstracted of all Shakespeare's impersonations, says : 'The character grows out of the soil where it is rooted, uncontrolled, uncouth and wild, uncramped by any of the meannesses of custom. It is of the earth, earthy. It seems almost to have been dug out of the ground, with a soul instinctively added to it, answering to its wants and origin.' Gervinus, in a too realistic interpretation of the offspring of the blear-eyed hag Sycorax, and still more of the wrathful hyperboles of Prospero, misses the full appreciation of this supernatural being, belonging to a wholly different order and genus from all the other varied conceptions of Shakespearean genius. Yet he, too, has aptly characterised Caliban as an embryonic being, defiled, as it were, by his earthly origin from the womb of savage nature.

The extreme contrast between the seventeenth and the nineteenth century's conception of the reasoning brute, with a brute-soul answering to its origin and desires, is most noticeable. Shakespeare's Caliban reasons throughout from the sheer animal point of view ; and his dam's god is a mere embodiment of power ; no object of faith or worship ; nor indeed a being with whom he claims to have any personal relations. There is no indication of belief in such unseen or spiritual agencies as is admittedly all but universal with the most degraded savages. We must, of course, except here the dramatic machinery, with Ariel and the spirits who bestow upon the eyes of the young lovers some vanity of Prospero's art ; and of whom he says presently—

> ' Our revels now are ended. These our actors,
> As I foretold you, were all spirits, and
> Are melted into air, into thin air.'

There is in the Caliban of Shakespeare no intellectual recognition of the supernatural, such as in Browning's Island Theologian makes him so essentially human. It is a distinction coinciding with what we re-affirm in relation to the present line of argument : that man in the very lowest stage of savage degradation does in so far recognise his immortal nature in the realisation, however vaguely, of some idea of the human soul as that which is the essence of the individual, and which survives the death of the body. To him the spirit means something wholly distinct from the breath; and death is very definitely the separation of soul and body. This perception has all the appearance of an innate, instinctive self-consciousness. It involves the belief in a future life, and includes the germ of a faith in immortality. It is the original endowment on which the ennobling belief in an omnipotent, omniscient God, and the vitalising faith in a divine Redeemer, are to be ingrafted in the fulness of time. It is 'the substance of things hoped for, the evidence of things not seen;' man's heritage as man; and wanting which he would fitly rank with the beasts that perish.

CHAPTER VIII.

THE SUPERNATURAL.

' A thousand fantasies
Begin to throng into my memory
Of calling shapes, and beckoning shadows dire,
And airy tongues that syllable men's names.'—*Comus.*

THE belief in the supernatural, however it may be explained, or even be sought to be explained away, appears to be universal among mankind. In the discussions which it has elicited in special reference to the distinctive elements of humanity, the important distinction between actual beliefs and their definition has not always been kept in view. One of the difficulties assigned by Sir John Lubbock in arriving at any clear conception of the religious systems of strange races, is traced by him to 'a confusion between a belief in ghosts and that in an immortal spirit.' Captain Burton notes this nice distinction in reference to the negro, that he believes 'in a ghost, but not in spirit; in a present immaterial, but not in a future;' and the essential diversity of the two opinions is accordingly assumed. 'The spirit is not necessarily regarded as immortal because it does not perish with the body.' This seems an altogether artificial refinement, based on the dogmatic creeds and beliefs of comparatively modern centuries; and in which the real significance of this admitted belief in a human spirit, or soul, absolutely distinct from the body, and capable of surviving it, is slighted if not entirely ignored. If the spirit is believed to survive after death, then any idea of its subsequent mortality can only be of a negative kind, the mere result of the incapacity to grasp with any clearness the idea of life immortal. In this respect it may aptly enough compare with our ideas on the limitation or infinity of space. M. Louis Figuier, who has undertaken, in his 'Day after Death,' to solve the mysteries of a future life, defines God as the Infinite in spirit, and the universe as the Infinite in extent; and then he locates this infinite God at the mathematical centre of the worlds which compose this infinite universe : which seems very much like undertaking to construct a circle which shall have no circumference, and yet finding for it a centre! The old doctrine of Anaximander of Miletus, whereby he accounted for the suspension of the earth in the centre of the universe, was that, being equidistant from the containing heaven in every direction, there was no reason why it should move in one direction rather than another. Anaxagoras modified this doctrine, and was accused of atheism, because of the physical explanations he assigned to celestial phenomena. The speculations of philosophy during all the later centuries have not achieved a solution of the problem of limited or unlimited space. Our ideas on such subjects are apt to vanish in the effort at definition, like cloud-castles when we attempt to draw them.

Religion and creed are by no means synonymous terms. The medieval controversies on the special nature and procession of the Holy Spirit, and the hopeless schism of the Eastern and Western Church represented by the single word *Filioque*, illustrate theological definitions forcing into concrete form such details of belief as no ordinary layman could define, or would probably recognise any necessity for defining, till challenged by the exactions of ecclesiastical orthodoxy. The modern scientific inquirer is apt at times to be little less dogmatic in his demands for concrete forms of thought than the old theologian. Our elaborated and long-defined ideas of the human soul, a future state, life, immortality, and God, are not only placed alongside the crude, wholly undefined, instinctive beliefs of the savage as to the survival of the spirit or soul of man after death : but a logical consistency of detail is demanded in reference to opinions which have been accepted like any other intuitive belief. So long as the savage recognises an immaterial spirit distinct from the body, surviving its dissolution, and perpetuating the personality and individuality identified with it, the precise conception he forms as to the duration of this immaterial life is of secondary significance. Experience has nothing to teach him in reference to it. While the memory of the dead is fresh, the idea of the surviving spirit will be strongly impressed on the mind. But as the recollection of the deceased fades away, the conception of his immaterial life will grow correspondingly dim, until the two disappear together.

The clearly-defined belief in the life and immortality of the Christian creed is due to the teachings of Christ Himself, and to the doctrine educed and taught by its first preachers, as the great lesson of the resurrection. Sir John Lubbock, after affirming that 'the belief in an universal, independent, and endless existence is confined to the highest races,' quotes, in confirmation of the absence of any belief in a future state, a reported endeavour to enforce the acceptance of this doctrine on a savage. The instructor 'tried long and patiently to make a very intelligent docile Australian Black understand his existence without a body, but the Black never could keep his countenance, and generally made an excuse to get away. One day the teacher watched, and found that he went to have a hearty fit of laughter at the absurdity of the idea of a man living and going about without arms, legs, or mouth to eat. For a long time he could not believe that the gentleman was serious, and when he did realise it, the more serious the teacher was the more ludicrous the whole affair appeared to the Black.' This narrative may perhaps fairly exhibit the actual condition of a savage mind to which the idea of life apart from bodily existence was absurd. But had the Australian been as subtle as Browning's Caliban, he might have appealed to good authority on 'the physical theory of another life,' and denied that the active existence of the soul is conceivable apart from some definite relation to space ; or he might have demanded an explanation of St. Paul's statement concerning 'the spiritual body' of the resurrection. Possibly enough, however, the teacher presented ideas which, in the sense in which they were interpreted by the poor Australian, were wholly ludicrous ; while, all the time, he held to the belief of his people in an immaterial life after death. The Swedenborgian ideal of a future state is to some minds so gross as to excite ridicule. But their mirth, however unseemly, would be very falsely construed into laughter at the supposed absurdity of all belief in a life beyond the grave. There is only too apt a tendency to treat any incomprehensible faith as folly. The doctrine of transubstantiation, or the real presence, appears to thousands not only untenable, but absurd ; to thousands more its denial is blasphemy and sheer atheism. The scientific sceptic who laughs at spirit-rapping and other kindred follies, exposes himself to denunciation as an infidel materialist. In truth the actual beliefs of the majority of men scarcely admit of logical analysis; and the 'foolishness' of the belief in a future life is neither confined to savages, nor to modern discovery.

In his poem of 'Cleon,' Browning has embodied, in the form of a letter from the Greek poet to his friend Protos, the longings of a pagan Greek of the first century for some revelation of that very immortality which, when presented as the doctrine of the resurrection, he rejects as folly. Reminded that he shall live as a poet, in the immortality of his verse, Cleon repels such consolation as a vain deception of mere words. As his soul becomes intensified in power and insight, the increasing weight of years warns him of life's close :—

> ' When all my works wherein I prove my worth,
>   Being present still to mock me in men's mouths,
>   Alive still, in the phrase of such as thou,
>   I—l, the feeling, thinking, acting man,
>   The man who loved his life so over much,
>   Shall sleep in my urn. It is so horrible,
>   I dare at times imagine to my need
>   Some future state revealed to us by Zeus,
>   Unlimited in capability
>   For joy, as this is in desire for joy,
>   To seek which, the joy-hunger forces us.
>   That, stung by straightness of our life made straight,
>   On purpose to make sweet the life at large—
>   Freed by the throbbing impulse we call death,
>   We burst there as the worm into the fly,
>   Who while a worm still, wants his wings. But, no!
>   Zeus has not yet revealed it; and alas!
>   He must have done so, were it possible! '

But Cleon, having thus given utterance to the earnest longings of a vain desire, adds a postscript on some trivial matters. The messenger of his correspondent, as it seems, is the bearer of a letter from him to one called Paulus, a barbarian Jew, who has much to say about one 'Christus' and this very immortality of which the poet fain would learn. But with true Greek contempt for all beyond the Hellenic pale, he writes—

> ' Thou canst not think a mere barbarian Jew,
> As Paulus proves to be, one circumcised,
> Hath access to a secret shut from us?
> .   .   .   .   .   Certain slaves
> Who touched on this same isle, preached him and Christ;
> And (as I gathered from a bystander)
> Their doctrines could be held by no sane man.'

The search for defined or consistent creeds on such matters of inquiry and belief, among nations in widely differing stages of progress, is apt to prove illusory, and among savage races is vain and deceptive. We transmute their ideas in the alembic of our own creeds and opinions, and obtain results unconsciously adulterated by prejudice and misconception. We are trying in prosaic literalness to do what the poet Browning has done with the Caliban of Shakespeare : to enter as it were into his brain, and think his own thoughts, wholly unaffected by those of the actual thinker. It seems to me sufficient for all that is attempted to be deduced from such beliefs, that the rudest savage does realise the idea of man's spirit as something at least ethereal, capable of leaving the body, of existing apart from it, of haunting the deserted dwelling, or hovering round the grave. With a very vague conception of what is implied in the idea of immateriality, his belief in the invisible ghost or spirit does realise the essential ideas of an immaterial existence, a spiritual life with the personality perpetuated apart from the body, and surviving death. Whether that survival shall be regarded as temporary or eternal is much more a matter of definition of the instinctive belief, than essential to its universality or significance as one of the most characteristic attributes of human reason.

So soon as we reach the stage of minutely defined beliefs and formulated creeds, they prove to be full of inconsistencies; and before the printing-press superseded tradition, and came provided with ready-made opinions for all, the interblendings of ecclesiastical dogma and popular folk-lore resulted in conceptions singularly quaint and even grotesque. The instinctive belief is one thing : the defined ideas, whether formulated into vulgar beliefs, or into written creeds, are of a wholly different nature. The medieval doctrine of purgatory, so curiously interwoven into Shakespeare's 'Hamlet,' is an illustration of the intermingling of those diverse elements ; and hence the strange extravagances which it involves. It had been adopted into the teachings of the early Church, had modified the whole prevailing ideas of a future life, and when developed by the opinions of successive generations, had been reduced to a dogmatic form by the teachings of centuries. This intermediate state of the soul accordingly affected the superstitions of thousands, long after it had ceased to be a part of their accepted creed.

It is curious, for example, to turn to the current popular ballads of Presbyterian Scotland, and to note how ineradicable have been the impressions produced on the popular mind by the ancient faith, in spite of the vigorous crusade of ecclesiastical discipline and public opinion conjoined, for upwards of three centuries. Pasch, Yule, Halloween, Fasternseen, Rudeday, Whitsunday, Candlemas, and other rustic anniversaries, all survive as relics of the ancient faith; and are mostly commemorated still by an unpremeditated yet universal consent, according to the Old Style. Such a faithful popular tradition thus running counter alike to modern almanacs and creeds, has not unreasonably been advanced as confirmation of the authenticity of the ballad-poems in which the same ideas have been transmitted, mainly by oral tradition. But there also the supernatural beliefs of earlier generations have proved no less tenacious than such ecclesiastical traditions. In 'Tamlane' and 'True Thomas' the apparition of the Queen of Elfland gives the special character to these old ballads. But the Scottish elves peopled the scaurs and dens of a wild country which for centuries had been the scene of bloody feud and violence, and reflect in their sombre hue the characteristics of their source. They were esteemed a capricious, irritable, and vindictive race, very different from the airy haunters of England's moonlit glades. The Scottish Elfin Queen is in part the embodiment of the same gloomy superstitions which begot the witch-hags and other coarse imaginings of the national demonology. Nevertheless the Queen of Elfland and her mischievous elves are generally designated the Good People: the canny prudence of the Scot leading him to apply fair words in the very naming of such testy and capricious sprites. Even in the indictments of ecclesiastical courts this is adhered to, as in that of Alison Pearson, convicted at St. Andrews, in 1586, of witchcraft, and consulting with evil spirits. She is charged with 'haunting and repairing with the gude neighbours and Queene of Elfland, thir divers years by-past, as she had confest;' and, among other things, she had been warned by one she met in Fairyland to 'sign herself that she be not taken away, for the teind of them are tane to hell everie year.'

The Scottish Elfin Queen is, accordingly, a very different character from the sportive Mab of Shakespeare's Mercutio, who gallops night by night over lawyers' fingers, courtiers' knees, and through lovers' brains; and

only becomes 'the angry Mab' when, as she drives o'er
slumbering ladies' lips she finds 'their breaths with
sweetmeats tainted are.' Still less does she resemble
that ethereal Queen of Shadows, Titania, in the 'Midsummer Night's Dream.' Her elfin court has indeed its
deceptive pleasures, its glamour, and its green-wood
revels ; but she and her elves are the vassals of Hell ;
and in the fanciful ballad, as in the prosaic indictment
for witchcraft, are described as paying their tithe, not
annually indeed, but every seven years to the devil.
Tamlane, for example, tells the Earl's daughter, who
meets this wanderer from Fairyland 'among the leaves
sae green '—

> ' And never would I tire, Janet,
>   In Fairyland to dwell;
> But aye, at every seven years,
>   They pay the teind to hell;
> And I'm sae fat and fair of flesh,
>   I fear 'twill be mysell.'

The ballad of ' Tamlane' is mentioned in the ' Com-
playnt of Scotland,' printed at St. Andrews in 1549, and
undoubtedly embodies the superstitions of a much
earlier date.

But it is more significant for our present purpose to
see reflected in the early Scottish ballads the popular
ideas of spirits, ghosts, and apparitions of the dead,
haunting the scenes of their unexpiated crimes, or the
grave where the murdered body had been laid. The
resemblance between these ill-defined incongruous ideas,
and some of those already referred to as characteristic of
the savage conception of death and the departed spirit,
is unmistakeable. But, besides the apparitions of the
dead who can find no repose in the grave till expiation
has been made for some deadly sin, or of the victim of
crime whose unresting spirit wanders abroad, like that

of the murdered Dane, demanding vengeance, there are characteristic types of national superstition : as where the dead are disquieted by the mourning of loving ones refusing to be comforted because they are not ; or again where rest is denied them till they recover their plighted troth. In ' The Wife of Usher's Well,' her three stout and stalwart sons, sent by her over the sea, are scarcely a week gone from her when she learns that they are drowned. In her agony at their loss, she prays that the winds may never again be still, nor the floods be calmed, till her sons return to her ' in earthly flesh and blood.' The dread prayer disturbs the rest of her sons, and the result is thus set forth in homely simplicity :—

> ' It fell about the Martinmas,
>   When nights are lang and mirk,
> The carline wife's three sons cam hame,
>   And their hats were o' the birk.
>
> It neither grew in syke nor ditch,
>   Nor yet in ony sheugh ;
> But at the gates o' Paradise,
>   That birk grew fair eneugh.'

And so the three drowned men remain, till the dawn approaches, with their mother tending on them in her short-lived joy, as seemingly her living sons restored to her. She lays them to rest with all a mother's tender care, wraps her mantle about them, and sitting down by their bedside, at length yields to sleep, ere the red-cock's crow warns them to begone. They cannot tarry longer from Paradise ; but their consideration for her is indicated with touching simplicity by their urging one another to linger to the latest moment on her account :—

> ' Up then crew the red red cock,
>   And up and crew the gray ;
> The eldest to the youngest said,
>   " 'Tis time we were away ;

> The cock doth craw, the day doth daw,
>   The channering worm doth chide;
> Gin we be miss'd out o' our place,
>   A sair pain we maun bide."
>
> "Lie still, lie still but a little wee while,
>   Lie still but if we may;
> Gin my mother should miss us when she wakes,
>   She'll gae mad ere it be day."'

In the confusion of ideas as shown in the birch
gathered at the gates of Paradise, the penance dreaded
in case of their absence being discovered, and the chiding
of the grave's channering, or fretting worm, there are
striking illustrations of the undefined blending of conceptions of an immaterial existence wholly apart from
the body; with the difficulty, as common to the mind
of the English peasant as to that of the Australian
savage, of conceiving any clear realisation of the disembodied spirit, or of death distinct from the 'wormy
grave.' The same homely pathos and tenderness intermingle with a like confused interblending of the grave
and the spiritual life, in 'Clerk Saunders,' 'William's
Ghost,' and other Scottish ballads of this class.   In
both the dead are represented as reclaiming their faith
and troth, without which they cannot rest in their graves.
In the former ballad, Clerk Saunders, a noble lover who
had been slain in the arms of May Margaret, the King's
daughter, returns after 'a twelvemonth and a day,' and
standing at her bower window an hour before the dawn,
addresses her :—

> 'Give me my faith and troth again,
>   True love, as I gi'ed them to thee.'

Before she will yield to his request, she insists on her
lover coming within her bower and kissing her, though
he warns her that his mouth is cold and smells of the
grave. She questions him about the other world, and

especially of what comes of women 'who die in strong travailing.' He replies in the same simple style of homely pathos as in the ballad already quoted :—

> 'Their beds are made in the heavens high,
>   Down at the foot of our good Lord's knee,
> Weel set about wi' gillyflowers ;
>   I wot sweet company for to see.
>
> O cocks are crowing a merry midnight,
>   I wot the wild-fowl are boding day ;
> The psalms of heaven will soon be sung,
>   And I ere now will be missed away.'

May Margaret returns her lover's troth by a curiously literal process, thereby freeing the disembodied spirit of a tie which still bound it to earth, and then he leaves her with the tender assurance that

> 'Gin ever the dead come for the quick,
>   Be sure, Margaret, I'll come for thee.'

But she follows the departing spirit without waiting to cover her naked feet ; and then there once more appears the same simple child-like confusion of ideas which makes the grave not merely the portal to the spirit-land, but the sole spirit-world :—

> ' "Is there ony room at your head, Saunders?
>   Is there ony room at your feet?
> Or ony room at your side, Saunders,
>   Where fain, fain, I wad sleep?"
>
> "There's nae room at my head, Margaret,
>   There's nae room at my feet ;
> My bed it is full lowly now :
>   Amang the hungry worms I sleep.
>
> "Cauld mould is my covering now,
>   But, and my winding-sheet ;
> The dew it falls nae sooner down
>   Then my resting-place is weet.
>
> "But plait a wand o' the bonnie birk,
>   And lay it on my breast ;
> And gae ye hame, May Margaret,
>   And wish my saul gude rest." '

Such confused ideas of Paradise and Purgatory, of the world beyond the grave, the final resting-place of the soul, and that where the body lies decaying in its 'wormy bed,' all illogically jumbled together without any conscious inconsistency, is of common occurrence in the early ballads. It represents the ideas of an age in which a belief in the immortality of the soul had been inculcated and inherited through many generations, and was entertained unquestioningly by all. Such embodiments of current popular thought may therefore be accepted as apt illustrations of how impossible it is to try by any standard of logical consistency the crude attempts of the savage mind to define its beliefs on the same subject. What shall we make—in view of such illogical opinions perpetuated for centuries in the most favourite popular forms, among a civilised Christian peasantry,—of such nice distinctions as that attempted to be drawn by Captain Burton, and quoted with highest approval, of the negro's belief in a ghost but not in a spirit ; in a present immaterial life, but not in a future one ? On evidence which seems far more indisputable than any definitions that he could possibly obtain of the negro's discriminating belief between ghosts and spirits, he may affirm that the Scottish peasantry of the sixteenth and seventeenth centuries believed that heaven and the grave were one and the same place.

Were our aim here to illustrate in detail the peculiarities of Scottish superstition and the national fairy-lore, the Gyre-Carline, or Scottish Hecate, the Kelpie, the Shellycoat, the Wraith, the Brownie, or Billie Blin of the ballads, the Daoine Shie or Men of Peace, as the fairies of the Highlands are styled, and other characteristic national fancies would come under review. But they are only referred to now in illustration of the mode in which such beliefs have been reduced to definite form in the traditions and popular rhymes handed down by the peasantry through many generations.

To a great extent the belief in the supernatural, as far as Scotland is concerned, has been transmitted to us unmodified by the refinements of a more critical age. It is otherwise with the corresponding superstitions and folk-lore of England. There the creative imagination of a rare group of poets who adorned her sixteenth century, selected the elfin creed and the darker super- stitions of popular belief as material on which their fancy should work its will. Shakespeare especially made them his own; and they have been transmuted into things of beauty which supersede the elves, witches, and lubber fiends that scared the old rustic hearth, and made darkness terrible. The Queen of Fairyland and all her elfin train are accordingly associated with the romantic epic of Spenser, and the elfin-dream of a midsummer's night to which Shakespeare has given enduring form.

But the distinction between the visions of the two Elizabethan poets is great. The former is wholly the romancer, and we must be content with the enjoyment of his epic as a minstrel's tale. The dramas of Shake- speare, on the contrary, present an inexhaustible vein of concrete philosophy ; though in a form so seductive that its profound wisdom is apt to elude the ordinary reader. They transmute some of the crudest incon- gruities of vulgar superstition into definite forms no less adapted for uses of pure science, than for the æsthetic requirements of the stage. They transform into ideal embodiments, available for all purposes of reasoning, fancies before intangible as the creed of the savage, which vanishes in the attempt to formulate it.

The Caliban of Shakespeare, as we have seen, realises the ideal of a being intermediate between brute and man, defined out of the vague beliefs entertained regarding the inhabitants of new-found lands in that sixteenth century. To the same conceptive genius we owe the no less definite realisations of popular folk-lore: the trafficker with Satanic powers, the communer with the dead, the disembodied intruder from the world of spirits, and the like impersonations of what formed the English counterpart to the superstitions embodied in early Scottish ballads. All this the most objective of poets accomplished for us in an age wholly unaffected by ideas which now influence our conceptions of the immaterial and the supernatural; and that in a way which renders them available for fresh inquisition into the innate ideas of the vulgar and the savage mind in relation to all that is supra-natural.

CHAPTER IX.

GHOSTS AND WITCHES.

'Why, what should be the fear?
I do not set my life at a pin's fee;
And for my soul, what can it do to that,
Being a thing immortal as itself.'—*Hamlet*.

THE ease with which Shakespeare sports at will in the purely ideal and supernatural world of his own fancy's creation, is only rendered less astonishing by that still greater marvel, the ease with which he moves amid the real world of humanity, compassing in exhaustless variety its every phase. Hence it is that we dwell, above all things, on the supreme naturalness of Shakespeare's dramatic art, his thorough truthfulness and verisimilitude, his ever-renewing modernness and universality. In a certain sense all this is simple enough, —simple as Hamlet's playing upon the pipe : 'Govern these ventages with your fingers and thumb, give it breath with your mouth, and it will discourse most eloquent music.' It is simple, since it springs from no mere transfixing of temporary fashions, either of dress or of thought, but is the impersonation of the human soul, its affections, its passions, its aspirations, its faith, hopes, and fears : things which can never grow old-fashioned or go out of date so long as humanity endures.

Hamlet's directions to the players are completed 'with this special observance, that they o'erstep not the modesty of nature ; for anything so overdone is from the purpose of playing, whose end, both at the first and now, was and is, to hold as 'twere the mirror

up to nature; to show virtue her own feature; scorn
his own image, and the very age and body of the time
its form and pressure.' He is, indeed, only dictating
the actor's part; yet in defining 'the purpose of playing,'
he has in view also that of the dramatist; and not less
so when, protesting against the strut and rant of the
player who oversteps the modesty of nature, he exclaims,
' I had thought some of nature's journeymen had made
men, and not made them well, they imitated humanity
so abominably.' It is from the lips of the wise Ulysses
that we listen to the familiar aphorism, 'One touch of
nature makes the whole world kin.' To this all Shakespeare's art is referred ; by this it is ever tested.

> ' This to our blood is born ;
> It is the show and seal of nature's truth.'

But though Shakespeare never oversteps the modesty
of nature, his genius has nowhere more strikingly exhibited its creative power than in his varied realisations
of beings lying beyond the pale of humanity, and
unfamiliar to all our experiences. The range in this
respect is no less ample than the wondrous variety
discernible in his delineations of men and women. They
have moreover not only as distinct an individuality, but
they have an equally impressive charm of verisimilitude.
They startle us less by any repelling strangeness than
his Shylock, Iago, Lady Macbeth, or Richard III. They
are not the mere offspring of an exuberant fancy wan-
toning in its wealth. Each has a purpose of its own,
and plays its needful and altogether fitting part in
relation both to the visible and spiritual world with
which man traffics here. 'Macbeth' has its witches—

> ' So withered and so wild in their attire;
> That look not like the inhabitants o' the earth,
> And yet are on't.'

They are the visible promptings of criminal desires, impersonated as the witches of popular folk-lore, in an age when King James deemed his ' Dæmonology' such an embodiment of wisdom that it was reprinted for the benefit of Shakespeare and his countrymen when that ' wisest fool in Christendom' succeeded to Elizabeth's throne. It was, no doubt, as his exquisite tribute of flattery to the sage king, that Shakespeare dramatised the legendary history of Macbeth, and brought on to the stage that Satanic agency in which his new sovereign had proclaimed such implicit faith. This popular belief was the very element on which Shakespeare delighted to work. His was not the weak fancy which takes refuge in that which is strange or unfamiliar, as therefore original. That the fancy he was to sport with was already familiar to the popular mind was one of the strongest reasons for its selection; and when he did embody the ' airy nothing,' the very charm and triumph of his art was that it seemed no more than the realisation of what all had known even from their cradle. The art is so perfect that no artifice could be discerned ; and as they looked from the cock-pit of the Globe or Blackfriars, into that wonderful dramatic mirror, Shakespeare's Englishmen fancied they saw no more than what they had been familiar with all their lives.

When the poet introduced ' the weird sisters' on the stage, as beings of that antique and legendary world of historic myth which it suited his purpose to dramatise, he dealt with what was as realistically present to the faith of his own age, as the fauns and satyrs, or the Olympian deities, with which Sophocles or Aristophanes peopled the Attic drama. His withered hags are surrounded with all the properties of current superstition ; and, with marvellous art, they are endowed with the highest supernatural agency of such malignant emissaries of Satan, yet with no over-refined idealism to rob them of their vulgar verisimilitude. Graymalkin and Paddock are their familiars. Their incantations are in perfect accordance with the folk-lore of the seventeenth and later centuries. The brinded cat, the hedge-pig and the toad, the potent charm of a wrecked pilot's thumb, and the sieve in which to outweather the storm ; while the bewitched sailor—for no better reason than that his wife has withheld her chestnuts from the hag,—

> 'Shall live a man forbid;
> Weary se'nnights nine times nine
> Shall he dwindle, peak, and pine:
> Though his bark cannot be lost,
> Yet it shall be tempest-tost,'—

as the king himself had been, on his homeward voyage with his bride ; and, as he doubted not, through just such agents of the powers of darkness. The very meanness of the vulgar agency by which Macbeth is seduced into disloyalty adds to the moral force of the drama. If he is to stoop to such baseness, it is fitting it should be at the promptings of such beldams as trade and traffic with him.

With just enough of the supernatural for their malignant vocation,—the distillation of the moon's 'vaporous drop,' the 'yew slivered in the moon's eclipse,' and the like mystic charms,— they 'hover through the fog and filthy air ;' or again, the 'secret, black, and midnight hags' surround the cauldron, with the boil and bubble of its hell-broth of newt and frog, toad and snake, adder's fork and blind-worm's sting,

> 'Tooth of wolf and maw of shark,
> Root of hemlock digg'd i' the dark,
> Liver of blaspheming Jew,
> Finger of birth-strangled babe,'

and all else that seems most loathsome and horrible, wherewith to work the incantations that are to lure their victim to perdition. Thus while seemingly introducing no more than the familiar accessories of the vulgar witch, Shakespeare elevates the weird sisters who haunt the blasted heath into Satanic spirits, more akin to the Eumenides of Greek tragedy: the agents of hell sporting with the doomed soul, which has welcomed temptation, and so made itself their prey.

In 'Hamlet' again another phase of popular folk-lore is transmuted with like ready art into the legitimate agency of 'gorgeous tragedy in sceptred pall.' The ghost of Hamlet's dead father haunts the old scenes of life's fitful fever; and, like vulgarest bugbear of the village rustic, vanishes at the cock-crow. But with this is interwoven another and more reverent dogma of the popular creed, not yet wholly eradicated. The purgatorial fires are rekindled to show by their light the disembodied spirit of the dead king. It is, as we know, a character which the author specially favoured. He personated it himself; revised its idealisation in the later versions of the tragedy; and perfected to his own high ideal the impalpable spirit in visible incongruity, late hearsed in death and quietly inurned, and now once again abroad, 'revisiting the glimpses of the moon, making night hideous.' It is, indeed, as this impersonation of the dead king that the ever-living poet reappears if we would recall him as the actor in his own dramas. The majesty of buried Denmark, in complete steel,—

> 'The very armour he had on
> When he the ambitious Norway combated;'

and yet 'as the air invulnerable.' With no other character can we so freely associate the personality of Shakespeare. We may think of him, with the help of

Cornelius Jansen's fine portrait, in rich lace collar and velvet doublet, such courtly dress as befitted the gentle-man of Elizabeth's or James's reign ; or in plainer, yet still becoming attire, as in the Chandos portrait, or the Stratford bust.   But with all of those the carping critic intermeddles with doubts and questionings, such as find no place when, to the mind's eye, the poet, impersonating one of his most marvellous imaginings,

> ' Armed at all points exactly, cap-à-pe,
> Appears before us, and with solemn march
> Goes slow and stately by.'

He has realised for himself how a spirit should walk ; how it should speak.   We hear for ourselves the voice of that unresting ghost ; the disembodied spirit, clothed in shadowy form and vestments of the dead father, as, in spite of fate, he tells 'the secrets of his prison-house ;' and all that is vulgar, grotesque, or incongruous, is at once exorcised from our minds.

> ' We do it wrong, being so majestical,
> To offer it the show of violence.'

But there is one appearance of the ghost in this subtle tragedy, which invites special study.   When first dis-covered, it comes on the startled watch, stalking as it were out from the void which lies beyond the castle parapet, 'that beetles o'er his base into the sea.' We look forth from the battlements of Elsinore Castle, into the still night, with the ocean far beneath ; while over-head

> ' Yond same star that's westward from the pole
> Has made his course to illume that part of heaven
> Where now it burns.'

Though challenged in vain by Horatio, as with martial stalk it has gone by, the ghost is visible to all.   It has, indeed, repeatedly appeared at the same dread hour, and been the wonder of fresh observers, ere it faded 'at the crowing of the cock.' But there is a later scene (Act iii. Scene 4), where Hamlet upbraids his mother with her complicity in the wrongs of his murdered father, until she exclaims—

> 'O Hamlet, speak no more;
> Thou turn'st mine eyes into my very soul,
> And there I see such black and grained spots
> As will not leave their tinct.'

As he presses home the charge to which her own conscience thus responds, in the midst of a contemptuous anathema at the new king, Hamlet suddenly breaks off, with the awe-struck invocation—

> 'Save me, and hover o'er me with your wings
> You heavenly guards!'

and then he demands, 'What would your gracious figure?' for the spirit of his dead father is once more present to his sight. But the queen sees nothing; hears only her son's words, addressed in deepest awe to 'the incorporal air;' is all unconscious of the awful presence and utterances of the visitant from the unseen world, who owns an interest in her still. Are we to understand that the disembodied spirit can be visible to whom it will; and that the love stronger than death, which survives in this ghostly compassion for her, manifests itself in such forbearance? In the midst of its charge to Hamlet, it suddenly breaks off :—

> 'But look, amazement on thy mother sits;
> O, step between her and her fighting soul;
> Conceit in weakest bodies strongest works;
> Speak to her, Hamlet.
> *Ham.*   How is it with you, lady?
> *Queen.* Alas, how is 't with you,
> That you do bend your eye on vacancy,
> And with th' incorporal air do hold discourse?
> Forth at your eyes your spirits wildly peep;

And, as the sleeping soldiers in the alarm,
Your bedded hairs, like life in excrements,
Start up and stand on end. O gentle son,
Upon the heat and flame of thy distemper
Sprinkle cool patience. Whereon do you look?
   Ham. On him! on him! Look you, how pale he glares!
His form and cause conjoin'd, preaching to stones,
Would make them capable. Do not look upon me;
Lest with this piteous action you convert
My stern effects : then what I have to do
Will want true colour; tears, perchance, for blood.
   Queen. To whom do ye speak this?
   Ham.   Do you see nothing there ?
   Queen. Nothing at all; yet all that is, I see.
   Ham. Nor did you nothing hear ?
   Queen.   No, nothing but ourselves.
   Ham. Why, look you there! look, how it steals away!
My father, in his habit as he lived!
Look, where he goes, even now, out at the portal!'

And as the ghost disappears, the queen all unconsciously
turns on Hamlet with the exclamation—

   'This is the very coinage of your brain :
This bodiless creation ecstasy
Is very cunning in.
   Ham.   Ecstasy!
My pulse, as yours, doth temperately keep time,
And makes as healthful music. It is not madness
That I have utter'd : bring me to the test
And I the matter will re-word; which madness
Would gambol from. Mother, for love of grace,
Lay not that flattering unction to your soul,
That not your trespass but my madness speaks.'

In the analogous scene in ' Macbeth,' where the ghost
of Banquo suddenly rises in the banquet hall—invisible
to all but the usurper, whose guilty soul it appals,—the
apparition utters no words ; and on the German stage,
where the dramas of Shakespeare excite an enthusiasm
akin to that of the old playgoers of the Elizabethan
Globe or Blackfriars, it is customary to introduce no
visible ghost, but to leave the effect to be realised as a

mere creation of Macbeth's fancy. In the realistic literalness of the English stage, the auditor has to reverse
the process, and assume the invisibility of Banquo to all
but the king. Lady Macbeth, after making light to
their 'worthy friends' of this strange fit of her lord as
momentary, 'but a thing of custom ; 'tis no other; only
it spoils the pleasure of the time,' turns on him with the
challenge—

       ' Are you a man?
  Macb. Ay, and a bold one, that dare look on that
Which might appal the devil.
  Lady M.   O proper stuff!
This is the very painting of your fear :
This is the air-drawn dagger, which, you said,
Led you to Duncan. O, these flaws and starts,
Impostors to true fear, would well become
A woman's story at a winter's fire,
Authorised by her grandam. Shame itself!
Why do you make such faces? When all's done
You look but on a stool.
  Macb. Prithee, see there! behold! look! lo! how say you?
Why, what care I? If thou canst nod, speak too.'

And so the scene proceeds, until at his

     ' Hence, horrible shadow
    Unreal mockery, hence!'

the ghost finally disappears, while the guests are sum-
marily desired by Lady Macbeth to stay all questioning
and go at once. To them it has been invisible throughout the scene. It is an added marvel to the conscience-
stricken Macbeth that they should 'keep the natural
ruby of their cheeks' in the presence of such a 'horrible
shadow.' To him it is too real to admit of a doubt that
it has glared on all alike. The impalpable apparition has
its ghostly presence anew impressed on our imaginations
by this capricious visibility. A discriminating criticism
can, indeed, assign other reasons for its invisibility to
the queen in 'Hamlet'; while to Lady Macbeth some

critics assume that the ghost of Banquo is not less manifest than to her husband; though she has gazed un-
blanched on that 'which might appal the devil,' being,
indeed, the very creature of his work and theirs. She
has schooled herself to the worst. To her 'the sleeping
and the dead are but as pictures;' and she coldly responds to her husband's passion : 'When all's done, you
look but on a stool.'

The ghost in 'Julius Cæsar' is still more nearly the
mere creation of a distempered fancy. It does, indeed,
speak, and tells the noble Roman of yet another meeting ;
but the ear may be as much 'made the fool o' the other
senses' as the eye ; and so it is with reason that Brutus
exclaims—

> 'I think it is the weakness of mine eyes
> That shapes this monstrous vision.'

As to the ghosts that haunt the couch of Richard on
the eve of Bosworth's fatal day,—though they also utter
words more horrible than the vision which appals the
eye,—they may be regarded, like other nearly similar
presentations, as 'false creations, proceeding from the
heat-oppressed brain,' the dramatic embodiments of the
tyrant's nightmare dream.

> 'Shadows to-night
> Have struck more terror to the soul of Richard
> Than can the substance of ten thousand soldiers
> Armed in proof.'

So far however we see that the poet moves with
equal ease and clearness of vision in that shadowy world
of dreams and enchantments, as in his own sublunary
sphere ; and at the waving of his incentive wand, the
sports of fancy and the creatures of vulgar folk-lore
come forth and reveal themselves in consistent harmony
with all the highest aims of dramatic art. But the ghosts

and the witches of this strange realm of fancy constitute but a small part of the supernatural elements in the Shakespearean drama ; and stand indeed in striking and purposed contrast to the wanderers from Fairy-land, the creatures of the elements, or the like airy sprites : beings as unsubstantial as 'the air-drawn dagger' of Macbeth, and yet each with an individuality as distinct as that of the usurping thane.

CHAPTER X.

FAIRY FOLK-LORE.

'Such sights as youthful poets dream
On summer eves by haunted stream.'—*L'Allegro.*

WHEN Puck is commanded by Oberon, 'the King of Shadows,' who rules supreme in the 'Midsummer Night's Dream,' to amend the mischief he has wrought, by wilful knavery or mischance, upon the rival Athenian lovers, and to work new pranks for their undoing, that fairies and mortals alike may be at peace, he replies—

'My fairy lord, this must be done with haste,
For night's swift dragons cut the clouds full fast,
And yonder shines Aurora's harbinger:
At whose approach, ghosts, wandering here and there,
Troop home to churchyards; damned spirits all,
That in crossways and floods have burial,
Already to their wormy beds are gone;
For fear lest day should look their shames upon,
They wilfully themselves exile from light,
And must for aye consort with black-brow'd night.'

In this the poet glances at those gloomier superstitions which are more or less characteristic of all rude conceptions of the invisible world. They constitute its predominating aspect in the savage mind, and were by no means wanting in English folk-lore. It is not to be supposed that the rude peasantry of England had fashioned out of the *Feld-ælfen* or *Dvergar* of their Saxon or Norsk fathers the airy haunters of their moonlit glades, devoid of all such repulsive features as survive in

the ballad-pictures of Scottish Elfland. To both they
were objects of vague apprehension. But the English
fairy, fashioned under more genial circumstances than
the wild social life and the rugged landscape of their
northern neighbours, was a tricksy and mischievous, but
not a malignant sprite. In Chaucer's 'Rime of Sire
Topas,' purposely written to ridicule the extravagances
of the romancers, the knight sets forth in search of ad-
ventures, and, in 'the countree of Faerie' meets with
the 'gret geaunt Sire Oliphant,' on whom his prowess
is to be shown. But, though it is a land of wonders,
where, as in Spenser's later visions, giants, dragons, and
monsters of all sorts may be looked for, its true fairy-
folk have no such repulsive characteristics; and of its
elfin queen we learn :—

> 'Here is the Quene of Faerie,
> With harpe, and pipe, and simphonie,
> Dwelling in this place.'

The charms of Fairyland, which were left in Scotland
to rude nameless ballad minstrels, who perpetuated
without disguise the current superstitions of the people,
thus early took the fancy of England's greatest poets;
and hence whatever was coarse, gloomy, and fit only to
'consort with black-browed night,' was eliminated from
its airy beings. But the gloom of this supernatural
element clung to the northern folk-lore. The persecu-
tions of the seventeenth century, and the grave aspects
of their later religious belief and forms of worship, doubtless helped to beget that mood of mind in the Scottish
peasantry which continued to find a charm in the
darkest superstitions of their forefathers.

Burns, in his 'Halloween,' perpetuates, towards the
close of the eighteenth century, with mingled humour
and gravity, the unsophisticated superstitions of the

peasantry with reference to that grand anniversary
of witches, fiends, and all the powers of evil, which
by a curious association of ideas had been assigned
to All Saints' Eve. Then also the fairies were reputed
to hold high festival, and to be specially active in their
good or evil doings for mankind. They had power to
prosper or blight according to their humour. Household,
flock and field were at their mercy ; and they were
believed never to overlook a slight or forget a favour.
But though 'Halloween' is specially noted by the
peasant bard as falling

> 'Upon that night, when faeries light,
>   On Cassilis Downans dance,
> Or owre the lays, in splendid blaze,
>   On sprightly coursers prance,'

yet the fairies are displaced by more prosaic and bane-
ful agents of darkness, in the incidents of the night.
They were already falling into disrepute ; while ghosts,
witches, and the emissaries of Satan were denounced,
but by no means discredited, by the ecclesiastical censors
of the age. With a curious definiteness, unusual in relation to such shadowy beings as the fairies of Scottish
Elfland, Allan Cunningham tells us, 'it is generally admitted that they left our land about seventy years ago.
Their mournings and moanings among the hills on the
Hallowmass night of their departure—according to the
assertion of an old shepherd,—were melancholy to hear.'
Allan Cunningham wrote thus in 1834 ; so that it is now
a full century since the rocky downs of Cassilis, and the
coves and moonlit valleys of Scotland, ceased to echo to
the ringing of the fairies' bridle-reins and the music of
their corn-pipes and bog-reeds.

But ere the last echoes of fairy music had died away,
another peasant poet shaped their most favourite legend-

ary prank into a rhyme of sweetest fancy and pathos. The dreaded mischief of the Scottish fairy was the transporting of children to Elfland, and leaving in their place the unsightly changeling which figures in many a village tale. But out of this rude superstition, common to the Scottish and Irish peasantry, the Ettrick Shepherd wrought his exquisite legend of 'Kilmeny,' a virgin pure, carried off to Fairyland, beyond the reach of sin and sorrow; and returning but for a month and a day, to charm all nature with a glimpse of perfect purity and peace.

> ' When seven lang years had come and fled,
>   When grief was calm, and hope was dead;
>   When scarce was remembered Kilmeny's name,
>   Late, late in a gloamin Kilmeny cam hame!'

But the vision of her return, though exceedingly beautiful, is wholly fancy-wrought, and need not detain us here. It is otherwise with Shakespeare's picturings of Fairyland. In his day the fairy held his unchallenged place in popular belief, and his bridle bells were still listened for in Charlecote chace. The poet accordingly pictured the actual Fairyland of his age, though whatever gloomy phantoms still haunted English glades and dells were banished from his poetic vision. Hence when the lord of Fairyland responds to the exhortation of Puck for needful haste, since night's fitting time, when ghosts and damned spirits alone venture abroad, is almost past, it is to disown all such affinities. He acknowledges no such restraints as those which made the ghost of buried Denmark haunt 'the dead vast and middle of the night,' and start 'like a guilty thing upon a fearful summons,' at the first morning cock-crow; and hence he thus repels Puck's reasons for haste, as wholly inapplicable to spirits such as they are. From choice they

court the paler light, and make their favourite haunts in
the moonlit glade :—

> ' But we are spirits of another sort;
> I with the morning's love have oft made sport;
> And like a forester, the groves may tread,
> Even till the eastern gate, all fiery-red,
> Opening on Neptune with fair blessed beams,
> Turns into yellow gold his salt green streams.'

The cock's shrill clarion has no warning dread for them ;
but when they hear the morning lark their pleasure is to
run before the dawn,

> ' Tripping after the night's shade
> Swifter than the wandering moon.'

They are shadowy beings, unsubstantial as the moon-
beam, and therefore such as soft stillness and the night
become ; but with no affinity to the murky gloom which
Macbeth associates with his 'secret, black, and midnight
hags.'   There is no confusion of the widely diverse elements of that supernatural world which played so familiar
a part in the realisations of popular credulity.   With
nicest delicacy the poet discriminates between the witches
and other traffickers with the powers of hell ; or the
'sheeted dead,' and the unresting spirits of murdered
men, which haunted the age with gloomy superstitions :
and those widely diverse creations wherewith the fanciful
folk-lore, inherited from elder generations, had peopled
grove and flowery dell, woodland, marsh and lake, with
goblins, sprites and fays, best fitted to sport in poet's
visions.   Of this wholly different class are such ethereal
imaginings as flit like rainbow gleams, playing their part
among the mortals who, 'in nightly revels and new
jollity' celebrate Hippolyta's nuptials in 'A Midsummer Night's Dream ;' or in 'The Tempest' help to light
Hymen's lamps for· Prospero's more gentle daughter.

They are the refined creations of an exquisite poetic fancy, working with the current material of what had doubtless charmed the boy in the familiar fairy-lore of the old Stratford ingle-nook, or haunted his moonlit wanderings among the glades of Charlecote Chase.

Among such familiar fairy-folk, Puck, or Robin Good-fellow, stands out with exceptional clearness and strongly marked individuality, playing his pranks on the odd 'human mortals'—

> 'The crew of patches, rude mechanicals,
> That work for bread upon Athenian stalls'—

who chance to cross the path of Oberon and Titania, amid their revels, and their chidings over the sweet changeling whom the fairy king would have as knight of his train. The elves and fays, with the jealous Oberon and his wilful queen, are beings such only

> 'As youthful poets dream
> On summer eves by haunted stream.'

But the Puck of this midsummer night's dream is such as could pertain only to one poet's vision. The 'drudging goblin,' is indeed introduced by Milton in the 'L'Allegro,' among the fire-side tales told over the spicy nut-brown ale. But the youthful poet is dreaming by no haunted stream; but only telling, daintily enough, the oft-told tale of

> 'How the drudging goblin sweat
> To earn his cream-bowl duly set,
> When in one night, ere glimpse of morn,
> His shadowy flail hath thrash'd the corn
> That ten day-labourers could not end:
> Then lies him down, the lubber fiend,
> And stretched out all the chimney's length,
> Basks at the fire his hairy strength;
> And crop-full out of door he flings
> Ere the first cock his matin rings.'

Here we have the popular conception of the rude
goblin, a huge, ungainly lubber fiend, hairy as a satyr,
drudging with loutish perseverance for his cream-
bowl; and when the bribe is earned, flinging his
unwieldy length before the chimney-log, like the
rudest toil-worn hind. But Shakespeare's Robin Good-
fellow is no lubber fiend, but a rare poetical embodiment of the comedy of mischief. 'My gentle Puck,'
as Oberon calls that merry wanderer of the night, is
a knavish elf, who esteems it choice sport to have set
the fondest lovers a-jangling by mistake. He delights
to play madcap pranks around the wassail bowl; or
even to lurk in it, 'in very likeness of a roasted crab,'
cozening the old gossip in her posset, or toppling the
spinster aunt, who in the midst of her saddest tale
has been cheated into fancying him a three-foot stool.
He is, in fact, the originator of all the mirthful mischances that seeming accident produces :—

> 'And then the whole quire hold their hips and laugh;
> And waxen in their mirth, and neeze, and swear
> A merrier hour was never wasted theie.'

The fairy messenger of Queen Titania does indeed
address him on their meeting as 'thou lob of spirits;'
but he has scarcely spoken ere she recognises Oberon's
henchman, who, at his bidding, 'will put a girdle round
about the earth in forty minutes.' The mad sprite
who frights the maidens of the villagery, and misleads
night-wanderers, laughing at their harm, is ready
to play his pranks on the Fairy Queen herself, now
that Titania and her fairy lord have quarrelled. For,
as he tells Titania's messengers—

> 'Oberon is passing fell and wrath,
> Because that she as her attendant hath
> A lovely boy, stolen from an Indian king;
> She never had so sweet a changeling;

And jealous Oberon would have the child
Knight of his train, to trace the forests wild;
But she perforce withholds the loved boy,
Crowns him with flowers, and makes him· all her joy.
And now they never meet in grove or green,
By fountain clear, or spangled starlight sheen,
But they do square: that all their elves for fear,
Creep into acorn cups and hide them there.
    Fairy. Either I mistake your shape and making quite,
Or else you are that shrewd and knavish sprite
Call'd Robin Goodfellow: are not you he
That frights the maidens of the villagery;
Skim milk, and sometimes labour in the quern,
And bootless make the breathless housewife churn;
And sometime make the drink to bear no barm;
Mislead night-wanderers, laughing at their harm?
Those that Hobgoblin call you, and sweet Puck,
You do their work, and they shall have good luck:
Are not you he?
    Puck.   Thou speak'st aright;
I am that merry wanderer of the night.
I jest to Oberon, and make him smile,
When I a fat and bean-fed horse beguile,
Neighing in likeness of a filly foal:
And sometime lurk I in a gossip's bowl.'

And so the madcap sprite gleefully recounts his mischief-makings, until Oberon summons him to spoil
Titania's moonlight revels, and bewitch her with
deceitful fantasies. The gravest meanings not infre-
quently lurk under the humours of Shakespeare's
comedy. The natural and supernatural are inter-
blended there, as in the living world and all the
simplest mysteries of life. 'Nothing happens by chance'
is a canon of the rustic creed; 'Every effect has
a cause,' says the village philosopher: in illustration
of which, the poet, sporting with the folk-lore of his
time, educes harmonious solutions in relation to incidents too homely for the theologian's care; and by
agencies as remote from his ample faith in the super-

natural as from the dynamics of modern philosophy. The mishaps of the dairy, the good luck of the barn, or the laughter-moving accident to the gossip by the hearth, are all the work of Hobgoblin or Sweet Puck. The graver mischances of seed-time and harvest, which perplex the husbandman and rob him of the fruits of his toil, are in like manner traceable to fairy brawls. Oberon and Titania have fallen out, and

> ' Therefore the winds, piping to us in vain,
> As in revenge, have suck'd up from the sea
> Contagious fogs : which falling in the land,
> Have every pelting river made so proud,
> That they have overborne their continents ;
> The ox hath therefore stretch'd his yoke in vain,
> The ploughman lost his sweat, and the green corn
> Hath rotted ere his youth attain'd a beard ;
> The fold stands empty in the drowned field,
> And crows are fatted with the murrion flock ;
> The nine men's morris is fill'd up with mud,
> And the quaint mazes in the wanton green
> For lack of tread are undistinguishable.
> The human mortals want their winter here ;
> No night is now with hymn or carol blest :
> Therefore the moon, the governess of floods,
> Pale in her anger, washes all the air,
> That rheumatic diseases do abound ;
> And thorough this distemperature, we see
> The seasons alter : hoary-headed frosts
> Fall in the fresh lap of the crimson rose ;
> And on old Hiems' thin and icy crown
> An odorous chaplet of sweet summer buds
> Is, as in mockery, set ; the spring, the summer,
> The childing autumn, angry winter, change
> Their wonted liveries ; and the 'mazed world,
> By their increase, now knows not which is which ;
> And this same progeny of evil comes
> From our debate, from our dissension ;
> We are their parents and original.'

And so, to amend such 'forgeries of jealousy,' Puck steps in with his glamour. Titania becomes the victim

of his pranks, and is beguiled of her Indian boy by
a fraud as simple as the roasted crab in the gossip's
bowl. The juice of the little western flower ' now
purple with love's wound,' is laid on her sleeping
eyelids; Bottom the weaver, ' shallowest thick-skin ' of
all the crew of rude mechanicals from Athenian stalls,
befitted with ' an ass's nowl ' instead of his own conceited pate, is laid to sleep near the bower where the
fairy Queen reposes in fitting state, on

> ' A bank where the wild thyme blows,
> Where oxlips and the nodding violet grows;
> Quite over-canopied with luscious woodbine,
> With sweet musk-roses, and with eglantine.
>
> .   .   .   .
> .   .   .   .   . And so it came to pass
> Titania waked, and straightway loved an ass.'

The harmonious interblending of such strange incongruities leads to ever-new phases of gracefullest fan-
tasy. The love-beglamoured fairy forthwith entertains
her monster-lover with all queenly courtesies. She
engages to purge his mortal grossness so that he shall
thenceforth be like airy spirit. A bevy of fantastic
sprites, more insubstantial than the gossamer-web—
Peaseblossom, Cobweb, Moth, and Mustard-seed, are
commissioned to tend on him with such services as
only fairies can render; and the incongruities of the
enamoured fairy and the gross Athenian mechanical,
are wrought out in details in which broad fantastic
humour and the most delicate grace interblend in perfect harmony. Peaseblossom and his fairy comrades answer
their mistress's summons, and receive her orders : —

> ' Be kind and courteous to this gentleman;
> Hop in his walks and gambol in his eyes;
> Feed him with apricocks and dewberries,
> With purple grapes, green figs, and mulberries;
> The honey-bags steal from the humble bees,

> And for night tapers crop their waxen thighs
> And light them at the fiery glow-worm's eyes,
> To have my love to bed and to arise;
> And pluck the wings from painted butterflies
> To fan the moonbeams from his sleeping eyes;
> Nod to him, elves, and do him courtesies.'

And so the airy shadows of this poet-dream disport themselves beneath the wandering moon, till the mortals have closed their revels and withdrawn; Oberon, reconciled to Titania, has followed with their fairy train; and Puck, ere he too vanishes, thus addresses us:—

> ' If we shadows have offended,
> Think but this, and all is mended,
> That you have but slumber'd here,
> While these visions did appear,
> And this weak and idle theme,
> No more yielding but a dream.'

It is the same sportive inexhaustible fancy which squanders its lavish wealth in 'Romeo and Juliet' when Mercutio describes the dream-freaks of Queen Mab, 'the fairy's midwife.' Yet Queen Mab and Queen Titania has each a realm of her own; and the two stand out in striking contrast, with equally diverse functions and individuality. Titania is, throughout, the refined ideal of the moon-lit dreamland over which she reigns. She looses none of her queenly dignity by the pranks which Robin Goodfellow is allowed to play on her. She yields herself so absolutely to the potent spell of that 'little western flower,' that under its glamour, she can disport herself with queenly grace in the very arms of her monster-lover. The charm of the comedy indeed lies in the curious interblendings of exquisite fancy and the sweetest glimpses of nature, with the lighter humour of the play : as when Oberon is moved to pity as he watches the favours which Titania is lavishing on the transformed lout. The elves over whom they reign are wont, like the bee, to 'murmur by the hour in fox-glove bells.' On duty bent, they 'hang a pearl in every cowslip's ear;' or, when affrighted by the wrath of Oberon and his queen, 'creep into acorn-cups and hide them there.' It is in exquisite harmony with such revellers among the zephyrs and the flowers, that their repentant fairy lord exclaims at sight of his queen toying with her Athenian swain, and sticking musk-roses on his ass's head :—

> ' Her dotage now I do begin to pity;
> For meeting her of late behind the wood,
> Seeking sweet favours for this hateful fool,
> I did upbraid her, and fall out with her;
> For she his hairy temples then had rounded
> With coronet of fresh and fragrant flowers;
> And that same dew, which sometimes on the buds
> Was wont to swell, like round and orient pearls,
> Stood now within the pretty flowerets' eyes,
> Like tears that did their own disgrace bewail.'

The incongruities of those 'four nights which quickly dream away the time' between the opening scene and the arrival of the fair Hippolyta's nuptial hour, are in perfect harmony with the wonderland of any midsummer night's dream. The fair Hermia betricked by Puck; Theseus of Athens and his Amazonian Queen entertained on their wedding-night with the interlude of 'Pyramus and Thisbe,' played by Quince, Bottom, Starveling, and poor Snug with his extempore roaring; and the Fairy Queen pursuing with the soul of love the transmogrified weaver, her ear not less enchanted with his singing than her eye with the grace of his hairy nowl : all blend together as in the gay romance of the dreamer.

The contrasts are equally striking, yet of a different kind, which furnish the bold dramatic antithesis of 'The Tempest.' The princely magician, Prospero, engrossed by his researches into the mysteries of nature and occult science, has been robbed of his dukedom by the perfidious brother whom he had appointed as his deputy. Escaping the death to which he had been consigned, we find him with the sharer of his 'sea-sorrow,' an only daughter, and his magical books, transported to that desert island the localisation of which has already been attempted in the geography of that ideal hemisphere where such enchanted islands are found. There Prospero reigns lord of nature and all her mysteries. His daughter Miranda, so peerless in her perfect innocency, has tempted us to some notice in a previous chapter. Not quite three years old when borne with her father to this lone retreat, she remembers only 'far off and like a dream,' the face of woman; and there she has grown up, her father's sole companion, like a pure lily, the unconscious embodiment of maidenly delicacy, a very child of nature. She is not indeed without some fitting education; for, as her father says,—

> 'Here
> Have I, thy schoolmaster, made thee more profit
> Than other princesses can, that have more time
> For vainer hours, and tutors not so careful.'

But though Miranda is her father's sole companion; and Shakespeare, or his first editors, have styled it an uninhabited island : they are neither its first settlers nor its sole inhabitants. The foul witch Sycorax, who with age and envy was grown into a hoop, 'for mischiefs manifold and sorceries too terrible to enter human hearing,' would have been put to death, but for some unnamed redeeming deed for which they would not take her life. So the sailors brought her from her native Argier and left her on the island. This blear-eyed hag, in the working of her unearthly spells, had enthralled an

ethereal being, too refined to be turned by her to any
serviceable account, and dying, left behind her that most
refined and daintiest of sylphs, Ariel. Prospero, in
whom he has found a more congenial master, and to
whom, therefore, he has done worthy service, is nevertheless the stern exacting lord, though he claims the
gratitude of his ethereal slave, and angrily taunts him
that he

> 'Thinks it much to tread the ooze
> Of the salt deep,
> To run upon the sharp wind of the north,
> To do me business in the veins o' the earth
> When it is baked with frost;'

and so Prospero demands—

> 'Hast thou forgot
> The foul witch, Sycorax?   .   .   .   .
> .   .   .   .   .   .   Thou, my slave,
> As thou report'st thyself, was then her servant;
> And, for thou wast a spirit too delicate
> To act her earthy and abhorr'd commands,
> Refusing her grand hests, she did confine thee,
> By help of her more potent ministers,
> And in her most unmitigable rage,
> Into a cloven pine; within which rift
> Imprison'd thou didst painfully remain
> A dozen years; within which space she died,
> And left thee there; where thou didst vent thy groans
> As fast as mill-wheels strike. Then was this island—
> Save for the son that she did litter here,
> A freckled whelp, hag-born,—not honour'd with
> A human shape.
>   *Ariel.*   Yes; Caliban, her son.
>   *Pros* Dull thing, I say so; he, that Caliban,
> Whom now I keep in service. Thou best know'st
> What torment I did find thee in: thy groans
> Did make wolves howl, and penetrate the breasts
> Of ever-angry bears; it was a torment
> To lay upon the damn'd, which Sycorax
> Could not again undo: it was mine art,

> When I arrived and heard thee, that made gape
> The pine, and let thee out.
>   *Ariel.*   I thank thee, master.
>   *Pros.* If thou more murmur'st, I will rend an oak,
> And peg thee in his knotty entrails, till
> Thou hast howl'd away twelve winters.
>   *Ariel.*   Pardon, master;
> I will be correspondent to command,
> And do my spiriting gently.'

And so the airy sylph, subject to the exactions of this imperious master, but now promised his liberty on the third day, joyfully departs to assume the character of a nymph of the sea, and in that shape to do his bidding.

Ariel is as ethereal as that other strange island-dweller, Caliban, 'the freckled whelp, hag-born,' is of the earth earthy. Yet he has a well-defined individuality among the beings of that airy world which is his natural element. He is a gay, sprightly, and even frolicsome spirit, not wholly without the mischievous qualities of Puck, but gentler and more refined in his spiriting, and of his own choice seeking his pastimes far from mortal haunts. His joyous nature does indeed derive a pleasure from the successful mischief-makings on which he is commissioned ; but all the while he is envying the free lark and butterfly, and rather sports with his poor dupes because of the commands of Prospero, than that, like the madcap goblin Puck, he finds his own delight in such pranks. For such 'earthy and abhorred commands' as the Argier witch alone had to lay on him, he was a spirit too delicate ; but, though all the while long-ing and thirsting for freedom, as we might fancy a captive butterfly or honey-bee, there is nothing repulsive to him in the quaintest of Prospero's tasks. He tells with manifest glee of his having performed to a point the tempest he was commissioned to raise ;

yea, to every article he has accomplished his strange bidding :—

> 'I boarded the King's ship; now on the beak,
> Now in the waist, the deck, in every cabin,
> I flamed amazement : sometimes I'd divide,
> And burn in many places; on the topmast,
> The yards and bowsprit, would I flame distinctly,
> Then meet and join.   Jove's lightnings, the precursors
> O' the dreadful thunder-claps, more momentary
> And sight-outrunning were not : the fire and cracks
> Of sulphurous roaring the most mighty Neptune
> Seem to besiege, and make his bold waves tremble,
> Yea, his dread trident shake.'

'My brave spirit!' Prospero responds, in admiration of such perfect fulfilment of his wishes, 'who was so constant, that this coil would not infect his reason?' to which Ariel thus gleefully answers :—

> 'Not a soul
> But felt a fever of the mad, and play'd
> Some tricks of desperation.   All but mariners
> Plunged in the foaming brine, and quit the vessel,
> Then all afire with me: the King's son, Ferdinand,
> With hair up-staring,—then like reeds, not hair,—
> Was the first man that leap'd; crying "Hell is empty,
> And all the devils are here!"'

And so, having thus fulfilled the utmost wishes of his master in relation to the tempest, he is now able further to report that all are safe, 'not a hair perished : on their sustaining garments not a blemish, but fresher than before ;' and all, as he had ordered, are dispersed in troops about the island, the king's son by himself 'cooling the air with sighs, in an odd angle of the isle.'

Again Ariel recounts with liveliest satisfaction the rougher play with which he has outwitted the drunken conspiracy of Trinculo and Stephano under the guidance of the poor monster Caliban.   They are such pranks as would have been peculiarly acceptable to Puck, and

seem to have proved in no way distasteful to the daintier
spirit to whom the commands of the Argier witch were
so abhorrent :—

> 'I told you, Sir, they were red-hot with drinking;
> So full of valour that they smote the air
> For breathing in their faces; beat the ground
> For kissing of their feet; yet always bending
> Towards their project. Then I beat my tabor;
> At which like unback'd colts, they prick'd their ears,
> Advanced their eyelids, lifted up their noses
> As they smelt music: so I charmed their ears,
> That, calf-like, they my lowing followed through
> Tooth'd briers, sharp furzes, pricking gorse, and thorns,
> Which entered their frail shins. At last I left them
> I' the filthy-mantled pool beyond your cell,
> There dancing up to the chins, that the foul lake
> O'erstunk their feet.'

Puck would have desired no choicer sport.   But with
Ariel, though done promptly, and with a pride in the
execution of it to his master's utmost wishes, it is at best
but pleasant task-work, performed under the promise
'thou shalt be free as mountain winds.'   His gentler
nature is shown in the child-like simplicity with which
he recalls to Prospero this promised boon :—

> 'I prithee,
> Remember that I have done thee worthy service;
> Told thee no lies, made thee no mistakings, served
> Without or grudge or grumblings; thou didst promise
> To bate me a full year.'

Miranda does not differ more clearly from Viola, Portia,
or the wilful and witty Beatrice, than Ariel does from
Puck, or any other of Shakespeare's airy creations.   He
is wholly incapable of the wanton mischief of that
knavish sprite, who on learning that by preposterous
mischance he has made Helena 'all fancy-sick and pale
of cheer,' by apportioning to her the wrong lover; and
set the whole wooers in the piece a-jangling: is even
more delighted at the mischief he has wrought, than

when anticipating the meeting of the charmed lovers, he exclaims—

> 'Shall we their fond pageant see?
> Lord, what fools these mortals be!'

In striking contrast to this, Ariel is touched by the human sufferings with which he can have no fellow-feeling. When he tells of the usurping duke and his companions driven to distraction by their griefs, and above all, the good old lord Gonzalo, with tears running down his beard, 'like winter's drops from eaves,' he thus addresses Prospero—

> 'Your charm so strongly works 'em,
> That if you now beheld them, your affections
> Would become tender.
> *Pros.*   Dost thou think so, spirit?
> *Ariel.* Mine would, sir, were I human.
> *Pros.*   And mine shall.
> Hast thou, which art but air, a touch, a feeling
> Of their afflictions, and shall not myself,
> One of their kind, that relish all as sharply,
> Passion as they, be kindlier moved than thou art?
> Though with their high wrongs. I am struck to the quick,
> Yet with my nobler reason 'gainst my fury
> Do I take part; the rarer action is
> In virtue than in vengeance: they being penitent,
> The sole drift of my purpose doth extend
> Not a frown further. Go, release them, Ariel.'

To Ariel we are plainly left to assume that this is the more welcome duty; to Puck it would have been altogether the reverse. Their troubles would have been sport to 'that shrewd knavish sprite,' who tells even Oberon, when he has challenged him for his blundering mischief—

> 'That must needs be sport alone;
> And those things do best please me
> That befal preposterously.'

And so, while we seem to feel a sympathetic joy at Ariel's own release, as at the freedom of a caged lark,

listening in fancy to his delighted song dying away as
he soars into the limitless blue ; we are all the more
fully prepared to enter into the feeling of Prospero :—

> Why, that's my dainty Ariel ! I shall miss thee ;
> But yet thou shalt have freedom.'

All other duties fulfilled, Prospero at the last com-
missions him to satisfy the promise already made, of
calm seas and auspicious winds to waft them homeward,
and catch the royal fleet far off, and so—

> ' My Ariel, chick,
> That is thy charge : then to the elements,
> Be free, and fare thou well !'

and with a swoop like that of the humming-bird-which
has dallied long over some favourite flower, and then
darts swift as thought out of sight, we seem to see
Ariel float and soar away into the golden light of the
setting sun.   The song of Ariel realises for us the very
thoughts and aspirations of such an embodied joy.   It
dies away on the mind's ear like the thrilling quiver of
the mounting lark :—

> ' Where the bee sucks, there suck I :
> In a cowslip's bell I lie ;
> There I couch when owls do cry.
> On the bat's back I do fly
> After summer merrily.
> Merrily, merrily shall I live now,
> Under the blossom that hangs on the bough.'

For this exquisite creation Shakespeare had no more
material to work upon than the same crude shapings of
popular fancy and rustic superstition which gave him
the lubber fiend out of which his Puck is fashioned. But
there is a higher art in ' The Tempest ' than in 'A Midsummer Night's Dream,' beautiful as both are.   The
pure poetry of richest fancy seems to entrance us into
the very spirit of fairy revelling, amid the marvels raised

for us by Prospero's potent wand; and then the poet dismisses all back to the realm of dreams. As in the lighter comedy of 'A Midsummer Night's Dream,' Puck lingers, after Oberon, Titania, and their fairy train have vanished, to suggest that offence is needless, since perchance you have but slumbered here; so, with a more solemn earnestness, suited to the dignity of the speaker and the incidents of the drama, Prospero tells us how all 'are melted into thin air;' and then, moralising on the 'insubstantial pageant,' the 'baseless fabric of this vision,' as but the type of all that seems to us most real: even 'the great globe itself,' yea all which it inhabit; he adds—

> 'We are such stuff
> As dreams are made on; and our little life
> Is rounded with a sleep.'

We have thus analysed certain objective creations that stand out with exceptional beauty or distinctive individuality of character, among the supernatural *dramatis personæ* which people the world of art created for us by the genius of Shakespeare. His witches, ghosts, and other impersonations of purely superstitious fancy, have their value in relation to the speculations of modern science; for the belief in unseen or spiritual agencies, and in sorcerers or wizards by whom they can be influenced or controlled, is acknowledged to be almost universal among the lowest savage races. As to his Oberon and Titania, his Mab, Puck, and Ariel; the king of shadows and queen of dreams, the fairy, goblin and sprite of popular folk-lore: they too have an interest for the modern student of science, who can value the transformation of the crude imaginings of rustic superstition into concrete forms of refined poetic art. Artistically they command our admiration by their realisation in clearly defined individuality of what, till Shakespeare embodied them, had flitted before the mind's eye as ghostly phantoms, vaguer than the creatures of our dreams. In this they only share with all the other characters of Shakespeare's drama, that charm of individual portraiture which makes each of them a study replete with hidden truth.

Hence the embodied zephyr of 'The Tempest' possesses a personality so consistently defined, that we feel, while entranced in the evolution of the drama, that the doings of Ariel are no whit more improbable than those of Ferdinand and Miranda, even in the exquisitely natural glimpse flashed on us in the midst of a scene which opens with Prospero in his magic robes, and Ariel acting out his most potent charms. The magician promises to Alonzo of Naples—

> 'I will requite you with as good a thing;
> At least bring forth a wonder to content you:'

and so he discloses to the glad father's eyes the two lovers seated at the chess-board :—

> '*Mir.* Sweet lord, you play me false.
> *Fer.*   No, my dearest love,
> I would not for the world.
> *Mir.* Yes, for a score of kingdoms you should wrangle,
> And I would call it fair play.'

Yet the moment we escape from the thrall of the poet's enchantment, and its world of fancy fades into the light of common day, we own to ourselves that 'our actors were all spirits, and are melted into air.' They are mere sports of fancy; things of beauty for a perpetual joy; but impossibilities in the sober reality of this world of fact and scientific realism.

So far we have dealt with Ariel, and the beings of which he is the type, as fit subjects for literary criticism.

Viewed as an illustration of synthetic power, this creature of a poet's fancy commends itself to every mind capable of appreciating the highest forms of art. Shakespeare had, as it were, the problem thus placed before him :— Assuming the four primary elements of the ancients ; and that they are peopled by such creatures as the Rosicrucian Sylphs, Gnomes, Naiads, and Pyroads,— beings endowed with natures each suited to the element which it inhabits : what would be the characteristics of an ethereal being, the dweller of the air ? The poet accepts the task, animates a zephyr, brings it into intimate relations with the philosophic impersonation of active human intellect, and places it alongside of the embodiment of perfect feminine purity. It is a marvellous creation of genius, which the longer it is studied yields the more admiration and delight at the perfectness of a conception so thoroughly self-originated. But what has science to do with Rosicrucian sylphs or gnomes : the airy nothings fashioned to people the elements of an obsolete creed, which chemical analysis long since dissipated ? So far from modern science accepting the antique creed of the four elements : its gases, metals, earths, and other simplest chemical constituents of the globe, already exceed sixty in number ; go on in ever increasing multiplicity ; and yet include among them as simple elements neither air, fire, earth, nor water. And for such elements as it owns, chemistry has its own spectrum analyses, eloquent in the truths they reveal. With its respirators, its diving bells, its balloons, and Davy lamps, science now makes its own sylphs, naiads, and gnomes : free enough from competition with the airy nothings begot in the fine frenzy of a poet's brain.

We resign, then, all claim to the scientific recognition of these poetic creations, and dismiss them back to the realm of fancy. But what of that being which the same creative genius has produced for us in clearly defined impersonation, as though he had received and accepted this other problem also :—Assuming that the highest forms of animal life and organisation are nothing more than the results of evolution from the lowest, what would be the characteristics of the brute when developed into that nearest approximation to man of which the mere animal is capable? It reads like the old enigma of the Theban sphinx ; and to it accordingly our modern Œdipus, the most objective of poets, bent all the powers of his genius. He has created for us a being fully realising the ideal of that seeming contradiction in terms, the rational brute ; and in doing so seems in all respects to anticipate that hypothetical product of evolution which modern science reproduces as the brute progenitor of man. Yet Shakespeare least of all dreamt of a human ancestor while working out this portraiture in minutest nicety of detail. To him of all men the distinction between man and his lower fellow-creatures seemed clear and ineffaceable. Hamlet, in his depreciatory self-torturings does indeed ask himself the question :—

> ' What is a man,
> If his chief good and market of his time
> Be but to sleep and feed? a beast, no more.'

But it is only that he may the more clearly infer that man is no such mere animal, but, on the contrary, is the sole living creature endowed with 'god-like reason ;' the one being that exists in conscious relationship to the 'before and after ;' and by virtue of such an inheritance is responsible for the use of it as a man, and not as a mere beast that feeds and sleeps. And so he thus replies to his own challenge :—

> 'Sure, he that made us with such large discourse,
> Looking before and after, gave us not
> That capability and god-like reason
> To fust in us unused.'

But, as Trinculo says, so soon as he casts eyes on
Caliban: 'Were I in England now, there would this
monster make a man; any strange beast there makes
a man.'

The new theory of the origin of species, after meeting
with the wonted reception of all great discoveries,—being
hastily and rashly condemned in its earlier stages, and
little less hastily accepted by many so soon as the shock
of its novel comprehensiveness had passed away,—has
proceeded by rapid process of evolution to the hypothesis
of the descent of man. It has found for us an ancestry
which by its antiquity puts the line of the Conqueror to
shame. Nor will it allow of any evasion of this pedigree.
Only a very few years have passed since ethnologists
were divided into monogenists and polygenists; and
the believer in the unity of the human race was laughed
at for his credulity. But all that is at an end. 'If the
races of man were descended, as supposed by some
naturalists, from two or more distinct species, which had
differed as much, or nearly as much, from each other,
as the orang differs from the gorilla, it can hardly be
doubted that marked differences in the structure of
certain bones would still have been discoverable in man
as he now exists.' So says Mr. Darwin; and so his
Caliban of evolution must needs find admission into
our pedigree as the undoubted progenitor and sole
Adam of the whole human race.

The Court of Heraldry has ever been wont to assume
an authority which admitted of no dispute. You shall
take its pedigree, or none. It had its three kings for

settling such matters, when England was apt to find
one rather more than she could manage in all the rest
of her affairs ; and our Garter King in the new Herald's
College of science has determined a pedigree for us
even more dogmatically than Garter, Clarencieux, and
Norroy combined. We are ready with the admission
that all life starts from a cell ; that the primary rule
of embryonic development is to all appearance common
to animal life ; that the human embryo in early stages
is not readily discernible from that of inferior animals
very remote from man ; and recognise the whole very
remarkable homologous structure in man and the lower
animals. We admit that, up to a certain stage, development proceeds with many striking analogies and some
startling homologies. But what we have to complain of
in the treatment of a question involving such far-reaching
results is that the modern evolutionist, leading us on
clearly, and on the whole convincingly, through many
remarkable evidences of development and seeming
evolution of species ; and recognising in so far the
essential element of humanity as to push research
beyond mere physical structure in search of intellect,
the social virtues, and a moral sense : just at the final
stage where the wondrous transformation is to be looked
for on which the verdict depends, we are directed solely
to physical evidence, as though brain, reason, mind, and
soul, were convertible terms.

Mind is the true standard of man. The perfection
of form is insignificant in comparison with the living
soul. We are not prepared to admit that the development of the brain of an orang or gorilla to a perfect
structural equality with that of man must necessarily be
followed by a corresponding manifestation of intelligence,
reason, and moral sense. Professor Huxley has come

to the conclusion that man in all parts of his organisation differs less from the higher apes than these do from the lower members of the same group. Consequently, says the evolutionist, 'there is no justification for placing man in a distinct order.' But may we not also say : Consequently something else than mere organisation must determine man's place, even according to the classification of the naturalist? But here it is, just at the all-important point on which the whole novel pedigree of humanity depends, that the needful links are assumed, and the supreme difficulties ignored. The conclusion is thus dogmatically stated :—'Man is descended from some less highly-organised form. The grounds upon which this conclusion rests will never be shaken, for the close similarity between man and the lower animals in embryonic development, as well as in innumerable points of structure and constitution, both of high and of the most trifling importance—the rudiments which he retains, and the abnormal reversions to which he is occasionally liable,—are facts which cannot be disputed. They have long been known, but until recently they told us nothing with respect to the origin of man. Now, when viewed by the light of our knowledge of the whole organic world, their meaning is unmistakeable.- The great principle of evolution stands up clear and firm, when these groups of facts are considered in connection with others, such as the mutual affinities of the members of the same group, their geographical distribution in past and present times, and their geological succession. It is incredible that all these facts should speak falsely. He who is not content to look, like a savage, at the phenomena of Nature as disconnected, cannot any longer believe that man is the work of a separate act of creation.'

'It may be so,' said Newton; 'there is no arguing against facts,' when Molyneux communicated to him a discovery by which he fancied he had upset the whole Newtonian system.   But the curious thing with Newton himself, as the type of man regarded from an intellectual point of view, is that as science proceeds on that path on which, to apply the words of his own epitaph, 'mathematics of his own invention have lighted the way,' it seems as if by intuition he had anticipated later discoveries at every step.   Lagrange's Calculus of Variations, Euler's Integrals, with other more recent and beautiful discoveries, appear to have been already his own.   He was wise beyond the capacity of his own generation ; and 'by an almost divine power of mind,' sounded the depths of philosophy, and revolutionised the world of thought.   And so is it with Shakespeare. He was wiser even than all the requirements of that grand era, which was in many respects so worthy of him ; and, in the Caliban of his 'Tempest,' anticipates and satisfies the most startling problem of the nineteenth century.

In the quaint setting of that beautiful comedy, amid the fanciful triumphs of a spurious science that once had its believers, and the creatures of the elements, which then commanded philosophic faith : his rational brute appears no less consistent and truthful to the ideal of his art, than the Ariel or the Miranda alongside of which it is placed.   But when the revels of the magician are ended, and the naturalist undertakes to deal with the transitional being in its relation to the sober realities of science and of fact, what place will he assign to this Caliban of fancy ; and what can we accord to the equally fanciful Caliban of evolution ?   Is not the latter rather a mere Frankenstein, still inanimate, the counterfeit presentment of undeveloped man, with its intellectual and moral possibilities an unsolved problem?

Whether we study Shakespeare's harmoniously consistent embodiment of the faith of the sixteenth century in beings native to the strange islands of the new-found world; or turn to that progenitor of man, limned so definitely by Mr. Darwin, so far as mere physical characteristics are concerned — a hairy quadruped, furnished with tail and pointed ears, arboreal in its habits, a creature which, if naturalists had then existed to examine it, would have been classed among the quadrumana, as surely us would the common, and still more ancient progenitor of the monkeys;—whether, I say, we study the one Caliban or the other, is it less a creature of the imagination; is it more a possibility of this world of our common humanity, than the Ariel of the poet's animated and embodied zephyr?

O

CHAPTER XI.

THE COMMENTATORS.

'Some have at first for wits, then poets, pass'd;
Turn'd critics next, and proved plain fools at last.'—*Pope.*

THE labours of a Shakespearean commentator take
a very modest and humble rank among the varied
products of literary adventure; and the reception they
have met with has too frequently been such as might
well deter any but the boldest from following in his
steps.

'If aught of things that here befall
Touch a spirit among things divine,'

it would be pleasant to think of Louis Theobald reading
the reversal of the old sentence which doomed him to
the literary pillory for his patient and useful critical toil.
It had been his habit to communicate the results of his
Shakespearean annotations to the weekly columns of
'Mist's Journal,' and hence the allusion, erased from later
editions of the 'Dunciad':—

'Nor sleeps one error in its father's grave;
Old puns restore, lost blunders nicely seek,
And crucify poor Shakespeare once a week.'

Theobald's patient diligence was unquestionable, but it
was sneered at as the mere grubbing among waste rub-
bish of a plodding antiquary.   He lived in an age when
the amenities of literary controversy were unknown;
and the friends of his great rival, recognising his inferiority in every element of wit and fancy to the satirist

with whom he had unhappily provoked comparison as
a writer of verse, adopted all Pope's prejudices in reference to his powers as a critic. Hence the disadvantage
at which he was placed in the battle of the books which
ensued. Warton styles him 'a cold, plodding, and
tasteless writer and critic.' But in this he confounded
two essentially distinct elements. As a would-be poet
and playwright Theobald undoubtedly merited the
epithets of cold and tasteless assigned to him. As the
claimant to the discovery of 'The Double Falsehood,'
included as a genuine production of Shakespeare's pen, in
his edition of the poet's works; and then as the blushing
confessor to the authorship of the one belauded passage
in its text, as his own finishing touch to what he still per-
sisted in assigning as a whole to the great dramatist : he
takes pre-eminence among the literary forgers of the
strange age to which he belonged. There is a touch of
sublimity in the apt impudence of the title, as though he
meant a bit of covert irony in his 'Double Falsehood'!
As a literary era it is difficult for us now to realise all
the strange inconsistencies of that Augustan age over
which Pope reigned supreme. There must have seemed
to Theobald's contemporaries and rival critics a fitness,
and even a poetical justice, in his advancement to the
dunce's throne, such as is lost sight of now. For nobody
thinks of Theobald as a poet, or recalls a single line of
his verse : unless, indeed, his own reclaimed forgery,
'Strike up my masters,' &c., in which he was supposed
to have added another hue to Shakespeare's rainbow !
But that, in spite of his promotion to that 'bad emi-
nence,' he should now be recognised as one of the most
judicious and even brilliant among all the Shakespearean
commentators, is a proof of how great his merit must
be in his own legitimate sphere. In place and point

of time he stands, as a critic of Shakespeare, between
Pope and the arrogant presumptuous Warburton.   In
point of merit he is the suggester of not a few ingenious conjectural emendations, now universally accepted, which the author of ' The Essay on Criticism '
might well have envied ; while his plodding industry,
in alliance with learning and critical discrimination, was
sufficient to have rescued the author of ' The Divine
Legation' from his undisputed claim to Mallett's 'Familiar Epistle to the Most Impudent Man living ' !

Bishop Warburton is a warning to all Shakespearean
critics. Of veneration, modesty, or diffidence, he took no
account.   His aim seemed less to produce a ' Shakespeare restored' than to create a remodelled Shakespeare,
reformed from what the poet did write to what, in the
superior judgment of his right reverend commentator,
he should have written. Without some reverential appreciation of the genius of the author, a revision of his
text can only lead to presumptuous impertinences ; and
not a few of Warburton's dogmatic recensions are sheer
nonsense, as where he declares of the line in Hamlet's
soliloquy,

> ' Or to take arms against a sea of troubles '—

' without question Shakespeare wrote " against *assail* of
troubles," i.e. assault '; or again, in Act iii. Sc. 4,
where Hamlet charges his mother with

> ' Such an act
> That blurs the grace and blush of modesty ; '

and in the same vein proceeds to a climax, which nevertheless leaves the act unnamed : the Queen demands
in reply—

> ' Ay me, what act,
> That roars so loud, and thunders in the index ? '

The sense and aptness of the last line seem obvious enough ; but in Warburton's hands it undergoes this ludicrous travesty :—

'That roars so loud, it thunders to the Indies!'

It is a warning to all who may venture where he so boldly trod. Yet whatever may have been the presumptions and shortcomings of the 'critical herd,' their labours have removed many obscurities and blemishes from the Shakespearean text ; while even the assumed authority of an annotated 1632 folio, seemingly in a contemporary hand, and edited with eulogistic confirmation by a veteran commentator, has failed to give currency to a single reading that cannot win general consent as a needful illumination of the original text.

But there is one class of corrections in which, in some cases a happy hit, in others a felicitous acumen, has led to valuable elucidations with the smallest amount of change in the literal text. The experience of every author much accustomed to proof-reading, familiarises him with that mischievous class of misprints which substitutes an apparent sense wholly different from the intended meaning. Among my own experiences in this way is the conversion of 'brutified savages' into ' *beautified* savages ;' or again the change of a sentence in which I had purposed to characterise certain plausible assertions as no better than ' clever guesses at truth' into the transformed statement of ' eleven guesses at truth '!— changes literally trifling, which nevertheless wholly destroyed the meaning. Shakespeare's text not only abounds with such ; but they go on, in certain cases, undergoing successive transformations in new editions, both by early and modern writers, until the blunder of a later edition is made the basis of an imaginary

restoration, very plausible at times, and yet altogether differing from what we have the means of shewing Shakespeare actually did write.   The temptation to the critic,
enamoured of his work, to fancy every ingenious literal
transformation not only an improvement, but an actual
discovery and restoration of the text, has of course to
be guarded against.   Examples of such fallacious discoveries are plentiful.   When Macbeth retorts to the
contemptuous upbraidings of his wife that he is

> ' Letting "I dare not " wait upon "I would,"
> Like the poor cat i' the adage,'

his reply is—

> 'I dare do all that may become a man;
> Who dares do more is none.'

Whereupon Lady Macbeth asks in the same contemptuous tone :—

> ' What beast was't then
> That made you break this enterprise to me?'

The antithesis of Lady Macbeth's *beast*, to what 'may
become a *man*,' in her husband's exclamation, is so
obvious and telling, that the passage might be thought
safe from any critical tampering.   But the amended
1632 folio converts the *beast* into *boast*; and its editor,
Mr. John Payne Collier, goes into ecstasies over the
happy correction of what, he says, 'reads like a gross
vulgarism.'   In similar fashion Warburton travesties
a simile which least of all might have been supposed
to lie beyond the appreciation of a bishop.   The dis-
consolate Rosalind, in 'As You Like It,' says of her
absent lover, 'His kissing is as full of sanctity as the
touch of holy bread.'   So at least read the folios.   But
not so, says the clerical censor; this is 'impious and
absurd,' and so he converts the beautiful allusion to

the holy touch of sacramental bread, into what he calls a 'comparison just and decent,' by rendering it *holy beard*, that is, the kiss of an holy saint or hermit'! In my own copy of the 1632 folio, some previous possessor has drawn his pen through the word *bread*, and written in the margin *hand:* a better reading than the bishop's, though poor as a substitute for the original text.

The editors of the 'Cambridge Shakespeare' remark in their final preface: 'The more experience an editor has, the more cautious he will be in the introduction of conjectural emendations : not, assuredly, because his confidence in the earliest text increases, but because he gains a greater insight into the manifold and far removed sources of error. The insertions, marginal and interlinear, and doubtless occasional errors, of the author's own manuscript, the mistakes, deliberate alterations and attempted corrections of successive transcribers and of the earliest printer, result at last in corruptions which no conjecture can with certainty emend.' It is one thing, however, to actually thrust into the most authoritative text of Shakespeare which we possess, the fancies and guesses of the student; another and wholly different course is to offer such guesses—when the results of careful and reverent study,— apart from the text, as hints for the consideration of fellow-students. In this fashion Theobald communicated his early notes to 'Mist's Journal'; and in our own day many a useful hint has been contributed to the columns of 'The Athenæum,' 'Notes and Queries,' or other literary periodicals.

In previous chapters certain of Shakespeare's dramas have been carefully reviewed under special aspects, and brought to bear on some points of interest in a novel field of criticism. As it has been my habit as a student of Shakespeare to note, from time to time, such conjectural emendations as occurred to me in the course of my reading, I venture to cull from these the notes on the text of the two comedies which have been chiefly referred to in the previous discussion. The principle is a sound one which admits no conjectural emendations into the text because they seem to make better rhythm, grammar, or sense, so long as the reading of the folio is a possible one. Were the prosaic rendering of Dame Quickly's description of Falstaff's death, as given in the marginal notes of Collier's 1632 folio, actually in the printed text, we should feel compelled to accept it in lieu of Theobald's felicitous suggestion, 'For his nose was as sharp as a pen, and a babbled of green fields.' But when the text actually reads, 'and a table of greene fields,' it is so obviously blundered that we are free to accept any good suggestion; and few indeed are likely to hesitate between Theobald's happy thought, and the poor commonplace of the unknown annotator: 'for his nose was as sharp as a pen on a table of green frieze.'

The case is reversed in another example of conjectural emendation. In 'The Taming of the Shrew,' Tranio says :—

> 'Let's be no stoics, nor no stocks, I pray;
> Or so devote to Aristotle's checks
> As Ovid be an outcast quite abjured;
> Balk logic with acquaintance that you have,
> And practice rhetoric in your common talk.'

Rowe converts *balk logic* into *talk logic*; while Capel, and an anonymous critic quoted in the Cambridge notes, respectively suggest *chop* and *hack*. But we owe to Blackstone the happy thought of converting *Aristotle's checks* into *Aristotle's ethicks*. 'Ethics' comes in so fittingly, along with logic and rhetoric, and the argument so obviously is—'Do not let us so austerely devote ourselves to philosophy as wholly to abjure love,' that the emendation seems one that might be welcomed by the most cautious editor. But *checks* makes good sense; and as it is found both in the folios and quarto, it is retained in the text of the Cambridge edition; while Blackstone's conjecture takes, its place as a foot-note.

This is at once the safe and true course. All such changes are open to diversity of opinion. The text of the folios, supplemented in certain cases by the quartos, excepting where the language is notoriously corrupt and meaningless, is the only authoritative one we can ever hope to appeal to; or at any rate must ever be of higher authority than any mere conjectural emendation. Nevertheless it may be thought at times that the Cambridge editors have carried their conservative adherence to the earliest text to an extreme: as where in 'A Midsummer Night's Dream,' a line in Lysander's well-known commentary on 'The course of true love,' is printed after the quartos, thus:—

> 'Making it momentany as a sound,
> Swift as a shadow, short as any dream;

though the folios render the word *momentarie*. Where so obvious a choice lay before them, the later text of the folio might safely be followed. The sole legitimate aim of the Shakespearean editor is to restore, and if needs be, to explain, but not to amend the actual text; to give, as far as possible, what Shakespeare did write, not to assume a censorship on his writings which would be presumptuous when dealing with far inferior authors.

Much of Pope's, as of Steevens' emendations of the metre of Shakespeare partakes of the censorial character. No two things professing to be the same could differ more widely than the heroic measure of Shakespeare and of Pope. The structure of Shakespeare's verse is strictly dramatic, prosody and all else being subordinated to the higher purposes of the dialogue. He displaced the rhyming couplets of the early drama ; and, following in the wake of ' Marlow's mighty line,' he constructed a free dramatic versification, partaking of the licence derived from the Old English decasyllables of Chaucer. Where the sense is better expressed by such means, the line frequently begins with an accent, making thereby the first foot a trochee instead of an iambus. A still more impressive effect is produced by adding on to the beginning of a full heroic line an extra emphatic syllable. Some editors adopt the plan of printing this in a line by itself ; as is done with the numerous half-lines purposely introduced. Marked pauses of different kinds break the monotony of a succession of heroic lines, and give pleasing irregularity and naturalness to the dialogue. In some cases the line is broken by the sense into two distinct parts, with an extra syllable at the break, so as to compel a pause in the voice. In others an unaccented syllable is omitted, so that the voice rests on the final accent preceding the cæsura, before starting on the first accent of the second half. Lines of twelve syllables are common, both with and without an accent in the superfluous syllables. An occasional verse occurs even with two additional feet, while others frequently want a foot. The licence of slurring or suppressing syllables is used to an extent which could not now be indulged in. Prose and verse intermingle, according to the subject, and the character of the speaker. A dialogue begins at times in prose, as in Act i. Sc. 3. of 'The Merchant of Venice,' where Shylock and Bassanio discuss the prosaic piece of business concerning the three-months' interest for three thousand ducats; but the moment that the entrance of Antonio awakens the jealous hatred of Shylock, the language becomes impassioned and metrical. Falstaff never speaks in verse but in his mock heroics, as where, in 'Henry IV' (Part II. Act ii. Sc. 4.) he plays the royal father to the prince, and 'will do it in King Cambyses' vein;' or again, where in loftiest fashion he addresses the new king, Henry V, with the purpose of showing Master Shallow how he can make 'King Hal' do him grace. The prince, on the contrary, passes from prose to verse, according as he condescends to the society of his boon companions, or unveils the traits of a noble nature, and gives expression to his higher emotions. Even so in 'The Tempest,' Caliban, though rude, is never prosaic; and except in the mere exchange of question and answer with Stephano and Trinculo, he speaks in verse, while they and the rude sailors are absolutely restricted to prose.

The rhythmical effect of varying pauses gives further variety to Shakespeare's dramatic verse; and additional freedom is secured by the frequent use of the hemistich, or imperfect line, not only at the end but in the middle of a speech. By such means particular passages are rendered more emphatic, and a natural ease is given to the language of dialogue, while retaining the elevated dignity which pertains to the measured structure of verse. Shakespeare in fact subordinates the sound to the sense, as he adapts the language to the character of the speaker. The rhythm is made in each case to respond to the exigencies of the dialogue, instead of forcing every variety of utterance to subject itself to the same artificial constraints of verse. The editors of the Cambridge Shakespeare remark, in reference to certain imperfect lines in 'The Tempest,' 'The truth is that in dialogue Shakespeare's language passes so rapidly from verse to prose and from prose to verse, sometimes even hovering, as it were, over the confines, being rhythmical rather than metrical, that all attempts to give regularity to the metre must be made with diffidence and received with doubt.'

Of all this, however, Pope, and the successors of his school who undertook the textual criticism of Shakespeare, had not the slightest appreciation. They dealt with him as an author of a ruder age than their own. Hanmer is more irreverent than Pope in the censorship exercised over the poet's metres ; and as to Warburton, who subsequently united his labours with those of the author of 'The Dunciad,' as a joint effort for the restoration of the genuine text: he coolly sets them forth as the fruits of his younger pastimes, when he 'used to turn over those sort of writers to unbend himself from more serious applications!' From such irreverent critics little that was good, and nothing that was trustworthy in the form of literary criticism, was to be looked for. But the condition of the text both in the quartos and folios invited to metrical reconstruction, for many passages of verse are there printed as prose. Guided by the artificial standard of their day, their vain efforts to force the measure of Shakespeare into the Procrustean bed of their heroic pentameters, tempt them to endless cobbling. Short lines are eked out with an added syllable, long ones are abbreviated, by elision, by omission, or change of words ; and after all, the baffled critics find that the 'native wood-notes wild' will not be constrained within their prescribed bounds. The increasing study of the elder poets, along with a truer appreciation of Shakespeare himself, as well as the familiarity with a freer line in the practice of our living poets, all combine to induce a juster estimation of the versification of the Elizabethan drama.

Amongst other progressive features in the development of Shakespeare's genius, certain characteristics of his verse clearly distinguish the earliest from some at least of his later dramas ; and have an interest for us here as adding further confirmation to the idea that the literary executors of the poet took the virgin manuscript of 'The Tempest' fresh from its author's pen, and placed it foremost in the collected works of their deceased friend. The Rev. Joseph Hunter, in his 'Disquisition on the Scene, Origin, Date, etc. of Shakespeare's Tempest,' enters into an elaborate argument to prove that 'The Tempest' is not only not Shakespeare's last work, but he aims from internal and other evidence at fixing the year 1596 as the date of its production. He indeed claims it to be the actual 'Love's Labour's Won' of Meres' 'Palladis Tamia, Wit's Treasury,' published in 1598, in which that writer commends Shakespeare as the most excellent among the English, alike for comedy and tragedy ; and, enumerating certain comedies in proof of this, he names his 'Gentlemen of Verona,' his 'Errors,' his 'Love Labours Lost,' his 'Love Labours Won,' his 'Midsummer Night's Dream,' and his 'Merchant of Venice.' Dr. Farmer imagined that the 'All's Well that Ends Well' is the play referred to. In reality there is no evidence, beyond such fancied fitness of the title to one or other of his known comedies, as may readily enough be assumed in the lóve's labour won of more than one of their plots.

The precise date of the production of 'The Tempest' is not a question of any moment in reference to the points chiefly discussed here; and indeed the attempts hitherto made to determine the order of production of Shakespeare's dramas from internal evidence have ended in very conflicting results. But it is worthy of note in reference to the verse of 'The Tempest,' that it bears a striking resemblance in one notable characteristic to that of 'Coriolanus,' another of the plays which appeared for the first time in the 1623 folio, and which is recognised on all hands as among the later productions of the poet's pen. It is indeed named by Mr. Joseph Hunter along with three, or possibly four others, of his latest plays, written when in his maturity 'his muse grew severe.' Professor Craik, in his 'English of Shakespeare,' dwells on the peculiarity now referred to, as a habit of versification very sparingly introduced in the earliest plays, and which seemed to grow upon the poet in his later works. This is the termination of the line on the tenth syllable, where ordinarily the true stress and most marked accent should be found, with a slight unemphatic monosyllable. Not only has this a certain unexpected effect, by the absence of that rest and dwelling on the syllable which the normal rhythm of the verse leads us to anticipate; but this effect is further heightened, and indeed owes its chief force, to the use generally of relative or conjunctive monosyllables, such as *and, have, that, with, for, is,* &c., words which lead mind and voice alike onward to the succeeding line. The effect is in some degree startling from the absence of the expected rest; but its true value lies in the increasing variety and flow of language, and the additional freedom of structure, in which dramatic verse legitimately deviates from the more stately epic. In this respect Shakespeare's first productions differed from those of earlier English dramatists; and the whole tendency of his mind was towards further change in the same direction. Professor Craik remarks of this specialty, 'it is a point of style which admits of precise appreciation to a degree much beyond most others; and there is no other single indication which can be compared with it as an element in determining the chronology of the plays.' It seems somewhat inconsistent with his idea that examples of this unemphatic tenth syllable are so rare in the 'Julius Cæsar,' that he cites seven as the whole which occur in that play. He does indeed use it as an argument for assigning an earlier date to this latter play than to the 'Coriolanus'; but the 'Julius Cæsar' is one of those which appears for the first time in the posthumous folio; and whatever its precise place may be in the chronological order of the plays, it certainly is not an early production.

Before citing from 'The Tempest' examples of this characteristic peculiarity of verse, it may be well to note that it is not to be confounded with the universal licence of ending a heroic line with the *-ly, -ing, -ness*, or other like termination of a large class of words; though more frequently this constitutes in Shakespeare's verse an extra unemphatic syllable following the fifth accent. In this, as in all other prolongations of the line beyond the final accent, the effect is to give richness and variety without interfering with the rhythmical pause at the end of the line. Below are a few instances of the kind of verse referred to, as it occurs in 'The Tempest.' The opening line of the second scene is one not of ten but twelve syllables, but it illustrates the peculiar effect resulting from the closing of a line with an auxiliary verb, constituting by grammatical structure a part of the verb with which the next line begins. In this respect it has some analogy to the terminating a line, and finding a rhyme, in the middle of a word : which, though now employed only as the extreme licence of burlesque extravaganzas, was used by Spenser in the mottoes of his 'Faerie Queen,' e. g.

> 'The Redcross Knight is captive made,
> By gyaunt proud opprest ;
> Prince Arthure meets with Una great-
> ly with those newes distrest.'

If the student of Shakespeare whose attention has not been hitherto called to this peculiarity in the verse of 'The Tempest,' compare it in this respect with the known early works of the dramatist, such as his 'Romeo and Juliet,' 'Love's Labour's Lost,' and 'A Midsummer Night's Dream,' he will perceive that it is a very noticeable characteristic of a change in the rhythmical structure of his dramatic dialogue, unquestionably pertaining to the latest structure of his heroic line, as in the following examples :—

> 'If by your art, my dearest father, you have
> Put the wild waters in this roar, allay them.'

> 'It should the good ship so have swallow'd, and
> The fraughting souls within her.'

> 'Thy mother was a piece of virtue, and
> She said thou wast my daughter.'

> 'I pray thee mark me, that a brother should
> Be so perfidious.'

> 'Some food we had, and some fresh water, that
> A noble Neapolitan, Gonzalo,
> Out of his charity, who being then appointed
> Master of this design, did give us with
> Rich garments.'

> 'From mine own library with volumes that
> I prize above my dukedom.'

'A freckled whelp, hag-born, not honour'd with
A human shape.'
                    'Would'st give me
Water with berries in't; and teach me how
To name the bigger light, and how the less.
                    'When thou didst not, savage,
Know thine own meaning, but wouldst gabble like
A thing most brutish.'
'Why speaks my father so ungently? This
Is the third man that ere I saw.'
'I will resist such entertainment, till
Mine enemy has more power.'

These examples, all culled from a single scene, abundantly suffice to illustrate the use of this peculiar metrical
licence throughout 'The Tempest.' In no case does
the final monosyllable admit of a rhetorical accent;
unless possibly in the eighth :—'and teach me *how* To
name the bigger light,' &c. But even here it is rather
the habit of resting on the tenth syllable, than the
meaning or structure of the sentence, that would suggest an accent; for indeed this is one of the numerous
specimens of dramatic dialogue specially adapted to the
character of the speaker, and which might be treated
as rhythmical prose. 'When thou camest first thou
strokedst me and madest much of me; wouldst give
me water with berries in't, and teach me how to name
the bigger light, and how the less, that burn by day and
night : and then I loved thee.' In all the other examples
the line terminates with a word on which the voice
cannot dwell without doing violence to the sense ; and
hence the unemphatic break, with the necessity of
passing on to the next line, gives a novel variety and
freedom to passages of the dialogue.

Of an opposite class of lines referred to above, in
which the line is broken, both by sense and metrical

structure, into two parts, by the omission of an unaccented syllable, the introduction of an extra syllable,
or the bringing of two accents together, so as to compel
the voice to rest between the one and the other, and so
make the first emphatic, examples abound in 'The
Tempest.' Of these a few may be quoted.

> 'But that the sea, mounting to the welkin's cheek,
> Dashes the fire out. O, I have suffered
> With those that I saw suffer!'—i. 2.

> 'Obey, and be attentive. Canst thou remember
> A time before we came unto this cell?'—i. 2.

> 'And executing the outward face of royalty
> With all prerogative. Hence his ambition growing.'—i. 2.

> 'We are such stuff
> As dreams are made on, and our little life
> Is rounded with a sleep. Sir, I am vex'd.'—iv. 1.

> 'Who most strangely
> Upon this shore, where you were wreck'd, was landed
> To be the Lord on't. No more yet of this.'—v. 1.

In both the characteristics specially illustrated in the
above examples, as well as in the general structure of
its verse, 'The Tempest' is distinguished from 'A Midsummer Night's Dream.' Much of the dialogue in the
latter is in rhyming couplets, and the regularity and
prevailing. uniformity of its measure recall the verse
of the 'Venus and Adonis' or others of the first heirs
of the poet's invention. Whatever be the precise date
of 'The Tempest' it is not to be doubted that those
two comedies so much akin in the fanciful originality of
their *dramatis personæ*, and the rich imaginative luxu-
riance of their verse, belong in point of time to two
widely separated eras of the poet's literary life.

CHAPTER XII.

THE FOLIOS.

'Prospero. So of his gentleness,
Knowing I loved my books, he furnish'd me
From mine own library with volumes that
I prize above my dukedom.'—*The Tempest.*

THE first folio of Shakespeare, which issued from the press in 1623, seven years after the poet's death, is the first complete and authorised collection of Shakespeare's dramas,—complete, with the one exception of 'Pericles, Prince of Tyre.' It is a handsomely printed volume, issued with all accompaniments which, according to the fashion of that age, could give eclat to such a literary monument of genius. One half of his dramatic works, and some of these among the very best, such as :—' Cymbeline,' ' Macbeth,' ' Measure for Measure,' ' The Tempest,' ' Julius Cæsar, ' Antony and Cleopatra,' ' Coriolanus,' ' King John,' and ' Henry VIII,' appeared there for the first time in print. The preface shows that its joint editors, John Heminge and Henry Condell, were actuated by all loving veneration for their deceased friend ; and when they there declare that those plays which had already appeared in print 'are now offer'd to view cured and perfect of their limbs : and all the rest, absolute in their numbers as he conceived them,' it is not to be doubted that they honestly believed what they affirmed. They were actors, not authors ; and apparently regarded the printer's share of the work as a thing with which they had nothing to do.

'It had beene a thing, we confesse, worthy to have beene wished, that the Author himselfe, had liv'd to have set forth, and overseene his owne writings. But since it hath been ordain'd otherwise, and he by death departed from that right, we pray you doe not envy his Friends, the office of their care and paine, to have collected and publish'd them.' So say the poet's literary executors in reference to their labour of love. They had, we may presume, obtained possession of all the manuscripts left by Shakespeare at his death; had added to these the original manuscripts, or copies of others, in the Blackfriars or Globe stage-libraries; and completed the series, as the text abundantly proves, by means of some of the very quartos which they denounce in their preface as 'stolne and surreptitious copies, maimed and deformed by the frauds and stealths of injurious impostors.' But all proof-reading was evidently left to the printers; and wild work they have made of it, as many an obscure or absolutely meaningless passage shews!

It has been a favourite idea of Shakespeare's commentators that the folios supply, on the whole, an authoritative critical text of Shakespeare; and unquestionably, as the earliest edition of the collected plays, and the sole original text for one half of them, the first folio must constitute the basis of all texts of the plays. Again, there is no doubt that the second, or 1632 folio, is corrected to some small extent from the first, though also it introduces blunders of its own. Yet it is, upon the whole, the highest authority where no quartos exist; and it is on the margins of a copy of this edition that the manuscript notes of Mr. J. P. Collier's famous text occur. It is not necessary to enter here on the vexed question of the genuineness or value of these notes.

But it will suffice to shew to how very limited an
extent the original text of the folio can be relied upon,
when it is remembered that the correction of minor
errors alone in this annotated copy are estimated by its
editor at twenty thousand. Many of these are palpable
blunders in spelling, punctuation, or such manifest transposition of letters or words as could scarcely escape
the eye of the first corrector, and had already been
amended by Rowe, Pope, Theobald, and other editors.
But besides those, the volume abounds in every kind
of error of omission or commission. The dialogue is
misplaced as to speakers, in part or whole. Verse is
printed as prose, and prose as verse. Words are
blundered and displaced, lines are transposed, words,
and it is believed whole lines, have been dropped out.
Sentences are cut in two by periods and capitals :
making in some cases a sort of bungling sense utterly
mystifying to the reader ; as in a well-known instance
in 'Henry VIII,' Act iv. Sc. 2, where Griffith, speaking
her best for the dead cardinal, says, according to the
folios :—

> 'This Cardinal,
> Though from a humble stock, undoubtedly
> Was fashioned to much honour. From his cradle
> He was a scholar, and a ripe and good one.'

To Theobald is due the simple but effective transposition of the periods which reconverted the plausible
nonsense of the printer into the true sense of the poet,
reading thus :—

> 'This Cardinal,
> Though from a humble stock, undoubtedly
> Was fashioned to much honour from his cradle.
> He was a scholar, and a ripe and good one ;
> Exceeding wise, fair-spoken and persuading.'

This being the condition of the best text we have to
appeal to, with such aid as the traduced quartos supply

for collation and correction of the folio misprints of
one half of the plays, it is obvious that abundant room
is left for the labours of the commentators. Their work
began in 1709, with the revised and corrected edition
of Shakespeare's plays by Nicholas Rowe, the first
attempt at a critical restoration of the text. A host
of zealous, if not always judicious critics have followed
in his steps. Poets, antiquaries, and scholars have
rivalled one another in the search for blemishes, and
exhausted their ingenuity in attempts to remove them.
Their joint labours and rival criticisms have accomplished much which is valuable. Yet even now, after
a century and a half devoted to such efforts, it cannot
be assumed that all has been done that patient diligence
and sagacity may hope to achieve. There are, doubtless, corruptions which no conjecture can with certainty
remove ; for even when the intelligent student is able
to offer a substitute for some meaningless phrase, which
illuminates the whole passage, it lies beyond possibility
of proof that this is what Shakespeare actually wrote.
But while a becoming reverence for the poet will restrain the most critical editor from unduly tampering
with the text, it need not preclude the most modest
student from communicating the results of his labours.
Any even plausible amendment of an obscure passage
may find admission into a foot-note, and be there left
to the judgment of the reader as a possible suggestion
or elucidation. Amendments in themselves inadmissible
have repeatedly suggested others of value ; and, even
when rejected as worthless, by tempting the reader to
renewed study, they often reward him with more comprehensive appreciation of the meaning of the original
text. In this sense alone are the following notes and
conjectural emendations put forth.

In general accuracy the text of 'The Tempest' com-
pares favourably with most of the plays in the first or
second folios; and as it appeared in the former of these
for the first time, it is not improbable that it may have
been printed as already suggested, from the author's own
manuscript. But from the little we know of Shakespeare's handwriting, it may be assumed that it was
not of the most readable character; and proof-reading
seems to have been carried on in the seventeenth century
under little or no editorial oversight, in a fashion which
admitted of very strange misprints passing muster in the
text. In truth the 1623 folio may be pronounced without hesitation to be one of the handsomest and worst
printed books that issued from the press in the whole
century. The persevering efforts to restore a pure
text have not been expended without a fair per-
centage of very happy results. Sometimes by the mere
change of a single letter sense has been found in what
was before meaningless, and Shakespeare's own text,
we can scarcely doubt, restored. That many textual
imperfections still remain is not to be doubted. The
majority of these, however, lie beyond the reach of any
such certainty of correction, since the hand of the
master has been, not merely blurred, but defaced beyond all decypherment by some careless blunderer. Yet
even with them carefully studied conjectural criticism
may still find room left for useful work: not indeed by
tampering with the text, but by supplementing it with
suggestive notes, which may at times restore the meaning, even if it leave doubtful the actual words of the
great master, 'whose mind and hand went together.'
The severe critical test to which every such suggestion
is certain to be subjected, is a sure guarantee that no
merely plausible change will secure general acceptance;

though where the text has been blundered into absolute meaninglessness, any sense is better than none.

In reference to 'The Tempest,' the version of it as revised by Dryden and D'Avenant has a certain value textually, though worthless in a literary point of view. Dryden was born only fifteen years after the death of Shakespeare at the comparatively early age of fifty-two. As to D'Avenant, a scandal of the time reputed him to be a son of the great dramatist. To such men, intimately acquainted with all the traditions of the stage, and to whom the language of Shakespeare was no less familiar in its colloquial freedom, than in its choicest phraseology, the correction of a misprint, or the substitution of a more intelligible or expressive word for a doubtful one, could be done with a confidence pertaining now alone to the diligent student of the Elizabethan literature. Yet, as we shall have occasion to note, the language was even then undergoing rapid change, and Dryden kept no critical eye on the points in which the usage of his own day already differed from that of the Elizabethan age. Rowe, Pope, and others of the earliest commentators, availed themselves of Dryden's amendments on the folio text, and some of them have been generally adopted. To him we owe the arrangement of portions, such as the talk of Caliban, into verse, in lieu of the prose of the folios. Of his verbal amendments an example may be quoted, where Caliban exclaims, on the entrance of Trinculo, according to the folio :—

> 'Lo, now, lo !
> Here comes a spirit of his, and to torment me.'

Pope reads '*now* to torment me,' thinking perhaps the repetition of the *now*, as of the *lo*, characteristic. Dryden had already rendered it 'sent to torment me.'

In similar points, more particularly noted hereafter, changes are due to Dryden's revision, but they are not of great importance, and some of them are not improvements. In the same scene, for example, Prospero, in describing to his daughter his brother's treachery, says—

> ' Whereon
> A treacherous army levied, one midnight
> Fated to the purpose, did Antonio open
> The gates of Milan.'

The idea manifestly is, that on that fatal or fated night Antonio accomplished his treacherous deed ; and, as Prospero proceeds to say,

> ' I' the dead of darkness
> The ministers for the purpose hurried thence
> Me and they crying self.'

But Dryden feebly substitutes *mated* for *fated*. Other emendations and suggestions will help to illustrate the condition of the text. Prospero, having narrated to his daughter the treacherous proceedings of his uncle, adds thus :—

> ' Mark his condition and the event ; then tell me
> If this might be a brother ;'

to which, according to the appropriation of the dialogue in the folios, Miranda replies :—

> ' I should sin
> To think but nobly of my grandmother :
> Good wombs have borne bad sons.'

Theobald proposed the transference of the last line to Prospero, as more consistent with the previous dialogue, and with the age and innocent simplicity of Miranda, as shown e. g. in the preceding interrogative : ' Sir, are not you my father ?' along with his response. When he describes their hurried banishment from Milan, he tells her, according to the original text—which may be given here, with orthography, capitals, and punctuation, as a sample of that of the folio :—

> ' In few, they hurried us a-boord a Barke,
> Bore us some Leagues to Sea, where they prepared
> A rotten carkasse of a Butt, not rigg'd,
> Nor tackle, nor sayle, nor mast; the very rats
> Instinctiuely have quit it.'

The *Butt* of the third line is rendered *boat* by Dryden, and in this he is followed by Rowe. The Cambridge editors, usually so conservative, adopt the alteration. Mr. Joseph Hunter, on the contrary, argues for a literal wine-butt cut in two, in spite of the inconsistency of its desertion by the rats; while Knight retains the *butt* as, at least, more strikingly conveying the idea of a vessel even less secure than the most rotten boat: as it is common enough now to speak of a poor, ill-appointed vessel as a tub. The '*nor* sayle' of the fourth line is a reading in which the second folio varies from the first ; and most editors adhere to the latter as equally indisputable in metre and sense ; but Mr. Joseph Hunter thinks ' the second *nor* is added to the reading of the first folio, to the improvement of the spirit.' It is an illustration of much else of the same kind ; for here a learned and most critical commentator adopts, I cannot doubt, a mere compositor's blunder, and finds in it the essence of Shakespeare's verse. Another example of doubtful appropriation of the dialogue occurs in the same scene. Prospero having described the services rendered to him at the last by Gonzalo, the speakers thus proceed, according to the folios :—

> ' *Mir.*   Would I might
> But ever see that man !
>   *Pros.*   Now I arise:
> Sit still, and hear the last of our sea sorrow.'

After the ' now I arise ' of Prospero, the stage direction,
' *Resumes his mantle,*' has been added by Rowe and
later editors. Collier's MS. notes render it ' *Put on robe
again*' ; but Blackstone regards the 'now I arise' as a
part of Miranda's remark, as though conceiving she has
heard all her father has to tell her ; and to this he
naturally responds ' sit still,' &c. Another example of
the original text will suffice to illustrate the orthography
and punctuation, in the slovenly fashion in which it remains uncorrected in the second folio, where Ariel tells
Prospero,

> 'Not a soule
> But felt a Feaver of the madde, and plaid
> Some trickes of disperation; all but Mariners
> Plung'd in the foaming bryne, and quit the vessell ;
> Then all a fire with me the Kings sonne *Ferdinand,*
> With haire up-staring (then like reeds, not haire)
> Was the first man that leapt; cride hell is empty,
> And all the Divells are heere.'

Dryden here changes the text to 'a fever of the mind,'
and is followed in this by Pope ; but the best later
editors retain it unchanged further than the indispensable correction of the punctuation. Again, Prospero,
according to the folio, addresses Caliban thus :—

> ' Thou most lying slave,
> Whom stripes may move, nor kindness !'

The substitution of *not* for *nor* by modern editors seems
to me a weakening of the text. Caliban is neither
moved by stripes nor kindness to any good purpose, in
Prospero's estimation. The address to him immediately
following, in the same vituperative style, beginning
' Abhorred slave,' is assigned in the folios to Miranda,
but modern editors have followed Dryden in transfer-
ring it to Prospero, of the correctness of which there

is no doubt. In this passage Prospero says, according
to the folio :—

> ' When thou didst not (sauage)
> Know thine owne meaning; but wouldst gabble, like
> A thing most brutish, I endow'd thy purposes
> With words that made them knowne: But thy vild race
> (Tho thou didst learn) had that in't, which good natures
> Could not abide to be with,' &c.

Vild is rendered *vile*, without the Cambridge editors
thinking it necessary to note the change.   It agrees
with the 'abhorred slave,' &c., of the opening part of
the sentence, but *wild* would accord as well, in some
respects, with the immediate context.   It may be worth
noting here a similar misprint in 'A Midsummer
Night's Dream,' Act i. Sc. 1, where, according to the
second folio, Helena, speaking of Demetrius, says—

> ' So I, admiring of his qualities:
> Things base and vilde, holding no quantity,
> Love can transpose to forme and dignity.'

Here Knight reads 'base and vild,' explaining the word
in a foot-note as *vile*.   No commentator, so far as I am
aware, has suggested another change, which appears to
me worthy of consideration, and may as well be noted
now as later, viz. *quality* for *quantity*.   I may notice
here also an example of the way in which the blunders
of one edition are liable to be made the basis of
false emendations in another.   In Act i. Sc. 2, where
Prospero suddenly changes his manner towards Ferdinand, 'lest too light winning make the prize light,'
Miranda demands, appealingly, 'Why speaks my father
so ungently?' but this, by a misprint in the second
folio, becomes *urgently*; and some former possessor of
my copy has drawn his pen through it, and written in
the margin *grudgingly*.   The paucity of stage directions
is another evidence of the absence of proper editorial

oversight in the folios, as where, in Act i. Sc. 1,
Prospero says—

> 'It works : come on,
> Thou hast done well, fine Ariel : follow me.
> Hark what thou else shalt do me.'

So it is printed in the folio, whereas the context clearly
shews that the first two words are an *aside*,—Prospero's
thought uttered audibly. The two commands, 'come
on,' and 'follow· me,' are addressed to Ferdinand, the
rest is for Ariel. Two alterations on Ariel's song were
made by Theobald, and have taken their place in the
current text, though neither is justified by any obscurity in the original. He reads, 'Where the bee sucks
there *lurk* I,' instead of '*suck* I,' and 'After *sunset*
merrily,' instead of *summer*, or, as it is in the folio
sommer. The associations with the fine music of Dr.
Arne have so familiarised all with the altered version ;
and both in sound, and in association with the bat's wing,
there is such an aptness in the latter change, that the
restored text is apt to be felt unacceptable at first. But
on any principle of sound criticism this seems an
attempt to change, so far as we know, what Shakespeare
did write, into what he ought to have written.

The following are the results of the author's own
reading and annotation of the two plays specially referred to. They are by no means produced as undoubted
emendations of the text, but merely as the conjectures
of a Shakespeare student, on points which are for the
most part admittedly doubtful or obscure.

CHAPTER XIII.

NOTES ON 'THE TEMPEST.'

'The best in this kind are but shadows; and the worst are no worse if imagination amend them.'—*A Midsummer Night's Dream.*

THE sole authority for the text of 'The Tempest' is the 1623 folio, with whatever editorial supervision or appeal to an original manuscript may be supposed to have guided the revisers of the second and subsequent folios. The text is, on the whole, free from gross blunders, and much more correct than other plays in the volume; but obscurities and undoubted errors do exist, with some of which the following notes attempt to deal conjecturally.

ACT I. SCENE I.

The rough dialogue of the first scene is purposely constructed in striking contrast to what follows, and is less open to rigid criticism. But Mr. Richard Grant White has not thought even the 'Boson,' or 'Boatswain,' undeserving of note in his 'Shakespeare's Scholar.' Following his example, a trifling change may be noted as perhaps admissible in the Boatswain's words: 'Bring her to try with main-course.' In the folio it is printed 'bring her to Try with Maine-course.' The capital suggests this as possibly the true reading : 'Bring her too. Try with main course.'

SCENE II.

' *Pros.* Being once perfected how to grant suits,
How to deny them ; whom to advance, and whom
To trash for overtopping.'

Knight explains *trash* as 'a term still in use among
hunters, to denote a piece of leather, couples, or any
other weight, fastened round the neck of a dog, when
his speed is superior to the rest of the pack ; i. e. when
he overtops them, when he hunts too quick.' This interpretation seems more like an afterthought, devised to
make the explanation fit on to the text. The meaning
seems rather that the crafty deputy had learned how
to grant and how to deny suits ; whom to promote and
whom to overtop, i. e. over whom to promote others, his
own creatures. The only other example of the use of
the latter word is where, in 'Antony and Cleopatra,'
Antony exclaims, 'All is lost,' and then adds, 'this pine
is barked that overtopped them all.' This is in accordance with the use ascribed to it in Prospero's allusion.
As to the doubtful word *trash*, it is repeatedly used by
Shakespeare in its ordinary sense of worthless. But
in one passage in which, as usually rendered, Knight's
interpretation of its special significance in 'The Tempest'
seems borne out, he finds an entirely new meaning for
it. In 'Othello,' Act ii. Sc. 1, where Iago is meditating
his purposed use of Cassio's name to awaken in the
Moor his fatal jealousy, he exclaims, according to the
Cambridge, as well as earlier texts :—

' Which thing to do,
If this poor trash of Venice, whom I trash
For his quick hunting, stand the putting on,
I'll have our Michael Cassio on the hip.'

In reality, however, the use of the same word in two

totally different senses is the work of the commentators. The first quarto has *crush* in place of the latter *trash;* while the second and third quartos and the folios have *trace*. Knight accordingly, adopting the latter reading, adds this note : ' The noun *trash*, and the verb *trace*, are used with perfect propriety. The *trash* is the thing *traced*, *put in traces*, confined—as an untrained worthless dog is held ; and hence the present meaning of *trash.*' This is not the only case where Knight seems to fit a meaning for the occasion. The commentators, dissatisfied with either of the old readings, have variously suggested *leash, train, trash, cherish;* the last, and most unsuitable one, being Warburton's. It is in its ordinary sense, as where Iago speaks of 'this poor trash of Venice,' that the word is everywhere else used by Shakespeare, unless in the reference by Prospero to his brother's perfidious policy. When, in a later scene (Act iv. Sc. i.), Stephano and Trinculo yield to the temptation of the 'glistering apparel' purposely hung up by Ariel ' for stale to catch these thieves,' Caliban exclaims, 'Let it alone ; it is but trash.' But the passage in Prospero's speech appears to have been recognised as obscure or faulty by the first editors ; and it is accordingly changed conjecturally in the second folio. As printed in the 1623 folio, the text reads 'who t'advance, and who to trash,' which suggests to me a very possible misprint for—

> ' Being once perfected how to grant suits,
> How to deny them ; who to advance, and who
> *Too rash* for overtopping.'

That is to say, who were fit to be promoted, and who were too rash to be advanced over old servitors. Prospero accordingly goes on to say that he ' new created the creatures that were mine ; ' either ' changed them, or else new formed them.' In this way the original text is adhered to more closely; and yet, by the alteration of a single letter, a clear meaning is given to what was formerly obscure.

> '*Pros.*   He being thus lorded,
> Not only with what my revenue yielded,
> But what my power might else exact, like one
> Who having into truth, by telling of it,
> Made such a sinner of his memory,
> To credit his own lie, he did believe
> He was indeed the duke.'

This passage has occupied the commentators with very diverse efforts at its elucidation. Hanmer reads, *loving an untruth, and telling 't oft;* Warburton, *having unto truth, by telling oft;* Musgrave, *having sinn'd to truth by telling 't oft;* the Collier folio, besides changing *lorded* into *loaded,* renders the later line, *Who having to untruth, by telling of it;* and its editor adds, 'There cannot be a doubt that this, as regards *untruth* at least, is the language of Shakespeare.'

Query :—

> Who hating an untruth.

Prospero says, 'My trust, like a good parent, did beget of him a falsehood.' It seems in the same vein of reasoning to say of him so trusted, that he resembled one who, originally hating an untruth, ended by believing his own lie.

> '*Me*, poor man, my library
> Was dukedom large enough; of temporal royalties
> He thinks me now incapable; confederates,
> So dry he was for sway, wi' the King of Naples
> To give him annual tribute, do him homage,
> Subject his coronet to his crown.'

It may be worth noting, that in the first folio it is *temporall roalties;* in the second folio it becomes *roialties.* But why 'temporal royalties'? There were no spiritual ones in question. The reference may be presumed to be to Prospero's supernatural rule, but to this he has made no allusion. He has only spoken of himself as 'rapt in secret studies,' and

> 'Neglecting worldly ends, all dedicated
> To closeness and the bettering of my mind
> With that which, but by being so retired,
> O'erprized all popular rate.'

Probably *royalties* is the true word ; but the change of a single letter, in the first folio, would give *realties*, a word contrasting with the supernatural things to which, by any interpretation, *temporal* must have reference ; and to which, as afterwards appears, the 'secret studies' refer.

'Subject his coronet to his crown.' As in Shakespeare's day *his* was the neuter, as well as the masculine possessive form, this may be read as equivalent to— 'Subject its coronet to his crown.' It was the coronet of Milan, but not yet of Antonio. There remains one other word, more clearly open to objection—'So dry he was for sway.' In the folios it is *drie*.

Query :—

> So *ripe* he was for sway.

> 'Pros.   Now the condition.
> This king of Naples, being an enemy
> To me inveterate, hearkens my brother's suit ;
> Which was, that he, in lieu o' the premises,
> Of homage and I know not how much tribute.'

Knight explains this, 'The *premises* of *homage*, &c.—the circumstances of homage *premised.*'

Query :—

> in view o' the promises
> Of homage.

' *Pros.*   Thou didst smile,
Infused with a fortitude from heaven,
When I have deck'd the sea with drops full salt,
Under my burthen groan'd; which raised in me
An undergoing stomach, to bear up
Against what should ensue.'

The commentators have manifested their recognition of some defect by proposing such changes as these: Hanmer reads for ' deck'd,' *brack'd* ; Warburton, *mock'd* ; Johnson, *fleck'd* ; and Reed, *degg'd.*

Query :—

Thou didst smile,
Infused with a fortitude from heaven,
When I have lack'd. The sea, with drops full salt,
Under my burthen groan'd; which raised in me, &c.

' *Pros.* This blue-eyed hag was hither brought with child.'

Sycorax is spoken of with every term of loathing : as a ' foul witch,' a ' hag,' a ' damned witch,' &c. There seems no propriety in coupling with these the term *blue-eyed*—one of the tokens, according to Rosalind, in ' As You Like It,' whereby to know a man in love. In the first and second folios it is ' blew ey'd.' Query :— *blear-eyed*, or *bleared.*

' *Pros.*   Thy groans
Did make wolves howl, and penetrate the breasts
Of ever-angry bears.'

Query :—*of even angry bears.*

' *Pros.*   Urchins
Shall, for that vast of night that they may work
All exercise on thee.'

Query :—*shall forth at vast of night.*

The term *vast* is sanctioned by its use in ' Hamlet,' where Horatio says, ' In the dead vast and middle of the

Q 2

night;' so at least it stands in three of the quartos, though in two others it is rendered *wast*. This becomes in the folios *waste*, and by Malone is converted into *waist*.

> '*Pros.*   One word more; I charge thee
> That thou attend me: thou dost here usurp
> The name thou owest not.'

Query :—

> One word more: I charge thee—
> Dost thou attend me?—thou dost here usurp, &c.

> '*Mir.*   O, dear father,
> Make not too rash a trial of him, for
> He 's gentle and not fearful.
> *Pros.*   What! I say,
> My foot my tutor?'

In this passage the former owner of my 1632 folio has changed *rash* into *harsh*—an ingenious, but certainly false conjecture; for Miranda, not less regardful of her father than her lover, says :—Do not too rashly put his forbearance to the test, for he is no churl, but of gentle blood and courage. Another correction by the same hand deals with a word already recognised as doubtful. Dryden changes *foot* into *child*; Walker suggests *fool*; the same unknown annotator corrects it thus :—'What, I say, foolish,—my tutor!'

ACT II. SCENE I.

> '*Gon.* How lush and lusty the grass looks! how green!'

The word *lush* is of doubtful origin and significance. Henley affirms it to mean 'rank'; Malone, 'juicy'; Knight quotes the word *lushy* as applied to a drunkard; R. Grant White suggests it to be a corruption of

luscious. Is it too simple a suggestion that the word
was *fresh*? The manuscript would readily admit of
such a misreading.

> ' *Seb.* Where she, at least, is banish'd from your eye,
> Who hath cause to wet the grief on't.
> *Alon.*   Prithee, peace.
>   *Seb.* You were kneel'd to and importun'd otherwise,
> By all of us; and the fair soul herself
> Weigh'd between loathness and obedience, at
> Which end o' the beam should bow.'

Query :—

>   to *weigh* the grief on't.
>
>   .   .   .   .
>   *Swayed* between loathness and obedience, at
>   Which end o' the beam *she'd* bow.

The folios have the word *waigh'd*, which I had noted
conjecturally on my own copy as a misprint for *sway'd*.
From the Cambridge Shakespeare it appears that S.
Verges has already suggested this, though its editors
overlook the suggestive orthography of the folio. The
she'd, instead of *should*, is Malone's, and adopted by
Knight. By dropping the *at* of the previous line, the
should would be more expressive. But, as has already
been shewn, the *at*, so placed, is highly characteristic of
the peculiar metre of this and one or two other of
Shakespeare's latest plays.

> ' *Ant.* I am more serious than my custom; you
> Must be so too, if heed me; which to do
> Trebles thee o'er.'

What does *Trebles thee o'er* mean here? Looking at it
in its relation to the context, it has to be borne in remembrance that Antonio, himself a traitorous usurper, is
making the first suggestion of treason, in purposedly
obscured hints, to Sebastian, the king of Naples' brother.
The king lies asleep; his son, the heir to the crown, is

believed to be drowned ; and a few sentences further on
the suggestion assumes this undisguised shape :—

> 'Here lies your brother,
> No better than the earth he lies upon,
> If he were that which now he's like, that's dead;
> Whom I, with this obedient steel, three inches of it,
> Can lay to bed for ever.'

In the folios the text reads—*Trebbles thee o're.*   Pope
renders it *Troubles thee o'er;* Hanmer, *Troubles thee not.*
Query :—

> I am more serious than my custom ; you
> Must be so too, if—heed me,—which to do't
> Rebels thee o'er.

The previous talk with Gonzalo, and the darker hints
since, have been carried on with quip, pun, and inuendo.
If we understand Sebastian's reply, 'Well, I am standing
water,' as a play on the word rebels, i. e. 'ripples thee
o'er' it is no worse pun than others which have preceded
it ; and hence follows metaphorical talk of flowing,
ebbing, and running near the bottom.

> '*Ant.*   She that from Naples
> Can have no note, unless the sun were post,—
> The man i' the moon's too slow,—till new-born chins
> Be rough and razorable; she that from whom
> We all were sea-swallow'd, though some cast again.'

Query :—

> She from whom we
> All were sea-swallow'd, though some cast again.

This is equivalent to 'She, coming from whom,' &c.
Otherwise it might read, 'She for whom we.'   The
earlier line, 'She that from Naples,' may have misled
the compositor in this subsequent line, as in similar
cases.   Mr. Spedding suggests to the Cambridge editors,
'She that—From whom? All were sea-swallow'd,' &c.,

making the ' From whom ' an interjectional reference to the previous ' She can have no note from Naples till new-born babies have beards to shave !' Rowe, Pope, Singer, and other commentators, all concur in recognising some defect in the text

> ' *Ant.* There be that can rule Naples
> As well as he that sleeps: lords that can prate
> As amply and as unnecessarily
> As this Gonzalo: I myself could make
> A chough of as deep chat.

Query :—

> A chough *give* as deep chat.

SCENE II.

> ' *Cal.* I'll bring thee
> To clustering filberts, and sometimes I'll get thee
> Young scamels from the rock.'

Scamels is the word in the folios It has been conjecturally amended, *seamalls*, *sea-mews*, *stannels*, and *shamois*; the last being Theobald's. Hunter thinks the word *scamels* genuine, because 'as it stands it gives us a very melodious line,' and also from ' the difficulty of finding a word which the printer may be supposed to have mistaken.' Nevertheless he suggests *samphire.* Caliban has said just before, ' I with my long nails will dig thee pig-nuts,' so that something simple may be assumed.

Query *muscles.* It fulfils one of Mr. Hunter's requirements, being nearly a transposition of the letters, and is more likely than either shamois or samphire. The special luxury of ' young muscles from the rock ' may also fitly contrast with the previous threat of Prospero to Ferdinand : ' Thy food shall be the fresh-brook muscles.'

ACT III. SCENE I.

> *'Fer.*   My sweet mistress
> Weeps when she sees me work, and says such baseness
> Had never like executor. I forget :
> But these sweet thoughts do even refresh my labours
> Most busy lest, when I do it.'

The reading of the last line has been the subject of a multitude of conjectures. The *lest* of the first folio becomes *least* in the second. Pope reads *least busy*, Theobald, *most busie-less*, and so on, through *busiest, busy felt, busy still, busiliest*, of a succession of commentators, crowned with Collier's folio marginal note of *most busy-blest*.

Query :—

> Do even refresh my labour
> Most *baseless* when I do it.

Baseless would thus stand in apposition to the *baseness* of his previous comment : 'Some kinds of baseness are nobly undergone,' &c.

> *'Fer.*   Would no more endure
> This wooden slavery, than to suffer
> The flesh-fly blow my mouth.'

In the first folio it is *wodden*, in the second it becomes *woodden*.

Query :—

> This *sudden* slavery.

SCENE II.

> *'Trin.* Why thou debosh'd fish, thou.'

The Cambridge editors, contrary to their usual adherence to the original text, undertake here to improve on the drunken talk of Trinculo, by the change of *debosh'd* to *debauched*—a questionable improvement.

SCENE III.

' *Gon.* By'r lakin, I can go no further, sir ;
My old bones ache : here 's a maze trod, indeed,
Through forth-rights and meanders ! '

The only other example of the use of *forth-right* occurs in ' Troilus and Cressida,' Act iii. Sc. 3, where Ulysses say's to Achilles :—

' If you give way,
Or hedge aside from the direct forth right.'

Here ' the direct forth right ' means undoubtedly the straight course, and so it is supposed to stand in the same sense, in Gonzalo's use of it, in apposition to ' meanders.' But treading a maze through direct courses does not seem the most likely expression. In the first folio it is *fourth rights*. According to the Cambridge editors it becomes *forth-rights* in the second, third and fourth folios. So far, at least, as my copy of the second folio is concerned, it is *forth rights* without the hyphen. Bearing in view the previous experiences, to which Gonzalo refers, I venture to suggest

Through *sore frights* and meanders.

' *Ariel.* You three
From Milan did supplant good Prospero ;
Exposed unto the sea, which hath requit it,
Him and his innocent child.'

Query :—

which hath *requited.*

ACT IV. SCENE I.

> '*Pros.* Now come, my Ariel! bring a corollary
> Rather than want a spirit; appear and pertly!'

What is a *corollary* here? Knight explains it as 'a surplus number.' In the folio it is printed with a capital, as though it were the name of some spirit. But capitals are employed too freely by the early printers to make this of much moment. The word is used nowhere else by Shakespeare, is unmusical where it stands, and is probably a misprint. The concluding word of the next line, *pertly*, seems also inapt. Ariel has just before asked if the masque is expected *presently*. This I imagine to be the word repeated, abbreviated probably in the original manuscript, at the end of a long line. As to the other conjectural change suggested here: it will be remembered that Prospero's command to Ariel is

> 'Go bring the rabble,
> O'er whom I give thee power, here to this place;
> Incite them to quick motion.'

Query :—

> Now come, my Ariel! bring a *whole array*
> Rather than want a spirit; appear, and *presently*.'

> '*Ceres* [*Song*]. Vines with clustering bunches growing;
> Plants with goodly burthen bowing;
> Spring come to you at the farthest
> In the very end of harvest.'

Spring can scarcely be the word here. Collier's folio notes substitute *rain*. But an apt change is suggested if we consider the nature of the invitation to which Ceres is responding : Juno says :—

> 'Go with me
> To bless this twain, that they may prosperous be,
> And honour'd in their issue.'

Query :—

> *Offspring* come to you at farthest.

> '*Fer.* Let me live here ever;
> So rare a wonder'd father and a wife
> Makes this place paradise.'

The Cambridge editors seem to imply that the word rendered *wife* here, is one of those in which different copies of the first folio vary, some giving it as *wife*, and some as *wise*; and they accordingly adopt the former, with the punctuation as given above. Judging from the photozincographic facsimile of the first folio, to which alone I have access, it reads *wise*. But owing to the use of the long *s*, the difference between the two letters is exceedingly slight; and where the printing is not perfectly clear, it is just one of the rare cases where the facsimile might mislead. In the second folio it is unquestionably *wise*, and is punctuated accordingly, thus :—

> So rare a wonder'd father, and a wise,
> Makes this place paradise.

This, I cannot doubt, is the true reading. Pope, who adopts *wife*, changes *makes* to *make*, to agree with the two nominatives. But it is common enough with Shakespeare to make the verb agree with the nearest nominative. Collier parades his folio annotator as giving what he assumes to be ' the final decision in favour of *wife.*' Prospero has just replied to a question of Ferdinand, that the majestic vision they have witnessed is the work of spirits, called forth by his art to enact his present fancies; and he naturally responds : ' Let me ever live in a place which so wonderful and wise a father converts into a paradise.'

> '*Ariel.* At last I left them
> I' the filthy-mantled pool beyond your cell,
> There dancing up to the chins, that the foul lake
> O'erstunk their feet.'

Feet cannot be the word here, when they were up to their

chins. Spedding suggests *fear*. Should it not be *fell*? Macbeth speaks of the time when his 'fell of hair would at a dismal treatise rouse and stir, as life were in't;' and Corin, in 'As You Like It,' speaking to Touchstone of the ewes, says 'their fells you know are greasy.'

> '*Cal.* The dropsy drown this fool!'

In the folio it is *dropsie*. Query *deep sea*.

> '*Pros.* Go, charge my goblins that they grind their joints
> With dry convulsions; shorten up their sinews
> With aged cramps.'

Query—

> *wry* convulsions . . . *agued* cramps.

ACT V. SCENE I.

> '*Pros.* My charms crack not; my spirits obey.'

Query:—*break* not. He says shortly after, 'My charms I'll break.'

> '*Ariel.*   The king,
> His brother, and yours, abide all three distracted,
> And the remainder mourning over them,
> Brimful of sorrow and dismay.'

So it is in the Cambridge and in other editions. But in the folios it is *brim full*, which makes better rhythm, and no worse meaning.

> '*Pros.* A solemn air, and the best comforter
> To an unsettled fancy, cure thy brains,
> Now useless, boil'd within thy skull!'

The folios have *boile* and *boil*. *Boil'd* is the suggestion of Pope.

Query '*now useless* coil,' as in Act i. Sc. 2,

> ' My brave spirit
> Who was so firm, so constant, that this coil
> Would not affect their reason.'

> ' *Pros.*   O good Gonzalo,
> My true preserver, and a loyal sir
> To him thou follow'st.'

Collier's MS. substitutes *servant* for *sir*. Query *suitor*. It is not his loyalty or service to the usurper that Prospero commends; but he may refer, in calling him a loyal suitor, to the fidelity with which he sued to Antonio, the usurping duke, on Prospero's behalf.

> ' *Pros.*   Their understanding
> Begins to swell ; and the approaching tide
> Will shortly fill the reasonable shore
> That now lies foul and muddy. Not one of them
> That yet looks on me, or would know me.'

The first and second folios both read : ' That now ly foule.' Assuming that some change is necessary, I should prefer adhering to this, and reading : ' The reasonable shores that now lie foul.' The repetition of *That* at the beginning of two successive lines suggests the possibility of a compositor's misreading here, as in similar instances. Query, ' E'en yet looks on me.'

> ' *Alon.*   You the like loss!
> *Pros.* As great to me as late ; and supportable
> To make the dear loss, have I means much weaker
> Than you may call to comfort you.'

Query *reparable*. Prospero is replying to Alonzo's exclamation ' Irreparable is the loss.' *Supportable* is unmusical and mars the rhythm.

'*Pros.* Mark but the badges of these men, my lords,
Then say if they be true . . . . . .
These three have robb'd me ; and this demi-devil—
For he's a bastard one—hath plotted with them
To take my life.'

My 1632 folio bears on its margin the substitution of
visages for *badges*. But the badges which shewed they
were not true, were, I presume, the stolen apparel in
which Stephano and Trinculo are decked. But as
Caliban would 'have none on't,' it should read 'these
two have robb'd me.'

'*Alon.* Where should they find this grand liquor that hath gilded 'em ? '

Shakespeare repeatedly uses the word *gilded*, but nowhere else in this sense. Query '*guiled*.

The epilogue which is appended to 'The Tempest'
seems an impotent afterpiece to this beautiful comedy.
It embodies in lame verse a feeble re-echo of the previous sentiments, without a single novel or apt idea. It
resembles in no respect Shakespeare's own epilogues,
and may be unhesitatingly assigned to some nameless
playwright of the seventeenth century.

CHAPTER XIV.

A MIDSUMMER NIGHT'S DREAM.

'Bottom. I have had a most rare vision. I have had a dream,—past
the wit of man to say what dream it was : man is but an ass if he go
about to expound this dream. Methought I was—— there is no man can
tell what.'—*A Midsummer Night's Dream.*

THE text of ' A Midsummer Night's Dream' rests on
different authority from that of ' The Tempest,'
which appeared for the first time in the 1623 folio, seven
years after its author's death. A quarto edition of ' A
Midsummer Night's Dream ' was printed for Thomas
Fisher, and ' soulde at his shoppe, at the Signe of the
White Hart, in Fleetestreete,' in the year 1600. It bears
the name of William Shakespeare on the title ; was duly
entered at Stationers' Hall ; and, though characterised
by the usual carelessness of the press at that date, was,
we may presume, set up from the author's manuscript.
This was followed during the same year by another, and
probably surreptitious reprint, by James Roberts, in which
the printer's errors of the first quarto are corrected, and
the stage directions somewhat augmented, but with a due
crop of misreadings of its own. The Cambridge editors
surmise that it was a pirated reprint of Fisher's quarto,
for the use of the players. As such it got into the hands
of those two special players who issued the first folio as
' Mr. William Shakespeare's Comedies, Histories, and
Tragedies. Published according to the True Originall
Copies ; ' and who, in the preface, pray their readers that
they ' doe not envy his friends the office of their care

and paine to have collected and published them.' They accordingly gave proof of their painstaking, so far as this comedy is concerned, by following the surreptitious copy. The first quarto thus appears to be the better authority for the text of 'A Midsummer Night's Dream;' and the folios have little more value than what is due to contemporary conjectural emendation. This is fully illustrated in the variations of the quarto and folio texts in a passage immediately to be noticed, from the first scene.

It is perhaps due to the. early place which 'A Midsummer Night's Dream' undoubtedly occupies among the dramatic works of Shakespeare, that in all the older texts it is divided into acts, but not into scenes. The stage directions also are meagre, and have been repeatedly confused with the text; and no list of *dramatis personæ* is given. Hence those points have remained to be supplied at the discretion of successive editors; and considerable diversity prevails. The same scene, for example, which Capell and other editors make the second scene in Act ii. becomes the third of Steevens and Knight, and the fifth of Pope.

In many ways it is apparent that this play is the work of a different period from that in which its author wrote 'The Tempest;' and it has even been supposed to embody recollections of the author's own boyish years. Young Shakespeare was in his twelfth year when the Earl of Dudley entertained Queen Elizabeth with the famous allegorical pageants produced at Kenilworth in honour of her visit. The preparations for this magnificent reception of royalty enlisted the services of the inhabitants of the surrounding country; and it is not to be doubted that those of Stratford, only a few miles distant, bore their full share alike in the labours and the pastimes of this grand local event. Among the characteristic allegorical devices introduced on the occasion, Triton, in likeness of a mermaid, paid obeisance to her Majesty ; and Arion, seated on a dolphin's back, enchanted her with a song, 'aptly credited to the matter.' It is a pleasant fancy to believe that the gifted boy actually witnessed this ; and recalling the delights of his youthful fancy at the enchanting scene, he reproduced it in the well-known piece of delicate flattery introduced into his 'Dream,' as a more lasting tribute to the Maiden Queen :—

> *Oberon.* My gentle Puck, come hither. Thou rememb'rest
> Since once I sat upon a promontory,
> And heard a mermaid, on a dolphin's back,
> Uttering such dulcet and harmonious breath,
> That the rude sea grew civil at her song ;
> And certain stars shot madly from their spheres,
> To hear the sea-maid's music.
>   *Puck.*   I remember.
>   *Oberon.* That very time I saw, but thou couldst not,
> Flying between the cold moon and the earth,
> Cupid all arm'd ; a certain aim he took
> At a fair vestal throned by the west ;
> And loosed his love-shaft smartly from his bow,
> As it should pierce a hundred thousand hearts :
> But I might see young Cupid's fiery shaft
> Quench'd in the chaste beams of the watery moon ;
> And the imperial votaress passed on,
> In maiden meditation, fancy-free.'

Malone, judging from internal evidence, regards this delicately fanciful drama as revealing all 'the warmth of a youthful and lively imagination ;' and therefore he concludes it to be one of his earliest attempts at comedy. But there is nothing crude or immature in it. On the contrary, much of its poetry is of the rarest beauty : yet dallying with the innocence of love, and fancifully interblending its mishaps with 'such sights as youthful poets dream.' Its light and airy, yet exquisitely charming verse, has received the highest meed of appreciation ; for

R

it has passed beyond the region of dramatic dialogue into that current popular poetry which is familiar as household words ; and is scarcely assigned to individual authorship, but rather constitutes a part of the living language, an universal property wherever the English tongue is spoken. The wonderful exuberance of fancy which characterises this comedy has already attracted our notice ; but many portions of the dialogue are in rhyme, and much both of the prose and verse is purposely wrought into a gay medley, which scarcely admits of the same strict critical analysis as 'The Tempest.' Indeed not a little of the charm of the prose dialogue lies in the unconscious blunderings of the Athenian mechanics. It has been subjected, nevertheless, to the same critical revision as others of the plays. Rowe, Pope, Theobald, Hanmer, Warburton, Johnson, and later commentators, down to Collier, with his antique MS. notes, have all tried their hands at the work of restoration. Some of their emendations are welcome elucidations of obscure or blundered passages. Others, especially those on the lighter dialogue of the 'hempen homespuns swaggering here,' are of a piece with the sage comments of the censorious Bottom himself on 'the tedious brief scene of young Pyramus and his love Thisbe : very tragical mirth.' Little more is attempted here than the production of a few notes and comments on obscure passages, the fruits of careful and reverent study of the play.

ACT I. SCENE I.

> *Dem.* Relent, sweet Hermia; and, Lysander, yield
> Thy crazed title to my certain right.'

Query *razed* title. The decision of Theseus has just

been given, by which all claim or title of Lysander to Hermia's hand is erased. The word *razed* repeatedly occurs in this sense in the dramas.

> ' *Lys.*   And she, sweet lady, dotes,
> Devoutly dotes, dotes in idolatry,
> Upon this spotted and inconstant man.'

Spotted is a Shakespearean word, the opposite of spotless : as Richard II. speaks of the spotted souls of his disloyal nobles. No one therefore would venture to disturb the text. But I may note here the conjectural change pencilled by me on the margin as harmonising, by antithesis, with Helena's 'devout idolatry' to her forsworn lover.

> '*Pon this apostate* and inconstant man.

The following example of variations in the quarto and folio texts will illustrate how little authority can be attached to the latter as fulfilling the promise of the editors that where the readers of Shakespeare had before been ' abus'd with divers stolne and surreptitious copies, maimed and deformed by the frauds and stealths of injurious impostors, even those are now offer'd to their view cured and perfect of their limbes.' The passage is here given according to the text of the 1632 folio, in which some attempts are made to remove the careless blunders of the first folio :—

> ' *Lysander.* How now my love? Why is your cheek so pale?
> How chance the Roses there do fade so fast?
> *Hermia.* Belike for want of raine, which I could well
> Beteeme them, from the tempest of mine eyes.
> *Lysander.* *Hermia* for ought that ever I could reade,
> Could ever heare by tale or history,
> The course of true love never did run smooth,
> But either it was different in blood.
> *Hermia.* O crosse! too high to be enthral'd to love

R 2

> *Lysander.* Or else misgraffed, in respect of yeares.
> *Hermia.* O spight! too old to be ingag'd to yong.
> *Lysander.* Or else it stood upon the choise of merit.
> *Hermia.* O hell! to choose love by anothers eye.'

The only other example of the use of the word *beteem* by Shakespeare, is where Hamlet, speaking of his father's loving care for his mother, says : ' He might not beteem the winds of heaven visit her face too roughly.' It can scarcely admit of any common meaning applicable in the two cases. But it is used by Spenser as equivalent to *bestow,* in which sense it suits the text, and as it has the authority both of the quartos and folios, must stand. I had noted *bestream* as a conjectural reading. *Bestow* would accord with another passage, where Henry V. in his prayer before the battle of Agincourt, says of the dead Richard's body—

> ' And on it have bestowed more contrite tears
> Than from it issued forced drops of blood.'

The quartos have ' Eigh me, for ought that I could ever read.' The first folio, omitting the ' Eigh me,' simply has : ' For ought that euer I could reade,' and the second folio replaces the ejaculation of the quartos with the name, nearly equivalent in sound, of *Hermia.*

The change of *love* (in the first folio *loue*) into *low*—

> ' O cross! too high to be enthrall'd to low '—

is due to Theobald, and commends itself to nearly every reader as a restoration of Shakespeare's own word.

> ' Or else it stood upon the choice of friends '

is the text of the quartos ; yet it is changed, undoubtedly for the worse, to *merit*, as shewn in the above version of the folio text. This example of variation between the quartos and folios serves to shew how little authority can be attached to the latter ; and at the same time illustrates the impossibility in some cases of amending undoubted errors by conjectural changes based on any probable misprint. Hermia's response perfectly accords with the original reading of the quartos, while it has little or no meaning in reply to 'the choice of merit,' which is nevertheless retained in the first and subsequent folios. Here there can scarcely be a doubt that the latter is an undesigned change for the worse. But nothing in the context helps to any conjecture as to the origin of the blunder, while its retention in the second and later folios indicates that the original quarto text was, so far at least, neglected in the corrections of the press. Collier's MS. annotator makes the feeble emendation of *men* for *merit*. It is a good illustration of the guesswork restorations based on supposed typographical errors ; and is an instance where, if the word *friends* had not the authority of the quartos to sustain it, the feebler word might have found favour, owing to its seeming resemblance to the objectionable *merit*. Mr. Collier, who does not seem to have been aware of the earlier authority for the received reading, says '*friends* has ordinarily been substituted for *merit*; but *men*, inserted in the margin .by the corrector of the folio, is likely to have been the real word, misheard by the copyist.'

> '*Hel.* Sicknesse is catching: O were favour so,
> Your words Ide catch, faire Hermia ere I go,
> My eare should catch your voice, my eye, your eye,
> My tongue should catch your tongues sweet melodie.'

So the text stands in the second folio ; and as it makes good sense, it might be allowed to remain. But alike in the quartos and first folio it reads, 'Your words I catch,' and Hanmer made on this the apt emendation, 'Yours would I catch,' which more fully accords with the whole context.

ACT II. SCENE I.

> '*Fairy.* And I serve the fairy queen,
> To dew her orbs upon the green.'

Knight, as his fashion is, explains the word *orbs* here
by devising a meaning suited to the context, and fitting
it to the word.   He accordingly says : ' *Orbs,* the *fairy
rings,* as they are popularly called.   It was the fairy's
office to *dew* these orbs, which had been parched under
the fairy feet in the moonlight revels.'   The word is repeatedly used by Shakespeare, but never in any such
sense ; and what follows in the fairy's speech implies
that it is the flowers that, in some way, he speaks of.
The cowslips are her special favourites, 'her pensioners' ;
and so he says—

> 'I must go seek some dewdrops here,
> And hang a pearl in every cowslip's ear.'

This is fitter work than dewing orbs, or parched fairy-
rings.   Grey suggests *herbs.*

Query—
> To dew her *cups* upon the green.

> '*Puck.* And now they never meet in grove or green,
> By fountain clear, or spangled starlight sheen,
> But they do square, that all their elves, for fear,
> Creep into acorn-cups and hide them there.'

Unless doubtfully in a passage in 'Titus Andronicus,'
the word *square* is not used in such a sense as would
suit the text, especially in reference to the fairy king
and queen.   Peck suggests *jar,* or *sparre.*

Query *quarrel.*

> '*Tit.* And never since the middle summer's spring,
> Met we on hill, in dale, forest, or mead.'

Knight explains 'the middle summer's spring' as the beginning of midsummer; but it seems a cumbrous tautology in this sense. Looking to the context, which describes, as the fruit of Oberon and Titania's brawls, contagious fogs, the green corn rotting in the drowned field, and 'the nine men's morris' filled up with mud, I had noted as a conjectural reading 'this *muddy* summer's spring.' But a slighter change would be 'the middle summer's *prime.*'

'*Tit.* The human mortals want their winter here;
No night is now with hymn or carol blest.'

Various conjectures have been offered in amendment of the somewhat pointless 'winter *here.*' Johnson changes it to *wonted year*; Warburton to *winter's heryed.* Theobald had already proposed the better amendment of *winter chear*, or *cheer*, which suits very well the context; and closely accords with the old spelling of the folios, *heere.* Looking to the previous statements, that 'The ox hath stretch'd his yoke in vain,' 'The ploughman lost his sweat,' 'The green corn hath rotted,' and 'The folds stand empty in the drowned field,' I am led to suggest *their winter hire.*

'*Dem.* Hence, get thee gone, and follow me no more.
Hel. You draw me, you hard-hearted adamant;
But yet you draw not iron, for my heart
Is true as steel; leave you your power to draw,
And I shall have no power to follow you.'

This passage has not hitherto been challenged; but the meaning of 'you draw not iron, for my heart is true as steel' is obscure. If it were rendered, 'But yet you draw not iron, *though* my heart is true as steel,' the idea might be that she had no heart of iron, hard as his was. But I suspect the *iron* to be a printer's blunder, suggested by the *steel* following. In the folios *Iron* is printed with a capital, which, in the second folio is somewhat displaced, and separated from the *ron*. This has apparently suggested to the former possessor of my copy an ingenious emendation, which he has written on the margin thus : *You draw, not I run, for,* &c. Among my own annotations are included this conjectural reading :—

> ' But yet you draw no truer ; for my heart
> Is true as steel.'

SCENE II.

> ' *Tit.* Come, now a roundel and a fairy song ;
> Then, for the third part of a minute, hence :
> Some to kill cankers in the musk-rose buds :
> Some war with rere-mice for their leathern wings,
> To make my small elves coats ; and some keep back
> The clamorous owl, that nightly hoots and wonders
> At our quaint spirits. Sing me now asleep ;
> Then to your offices, and let me rest.'

The idea of the third part of a minute dedicated to the fulfilment of the fairy queen's behests, by the companions of Puck, who could 'put a girdle round the earth in forty minutes,' admirably accords with the movements of such airy beings, swift as thought. But Warburton so utterly misses the meaning, that he converts such fairy pastimes into a toil *for the third part of the midnight.*

> ' *Her.* Lie further off : in human modesty,
> Such separation as may well be said
> Becomes a virtuous bachelor and a maid.'

Titania's use of the phrase 'human mortals' is very expressive, but 'human modesty' seems a needless pleonasm. The word stands *humane* in the quartos, and in three out of the four folios. Nicholas Rowe, the earliest reviser of Shakespeare's text, made the fourth folio the basis of all his restorations, and no doubt adopted this without being aware of any variation. The elder form of *humane* would be preferable, though it can scarcely be claimed as a purposed change, for this is the usual mode of spelling *human* in Shakespeare's day. If any change is to be made, *common modesty* would better suit the context.

ACT III.   SCENE II.

> '*Obe.* This falls out better than I could devise;
> But hast thou yet latch't the Athenian's eyes
> With the love-juice, as I did bid thee do?'

The word is variously *latcht, lacht,* in the quartos and folios. Hanmer makes it *lech'd,* another commentator *laced*; while Knight, seeking as usual a meaning in the context, explains it *licked o'er.* But is there any such word? Puck is elsewhere commanded to 'anoint his eyes;' or he is to 'crush this herb into Lysander's eye.' Oberon speaks of the juice as 'on sleeping eye-lids laid,' and himself undertakes to 'streak' Titania's eyes with the same potent fluid. But no such word as *latch't* is used elsewhere in any similar sense. Oberon's term, *streak'd,* would here also suit the rhythm. But *latch't* may possibly be a misprint for *bath'd.*

> '*Her.*   I'll believe as soon
> This whole earth may be bor'd; and that the moon
> May through the centre creep, and so displease
> Her brother's noontide with the Antipodes.'

Hanmer suggests *disease* in lieu of *displease.* The idea in relation to which Hermia introduces this quaint analogy is the substitution of Demetrius for her favoured lover Lysander, of whom she says, 'The sun was not so true unto the day as he to me;' and therefore she will as soon believe that at this very time of night, while the moon is here, the sun may be supplanted by it, on the other side of the world.

Query :—

> ' That the moon
> May through the centre creep, and so *displace*
> Her brother's noontide with the Antipodes.'

> ' *Hel.* Can you not hate me, as I know you do,
> But you must join in souls to mock me too ? '

' Join in souls' has been recognised as, in some way or other, wrong. Hanmer substitutes *flouts* for *souls*, and probably some such word is the true reading. Warburton renders it *must join insolents ;* Tyrwhitt, *must join ill souls ;* and Mason, with the slightest change on the text, *You must join in soul.*

Query :—*join in sports.* She accuses them of being all set against her for their merriment ; 'all to make you sport ;' and when Hermia enters, she charges her as one of this confederacy, joined 'all three to fashion this false sport.'

> ' *Her.* Dark night, that from the eye his function takes,
> The ear more quick of apprehension makes ;
> Wherein it doth impair the seeing sense,
> It pays the hearing double recompense.'

The *his* in the first line is undoubtedly the old Anglo-Saxon neuter genitive, and is as Shakespeare wrote it. Where, however, in this and many other lines, there is obviously no rhetorical gender, and the nominative *it* follows close at hand, it would be no greater liberty with the text to substitute the modern form *its*, than many orthographical changes universally approved of. Another passage in this comedy will serve to illustrate

the old use of *his*. Titania is detailing to Oberon the
fruits of their brawls :—

> ' The ox hath therefore stretch'd *his* yoke in vain,
> The ploughman lost *his* sweat; and the green corn
> Hath rotted, ere *his* youth attained a beard.'

The new form was adopted in a single generation.
Milton evades the obscurity in rhetorical impersonation consequent on *his* being in use as a neuter form, by
falling back, whenever he can do so, on the gender of
the Latin derivative ; e. g. 'Paradise Lost,' Bk. I, Lat.
forma :—

> ' His form had not yet lost
> All her original brightness.'

But by the time that Dryden succeeded him as the
poet of a new era—though he was in his forty-fourth
year at Milton's death,—the change had been so universally adopted, that in challenging the grammatical
English of Ben Jonson he quotes this line from his
' Catiline '

> ' Though heaven should speak with all his wrath at once,'

and says of it ' *Heaven* is ill syntax with *his*.'
This proof of how thoroughly a grammatical usage
of Shakespeare's age had passed out of knowledge in a
single generation, shews that Dryden's emendations on
the text of ' The Tempest ' rest on little better authority
than the guesses of modern commentators. He would
have converted the *his* into *its*, not as a change rendered
desirable by altered grammatical forms, but as the
correction of a positive blunder. But many passages
occur where the retention of the old neuter form is apt
to mislead ; and as Shakespeare does occasionally employ the new form, its substitution in other cases is
allowable. Take, for example, the following lines from
Oberon's directions to Puck :—

> ' Then crush this herb into Lysander's eye;
> Whose liquor hath this virtuous property,
> To take from thence all error with his might,
> And make his eyeballs roll with wonted sight.'

' With *its* might' would be a legitimate emendation. The first *his* undoubtedly refers to the liquor, the second to Lysander; yet as the text stands, it suggests the idea that, along with Lysander's ' error,' the liquor was to take away his might.

> ' *Hel.* We, Hermia, like two artificial gods,
> Have with our needles created both one flower,
> Both on one sampler, sitting on one cushion.'

Pope needlessly takes in hand to amend the harmony of the second line, which is thoroughly Shakespearean. He reads ' Created with our needles both one flower.' Steevens, with the same object in view, abbreviates *needles* to *neelds*. But no commentator notices the extravagant simile, ' like two artificial gods.' I had noted on my own annotated copy the conjecture, *like to artificer gods*. But *gods* seems altogether alien to the general current of Helena's thoughts. Query, *two artificial buds*.

> *Hel.*　　　　　　So we grew together,
> Like to a double cherry, seeming parted,
> But yet a union in partition;
> Two lovely berries moulded on one stem;
> So with two seeming bodies, but one heart;
> Two of the first, like coats in heraldry,
> Due but to one, and crowned with one crest.'

To any one acquainted with heraldry, the phrase ' two of the first' seems such unmistakeable heraldic language, that he is apt to fancy he understands the whole allusion. But reduced to a defined solution, it does not appear by any means so clear. Monk Mason says ' two of the first means two coats of the first house, which are properly due but to one;' and Knight says, 'there is a double comparison here—first, of the two bodies compared to two coats of heraldry; and secondly, of the one heart compared to the one crest, and the one owner.' But this can only end in the impaling of two similar coats of arms, and leaves the 'due but to one,' on which the whole force of the simile rests, unaccounted for. Douce and Grant White reject the heraldic significance of 'first,' and hold it to be used in its ordinary sense, referring to two bodies. Of the general meaning there can be no doubt. Helena tells Hermia that, with their 'sisters' vows' and closest friendship, they had been as if with two bodies, yet but one heart. As, however, the heraldic interpretations seem to fail according to the received version, it may be worth while reconsidering the original text. The first folio reads, 'Two of the first life coats in heraldry.' The only change in the second folio is the insertion of a comma after *life.* Theobald changed the *life* to *like.* It seems to me that the text as it stands in the second folio, makes at least as good sense as the other, and no worse heraldry. Two bodies of the first life, would be moulded on one parental stem, and two coats in heraldry of the first life, would be due to one and the same descendant.

'So with two seeming bodies, but one heart,
Two of the first life : coats in heraldry
Due but to one, and crowned with one crest.'

* * *

'*Her.* I understand not what you mean by this.
Hel. Ay, do, persever, counterfeit sad looks,
Make mouths upon me when I turn my back.'

The first quarto, according to the Cambridge editors, reads, *I doe. Persever.* The second quarto and the follos are stated, on the same authority, to read *I, do, persever.* The first folio, in so far as the photozinco-graphic facsimile may be appealed to, reads—

> 'I, doe, perseuer, counterfeit sad lookes,
> Make mouthes vpon me when I turne my backe.'

In the second folio it becomes, *I, do, persever,* &c. The capital *I*, however, is the usual way of rendering the *ay* of our later orthography, and is not, therefore, any sure guide to the true reading. Rowe rendered it, *Ay, do, persevere* ; but modern critical editors have restored the *persever*, as essential to the rhythm. It seems to me more effective, as Helena's answer to Hermia, and not without some justification from the original text, to read—

> 'I do ;—perceive you counterfeit sad looks.'

She has already exclaimed shortly before, ' Now I perceive they have conjoin'd, all three ;' and when he says, ' I understand not what you mean,' she replies, ' But I do ; I perceive you counterfeit sad looks, make mouths upon me,' &c.

> ' *Her.* Lysander, whereto tends all this?
> *Lys.* Away, you Ethiope!
> *Dem.*   No, no ; he'll
> Seem to break loose; take on as you would follow,
> But yet come not: you are a tame man, go ! '

This passage has given the commentators no little trouble. In the first quarto it is *No, no ; heele Seeme to breake loose.* The second, finding something wrong, renders it as one line—*No, no, hee'l seeme to breake loose.* The folio editors, or press reader, try another change, and it there reads, still as one line—*No, no, Sir, seeme to breake loose.* Pope rearranges the verse, and reads, *No, no he'll seem To break away ;* Capell makes it, *No, no ; he'll not come. Seem to break loose ;* Malone, *No, no ;*

he'll—sir, Seem to break loose; Steevens, *No, no; sir:—he will,. Seem to break loose;* while Jackson furnishes an amusing example of the misspent ingenuity which so often makes the error of one editor or commentator the basis of another's conjectures. Taking the *sir* of the folios as his guide, he renders it, *No, no, he'll not stir; Seem to break loose.* The Cambridge editors, distracted with the multitude of counsellors, after exhausting a long foot-note, take up the question anew in the appendix, where they say, 'In this obscure passage we have thought it best to retain substantially the reading of the quartos. The folios, though they alter it, do not remove the difficulty, and we must conclude that some words, perhaps a whole line, have fallen out of the text.' They accordingly indicate the supposed hiatus thus :—

> No, no; he'll . . .
>   Seem to break loose; &c.

It seems presumptuous to follow such varied and high authorities with a new suggestion; and still more, to fancy, as I am tempted to do, that a very trifling alteration clears up the whole difficulty, without any missing line. A pair of distracted lovers, set at cross purposes by Puck's knavish blundering, are giving vent to the most extravagant violence of language. Helena says, a very little before—

> 'O spite! O hell! I see you all are bent
>   To set against me for your merriment.'

In like fashion, as it appears to me, Demetrius now exclaims, in language perfectly consistent with the rude epithets Lysander is heaping on Hermia—

> 'No, no ; hell
>   Seems to break loose; take on as you would, fellow!
>   But yet come not; you are a tame man, go!'

Lysander's reply, though addressed seemingly to Hermia, is amply consistent with such violent hyperbole :—

> ' Hang off, thou cat, thou burr ! vile thing, let loose,
> Or I will shake thee from me like a serpent.'

ACT IV. SCENE I.

> ' *Obe.* And gentle Puck take this transformed scalp
> From off the head of this Athenian swain ;
> That he awaking when the others do,
> May all to Athens back again repair.'

All may to Athens is suggested by the context, but it is more musical as it stands.   Query *transforming scalp*.

It cannot but seem presumptuous to venture on any emendation of Nick Bottom's exquisite soliloquy, which he places far beyond reach of all carping critics by his solemn decision that ' man is but an ass if he go about to expound this dream.' Yet one little particle does seem to admit of change.   His resolution is, ' I will get Peter Quince to write a ballad,' or, as the folios have it, a ballet, ' of this dream.   It shall be called Bottom's Dream, because it hath no bottom, and I will sing it in the latter end of a play, before the duke.   Peradventure, to make it the more gracious, I shall sing it at her death.' *At her death* is doubtless at the death of Thisbe, when he, being already the dead Pyramus, would all the more characteristically turn up again with his own ballad, instead of the Bergomask dance which he does actually volunteer.   Whether it be safe to venture on the change of a single letter in his inimitable confusions of all the senses may well be questioned ; but doubtless he means ' in the latter end of *the* play ' of Pyramus and Thisbe, with a view to add one more climax to its ' very tragical mirth ' : and not at the close of some possible future appearance before the duke.

ACT V. SCENE I.

The comedy closes with a fairy dance and song, which the Cambridge editors, following the quartos, assign to Oberon. But this is obviously an error, though parts of it may be properly enough assigned to him to sing in *solo*. Johnson preceded them in restoring the song to Oberon. But having by this means converted it into a part of the dialogue, he proceeds naively to enquire after the song which Titania calls for, and comes to the conclusion that ' it is gone after many other things of greater value. The truth is that two songs are lost,' one called for by Oberon and the other by Titania, because, as Johnson supposes, ' they were not inserted in the players' parts, from which the drama was printed.' All this is a mistake, founded on the revival of the original error of assigning the song to Oberon. On the contrary, his orders are given to ' every elf and fairy sprite ' to perform various favouring services within the hallowed house of Duke Theseus and his bride, and then he adds :—

> ' And this ditty after me
> Sing and dance it trippingly.'

Titania thereupon joins in with her commands to their fairy train :—

> ' First rehearse your song by rote,
> To each word a warbling note ;
> Hand in hand with fairy grace,
> Will we sing and bless this place.'

In the folios the song immediately follows this, printed

S

as such in italics, and headed *The Song.* It was no doubt at the date of the first folio, if not at that of the quartos, set to music, with its various parts apportioned to different fairy singers. Oberon and Titania doubtless had a prominent share assigned to them; and the fairy chorus taking up alternate lines, repeating, and singing in parts, the verse would be arranged, in accordance with the exigencies of the music, and in all probability transcribed therefrom with no very critical attention to the order of the lines. In the folios the closing lines stand thus :—

> ' With this field dew consecrate,
> Every fairy take his gate,
> And each .severall chamber blesse,
> Through this pallace with sweet peace,
> Ever shall in safety rest,
> And the owner of it blest.
> Trip away, make no stay;
> Meet me all by breake of day.'

It has been seen from the first that some change is needed here. Mr. R. Grant White says : ' " Ever shall in safety rest " is neither sense nor English, ancient or modern.' Rowe renders the line *Ever shall it safely rest;* Malone, *E'er shall it in safety rest;* Warburton, *Ever shall it safely rest.* Staunton appears to have first detected the true source of error, and suggested the transposition of the fifth and sixth lines, after attempting amendment in another way, by changing *Ever shall* into *Every hall.* Without being aware of his proposed transposition, I had already noted on the margin : ' These lines to be sung by different fairies'; and assuming them thus to be taken up by different singers, whereby the logical sequence might be disarranged, I had marked a more comprehensive re-arrangement. At the point where these lines begin there is a change of theme. Oberon and Titania may be assumed to take the lead, up to this point, with their special blessings on the bridal bed and the promised issue. The earlier portion correctly arranges itself in couplets, and may be supposed to be sung as a duet by Oberon and Titania. The scene lies in the palace of Theseus. 'The iron tongue of midnight hath told twelve;' and the irrepressible Bottom, whose death-stab

> 'In that left pap,
> Where heart doth hop,'

was supposed to have made an end of him in a previous scene, has in vain come alive again with his proffered epilogue. 'No epilogue, I pray you,' exclaims the Duke, 'for your play needs no excuse. Never excuse; for when the players are all dead, there need none be blamed:' and so his commands are—

> 'Lovers to bed; 'tis almost fairy-time,
> I fear we shall outsleep the coming morn.'

Puck accordingly appears forthwith, broom in hand, to prepare 'the hallow'd house' for its supernatural visitants:

> 'The fairies that do run,
> By the triple Hecate's team,
> From the presence of the sun,
> Following darkness like a dream.'

Oberon despatches 'every elf and fairy sprite' to illumine the palace with their glimmering light. Titania invites them first to a rehearsal of their song of blessing; and then, the whole fairy band being commissioned to wander through the house and fulfil their errand there till break of day, Oberon says:

> 'To the best bride-bed will we,
> Which by us shall blessed be;'

and so he proceeds with a succession of fairy benedictions in rhyming couplets. But now, at the close,

S 2

the fairy train are anew commissioned to go through
the palace of Theseus and bless every chamber, conse-
crating it with their elfin field-dew.   Arranged in the
following order, the consecutive relation of ideas seems
to be more clearly expressed :—

> 'Through this palace with sweet peace
> Every fairy take his gait,
> And each several chamber bless,
> With this field-dew consecrate;
> And the owners of it blest,
> Ever shall in safety rest;
> Trip away;
> Make no stay;
> Meet me all by break of day.'

Oberon begins his part of this elfin consecration-
service thus :—

> 'Through the house give glimmering light
> By the dead and drowsy fire,
> Every elf and fairy sprite,
> Hop as light as bird from brier.'

We have accordingly spoken above of Oberon despatch-
ing his train to illumine the palace thus.   But the first
couplet seems to involve a confusion of ideas, which
early attracted the attention of the commentators.
Warburton makes the first line, *Through this house;*
Johnson further changes it to, *Through this house in
glimmering light;* while Mr. R. Grant White offers the
slight but apt change of *Though*, for *Through*.   My own
conjectural reading suggests a different change, also involving no great literal variation :—Through the *house-
wives'* glimmering light.   The couplet of Puck which
immediately precedes, sufficiently harmonises with such
an idea, where with broom he sweeps the dust behind
the door.

It seems a piece of hypercriticism to subject the light

fairy songs and the epilogue of Puck, with its rhyming couplets, to any severe verbal analysis. Where, however, the language seems obscure, the efforts at amending the text are sometimes rewarded by catching its meaning, without the necessity for any change. The notoriously careless way in which this comedy appears to have been edited from the first justifies suspicion of blundering whenever a difficulty occurs ; for none of all the plays of Shakespeare surpass 'A Midsummer Night's Dream' in the simple beauty of its charming verse. What, then, is the meaning of this line—'*No more yielding but a dream*'? Like other readings where the text has been corrupted, it has a seeming significance in relation to the context till the meaning is challenged. Not a little of the beautiful fancy of the whole comedy turns on the way in which the supernatural elements seem to hover indefinitely between reality and a dream; and so Puck says at parting, with this slight conjectural emendation :—

> 'If we shadows have offended,
> Think but this, and all is mended,
> That you have but slumber'd here,
> While these visions did appear;
> And this weak and idle theme,
> No *mere idling*, but a dream,
> Gentles do not reprehend.'

So much for conjectural revision and emendation of 'A Midsummer Night's Dream.' In this, as in all other of the great master's works, the beauties are so manifold and so striking, that the few undoubted blemishes with which the textual critic is free to deal, are but as motes in the sunshine ; and Shakespeare can be enjoyed, with little sense of imperfection, in the most corrupt text of old quarto or folio.

The marvellous piece of fancy thus subjected to cold critical supervision, is so wonderful an embodiment of

sportive idealism; such a happy blending of the utmost
extremes of incongruity : that it seems as much to set
analytical acumen at defiance as if it were an actual
dream. That Lysander and Demetrius, Hermia and
Helena, should so disport themselves, so woo, so rail,
scorn and anathematise each other, prove faithless,
proclaim loathing, and yet, after all, share in the fairy
blessings whereby

> 'Shall all the couples three
> Ever true in loving be,'

would seem inconceivable, had not Shakespeare wrought
the whole into such perfect consistency, that the imagination welcomes it as the realisation of its own rarest
fancy-flights, and claims for it a charmed circle within
which imagination shall hold its own, and reason dispense
with all censorious anatomisings. We yield ourselves to
the charm, and then imagination sees no more incongruity in the perverse wooings of the Athenian lovers,
than in the pranks of Puck, and the quaint devices of
Oberon for outwitting his wilful Queen of Shadows.
Shakespeare once believed it all himself, when by the
Stratford ingle-nook he listened as a boy to nursery
tales of elves and fairies, such as doubtless some of the
narrators were ready to swear they had themselves seen
when the moonlight glanced through the oak-branches,
and played with flitting light and shadow among the
cowslips and daisies of Charlecote Chace.

But there is one character least of all seemingly fitted to
consort with beings light as air : that most prosaic of
'rude mechanicals' and 'human mortals,' Nick Bottom.
Yet what inimitable power and humorous depth of irony
are there in the Athenian weaver and prince of clownish
players ! Vain, conceited, consequential : he is nevertheless no mere empty lout, but rather the impersonation of

characteristics which have abounded in every age, and find ample scope for their display in every social rank. Bottom is the work of the same master hand which wrought for us the Caliban and Miranda, the Puck and Ariel, of such diverse worlds. He is the very embodiment and idealisation of that self-esteem which is a human virtue by no means to be dispensed with, though it needs some strong counterpoise in the well-balanced mind. In the weak vain man, who fancies everybody is thinking of him and looking at him, it takes the name of shyness, and claims nearest kin to modesty. With robust insensitive vulgarity it assumes an air of universal philanthropy and good-fellowship. In the man of genius it reveals itself in very varying phases : gives to Pope his waspish irritability as a satirist, and crops out anew in the transparent mysteries of publication of his laboured-impromptu private letters ; betrays itself in the self-laudatory exclusiveness which carried Wordsworth through long years of detraction and neglect to his final triumph ; in the morbid introversions of Byron, and his assumed defiance of 'the world's dread laugh'; in the sturdy self-assertion of Burns, the honest faith of the peasant bard, that

> 'The rank is but the guinea stamp,
> The man's the gowd for a' that!'

In Ben Jonson it gave character to the whole man. Goldsmith and Chatterton, Hogg and Hugh Miller only differed from their fellows in betraying the self-esteem which more cunning adepts learn to disguise under many a mask, even from themselves. It shines in modest prefaces, writes autobiographies and diaries by the score, and publishes poems by the hundred—

> 'Obliged by hunger and request of friends.'

Nick Bottom is thus a representative man, 'not one, but all mankind's epitome.' He is a natural genius. If he claims the lead, it is not without a recognised fitness to fulfil the duties he assumes. He is one whom nothing can put out. 'I have a device to make all well,' is his prompt reply to every difficulty, and the device, such as it is, is immediately forthcoming. A duke is but a duke after all; and we may be well assured, when Theseus tells the Queen of the Amazons of his welcomers collapsing in 'the modesty of fearful duty,' Nick Bottom had no place in his thoughts :—

> 'Where I have come, great clerks have purposed
> To greet me with premeditated welcomes;
> Where I have seen them shiver and look pale,
> Make periods in the midst of sentences,
> Throttle their practised accent in their fears,
> And in conclusion, dumbly have broke off,
> Not paying me a welcome.'

As to Bottom, were he the duke, and Theseus the clown, he could not take it more coolly. He comes back from the fairy brake, ready as ever for the minutest details, and prompt for action. No time for talk now. 'The duke hath dined; get your apparel together, good strings to your beards,'—for a pretty thing it were, if your aptly-chosen orange-tawny or French-crown-coloured beard were to drop off in the very crisis of the tragedy! 'In any case let Thisby have clean linen;' and poor Snug, the extempore lion, beware of paring his nails. 'And, most dear actors, eat no onions nor garlic, for we are to utter sweet breath, and I do not doubt but to have them say it is a sweet comedy.' Bottom is as completely conceived, in all perfectness of consistency, as any character Shakespeare has drawn : ready-witted, unbounded in his self-confidence, and with a conceit nursed into the absolute proportions which we witness by the admiring deference of his brother clowns. Yet this is no more than the recognition of true merit. Their admiration of his parts is rendered ungrudgingly, as it is received by him simply as his due. Peter Quince appears as responsible manager of the theatricals, and indeed is doubtless the author of 'the most lamentable comedy.' For Nick Bottom, though equal to all else, makes no pretensions to the poetic art. He is barely awakened out of his fairy-trance, when he begins to cudgel his brains. 'Methought I was—there is no man that can tell what. Methought I was, and methought I had—but man is but a patched fool if he will offer to say what methought I had. The eye of man hath not heard, the ear of man hath not seen, man's hand is not able to taste, his tongue to conceive, nor his heart to report, what my dream was. I will get Peter Quince to write a ballad of this dream ; it shall be called Bottom's Dream, because it hath no bottom ; and I will sing it in the latter end of a play, before the duke.' Here there is no mistaking the poet of the company. All due recognition of his powers is conceded as a matter of course ; but the result leads none the less to Bottom's own pre-eminence. The ballad is to be 'Bottom's Dream,' and with it he is to come in as the climax of the whole performance, before the admiring duke.

Peter Quince is as it were proprietor or lessee of the improvised theatre, and assumes accordingly such authority as 'the only begetter' of their comedy must needs do. He apportions to Bottom his part of Pyramus, and persists in his cast of the play in spite of the weaver's ambition to hide his face and play Thisbe ; or shew his face and roar in the lion's part, till the duke shall say, 'Let him roar again ! let him roar again !' But it is a point manifestly conceded by all as beyond dispute, that without Nick Bottom nothing can be done. To the very colour of his beard he is ready for the perfect discharge of the lover's part, much as he should prefer to play the tyrant. He is prepared for any daring, any sacrifice ; if needs be, can undertake Thisbe, and speak her to the very life, 'in a monstrous little voice'; or, since his threatened roarings were enough 'to fright the duchess and the ladies, and to hang us all,' he 'will aggravate his voice so, that he will roar you as gently as any sucking dove ; he will roar you an 'twere any nightingale.' As to his own specialty of Pyramus, 'a lover that kills himself most gallantly for love,'—rather than the ladies shall be put beside themselves with fear at the sight of a drawn sword, or the grave tragical suicide omitted, he is prepared to announce.to the duke and his noble auditors, 'for the more better assurance, that I Pyramus am not Pyramus, but Bottom the weaver.'

Quince is throughout the literary man. He is to 'draw a bill of properties such as our play wants ;' and to him Bottom turns, as a matter of course, to 'write me a prologue, and let the prologue seem to say' what he forthwith dictates. As to the weaver himself, he doubt-less does not use to write his name, but has a mark to himself, like an honest plain-dealing man. Nevertheless poets must be content to be guided by their betters. He will dictate the very measure of his prologue, in spite of Peter Quince's vocation as laureat. He will have none of your alternating eights and sixes ; nothing will please him but that it be written in verses of eight and eight. He anticipates every difficulty, and is ever equal to the occasion. 'To bring in, God shield us ! a lion among ladies, is a most dreadful thing ; for there is not a more dreadful wild-fowl than your lion living, and we ought to look to 't ;' and so he decides that Snug must name his name, and shew half his face through the lion's neck, and with all soothing entreaties to the ladies not to fear, not to tremble, he is to tell them plainly he is Snug the joiner. He looks into the almanac, and finds moonshine for them just when wanted ; devises a wall for Pyramus and Thisbe, and a cranny through which they may whisper ; and when at last Puck sends him back from his tiring-room in the thorn-brake, translated with the ass's head, the scare of the whole company leaves him wholly unaffected. ' I will not stir from this place do what they can ; I will walk up and down here and I will sing, that they shall here I am not afraid.'

No wonder, when Bottom could nowhere be heard of, all further hope of the performance was at an end. There are those in every rank in life whose self-reliance is a prop on which all lean. ' If he come not,' says Flute, ' then the play is marred. It goes not forward, doth it ? ' ' It is not possible,' is Quince's reply. He doubtless had him in his eye when he wrote the character. ' You have not a man in all Athens able to discharge Pyramus but he.' There is neither dubiety nor jealousy as to his pre-eminent abilities. ' No,' says Flute, as spokesman for the whole, ' he hath simply the best wit of any handicraft man in Athens ; ' and indeed the only point of difference between them is whether ' sweet bully Bottom ' shall indeed be pronounced, according to Peter Quince's eulogium, ' a very paramour for a sweet voice ; ' or whether, as Flute will have it, they should not rather call him a paragon ; for ' a paramour is, God bless us, a thing of naught !' Had their sport but gone on, they were all made men. Sixpence a day had been the undoubted award of such a genius. ' Sixpence a

day during life; he could not have 'scaped sixpence
a-day.   An the Duke had not given him sixpence a-
day for playing Pyramus,' says the admiring Bellows-
mender, ' I'll be hanged! He would have deserved it.
Sixpence a-day in Pyramus, or nothing.'   But now
all is ruined without him, when—' O most courageous
day ! O most happy hour !'—to the unbounded delight
of Quince and his whole company, the transmogrified
weaver turns up again, and all is well.

But fully to appreciate the ability and self-posses-
sion of Nick Bottom in the most unwonted circumstances, we must follow the translated mechanical to
Titania's bower, where the enamoured queen lavishes
her favours on her strange lover.   His cool prosaic
commonplaces fit in with her rhythmical fancies as
naturally as the dull grey of the dawn meets and em-
braces the sunrise.   His valiant song awakes Titania
from her flowery bed amid the fragrance of the wild
thyme and the nodding violets, while woodbine, sweet
musk-roses and the eglantine overcanopy her couch ;
and to her charmed eye the transformed weaver, with
his ass's nowl, appears an angel.   'What hempen homespuns have we swaggering so near the cradle of the
fairy Queen ?' is Puck's exclamation when he first gets
sight of Quince's company.   Titania, on the contrary,
awakened by Bottom's carol, exclaims, 'What angel
wakes me from my flowery bed ?' and so she forthwith
addresses him :—

> ' I pray thee, gentle mortal, sing again ;
> Mine ear is much enamour'd of thy note,
> So is mine eye enthralled to thy shape ;
> And thy fair virtue's force perforce doth move me,
> On the first view, to say, to swear, I love thee.'

' Methinks, mistress,' he replies,—in no way put out by

such advances,—'you should have little reason for that. And yet, to say the truth, reason and love keep little company together now-a-days. The more the pity that some honest neighbours will not make them friends.' He is at home at once with the whole fairy court, and condescends to his airy attendants with an easy gracious familiarity worthy of one to whom the favours of Queen Titania come as though they were his by right. 'I shall desire more of your acquaintance, good Master Cobweb,' he says, with a play upon his name. Turning to another of the fairy train, 'Your name, honest gentleman?' is his easy salutation. With him, in like manner, he has his jest; as apt as that of the wise King James, when it pleased him to pun in learned fashion with admiring courtiers at Holyrood or Whitehall. 'I pray you commend me to Mistress Squash, your mother, and to Master Peascod your father. Good Master Peaseblossom I shall desire you of more acquaintance;' and presently the whole delicate fairy band are engaged in scratching his ass's muzzle. For, as he says to good Monsieur Mustardseed, 'I must to the barber's, monsieur; for, methinks I am marvellous hairy about the face; and I am such a tender ass, if my hair do but tickle me I must scratch.'

Here we cannot but note the quaint blending of the ass with the rude Athenian 'thick-skin': as though the creator of Caliban had his own theory of evolution; and has here an eye to the more fitting progenitor of man. Titania would know what her sweet love desires to eat. 'Truly a peck of provender: I could munch your good dry oats. Methinks I have a great desire to a bottle of hay. Good hay, sweet hay, hath no fellow.' The puzzled fairy queen would fain devise some fitter dainty for her lover. 'I have a venturous fairy,' she tells him, 'that shall seek the squirrel's hoard, and fetch thee new nuts.' But no! Bottom has not achieved the dignity of that sleek smooth head, and those fair large ears, which Titania has been caressing, and decorating with musk-roses, to miss their befitting provender. 'I had rather have a handful or two of dry peas.' It comes so naturally to him to be an ass! As for the coying of his amiable cheeks, and all the other choice attentions of fairy royalty, he takes them as a matter of course. 'I pray you, let none of your people stir me; I have an exposition of sleep come upon me;' and so he dozes off to sleep, with a gentle bray, enwound in the doting fairy's arms. When he awakes again, he is all alone in the hawthorn brake. His first thought is his cue; as though he had, but the moment before, gone, as Peter Quince says, 'to see a noise that he heard, and is to come again.' But as he finds that all have stolen hence, and left him to his sleep, he falls back on his experiences in Wonderland. 'I have had a most rare vision. I have had a dream, past the wit of man to say what dream it was. Man is but an ass if he go about to expound this dream.'

Yet though Bottom is an ass, he is no fool. He is indeed wrapped up in the supremest ignorance of 'rude mechanicals that work for bread upon Athenian stalls.' Of such wisdom as belongs to the schools, or was taught in the porch, he makes no pretence; but of mother wit he has his full share. His sublime conceit rests in part on a certain consciousness of innate power. He is unabashed by rank, undaunted by difficulties, ready at a moment's notice for all emergencies, thoroughly cool and self-reliant. No wonder that he can look a duke in the face. He has been accustomed to take the lead among his fellow mechanics, and to have his counsels followed as a matter of course. Nick Bottom is a natural genius, of a type by no means rare. There is a consequential aldermanic absolutism about him, familiar to many a civic council-board. He gives his opinions on the play, in all its intricacies and perplexities, with an infallibility which no Shakespearean commentator could surpass. 'Tis a very good piece of work, and a merry;' though his own part 'will ask some tears in the true performing of it.' Duke Theseus, when witnessing the actual performance, ventures on a comment ; but Bottom, in the midst of his most tender Pyramus-vein, is ready with his 'No, in truth, sir,' and will play, not only actor, but commentator too.

There are Bottoms everywhere. Nor are they without their uses. Vanity becomes admirable when carried out with such sublime unconsciousness ; and here it is a vanity resting on some solid foundation, and finding expression in the assumption of a leadership which his fellows recognise as his own by right. If he will play the lion's part, 'let him roar again!' Look where we will, we may chance to come on 'sweet bully Bottom.' In truth there is so much of genuine human nature in this hero of 'A Midsummer Night's Dream,' that it may not always be safe to peep into the looking-glass, ·lest evolution reassert itself for our special behoof, and his familiar countenance greet us, 'Hail fellow, well met, give me your neif!'

INDEX

T

For EU product safety concerns, contact us at Calle de José Abascal, 56–1°,
28003 Madrid, Spain or eugpsr@cambridge.org.

www.ingramcontent.com/pod-product-compliance
Ingram Content Group UK Ltd.
Pitfield, Milton Keynes, MK11 3LW, UK
UKHW010347140625
459647UK00010B/897